Advance Praise for *Campus CEO*

"Randal is a business-savvy scholar. He knows how to make the most of his time, which is a crucial lesson for all aspiring entrepreneurs. *Campus CEO* is based on experience, and I would recommend it to anyone in school or out of school. Randal knows the ropes on both sides—and he's a great guy!"
—**Donald J. Trump**

"It's imperative that the student entrepreneur uses all resources available to him or her. Not only does Randal Pinkett's *Campus CEO* identify such resources, but it also gives you key information to maintain a healthy educational and financial future."
—**Earl G. Graves Sr., Founder, Chairman, and Publisher,** *Black Enterprise Magazine*

"Filled with useful materials and detailed advice, *Campus CEO* is a thoroughly researched guide for the aspiring student entrepreneur. Chronicling his days creating several campus ventures, Randal Pinkett describes the intricacies of taking advantage of numerous resources for the student entrepreneur. Pinkett has authored an invaluable reference for students of all ages who want to start their own business without compromising their academic performance."
—**Carl J. Schramm, President and CEO, Kauffman Foundation, and Author,** *The Entrepreneurial Imperative*

"Few people have made better use of their college years than Randal Pinkett, who excelled at Rutgers in the classroom, on the athletic field, and in the business he launched as an undergraduate. His practical advice and inspiring ideas in *Campus CEO* give a new generation of student entrepreneurs a great start toward that same kind of success."
—**Richard L. McCormick, President, Rutgers, The State University of New Jersey**

"Randal Pinkett's *Campus CEO* enables students to take their passion beyond the walls of formal education by turning potential into action."
—**Douglas E. Schallau, President, Junior Achievement of New York, Inc.**

"Randal Pinkett's *Campus CEO* helps students take their passion above and beyond the four walls of formal education."
—**Gabriella Morris, President of the Prudential Foundation, which sponsors The Prudential Young Entrepreneur Program**

"Randal Pinkett's *Campus CEO* is an indispensable tool to help the student entrepreneur create a multimillion-dollar business enterprise, while striking a healthy balance between work and school to also maintain good grades."
—**"The Three Doctors"—Sampson Davis, MD, Rameck Hunt, MD, and George Jenkins, DMD, Authors of *The Pact***

"Entrepreneurship has no age limits. Randal Pinkett's *Campus CEO* helps the young entrepreneur get a head start along the road to a successful business."
—**Melanie McEvoy, President, National Association of Women Business Owners (NAWBO), New York City**

"Entrepreneurs are individualists by definition, but it always helps to find good ideas such as in this book."
—**Jim Rogers, Author of *Adventure Capitalist***

"Randal Pinkett's *Campus CEO* is an indispensable tool to help the student entrepreneur create a successful business plan for life, both in and out of school. It helps students take their passions above and beyond the four walls of formal education and into a promising future of business excellence. I highly recommend this book"
—**Sean Covey, Author of *The 7 Habits of Highly Effective Teens***

"A great book with a timely message. Our education system produces employees—that's why *Campus CEO* will create more millionaires!"
—**Robert Kiyosaki, Entrepreneur, Investor, Educator, and Author of *Rich Dad, Poor Dad***

CAMPUS CEO

THE STUDENT ENTREPRENEUR'S GUIDE TO LAUNCHING
A MULTIMILLION-DOLLAR BUSINESS

RANDAL PINKETT

KAPLAN PUBLISHING

This book is dedicated to: my fellow Campus CEOs—Dallas, Jeffrey, Aldwyn, Raqiba, and especially Lawrence—for turning a dream into reality and, most important, for your true brotherhood and sisterhood at every step along the way; all of the members of my family, including my mother, Elizabeth, my brother, Daniel, and my late father, Leslie, for shaping me to become the man I am today; and my loving wife, Zahara, for your commitment to me and your vision in encouraging my pursuit of *The Apprentice.*

Editorial Director: Jennifer Farthing
Acquisitions Editor: Karen Murphy
Senior Managing Editor, Production: Jack Kiburz
Typesetter: Todd Bowman

Published by Kaplan Publishing,
a division of Kaplan, Inc.

Printed in the United States of America

07 08 09 10 9 8 7 6 5 4 3 2 1

Library of Congress Cataloging-in-Publication Data

Pinkett, Randal.
   Campus CEO : the student entrepreneur's guide to launching a multimillion-dollar business / Randal Pinkett.
     p. cm.
   Includes index.
   ISBN-13: 978-1-4195-9371-0
   ISBN-10: 1-4195-9371-4
   1. New business enterprises. 2. Student-owned business enterprises. 3. Entrepreneurship. I. Title.
   HD62.5.P556 2007
   658.1'1--dc22   2006038087

Acknowledgments

Because *Campus CEO* is a reflection of my life and the lives of others, it represents more than just a book to me. It is also a tribute to the noteworthy efforts of countless men and women who contributed both directly and indirectly to its content and its ethos. So while I recognize several of these individuals below, these acknowledgments are but a fraction of all those who truly deserve my thanks.

To my book agent, Earl Cox, thank you for your vision, experience, and acumen in putting all of the pieces of the puzzle together to bring this book to fruition. To Lynette Khalfani, thank you for your tireless efforts, dedication, and genuine enthusiasm for this book. To my public relations manager, Tuwisha Rogers, thank you for your capable leadership in coordinating the numerous moving parts associated with this book and far beyond. To the great team at Kaplan, including John Polstein, Barry Tonoff, Courtney Goethals, Jack Kiburz, Jennifer Farthing, Carina Wong, and Todd Bowman, thank you all for your dedicated efforts; and special thanks to Karen Murphy, for your outstanding editorial support and camaraderie throughout the entire process; Dino Battista, for your strong marketing direction; and Maureen McMahon, for your overall leadership and sincere interest in supporting this project. To the wonderful team at Rose Communications including Victoria Grantham and Rosemary Ostmann, thank you for your hardworking efforts to promote this book to students everywhere. To Michael Simmons, Josh Shaw, and Erike Mayo, thank you for your editorial feedback as fellow Campus CEOs and entrepreneurs. To the Dowd Agency led by Jim Dowd, and Noelle-Elaine Media led by Renée Warren, Kirsten Hill, and Danielle Grassi, thank you for your continued work as the best public relations team in the business. To all of the Campus CEOs who willingly offered their experiences, thank you for sharing your stories for the benefit of others. To the professors, administrators, and staff at Rutgers, Oxford, and MIT, thank you for supporting my academic and entrepreneurial aspirations. To the talented men and women from MBS and BCT, including Dallas, Aldwyn, Raqiba, Shawn, Sekou, Desira, Shantell, Taifa, Michelle, Melissa, Andrea, Rodney,

Barry, Marlon, Ian, Shawn, Tara, Kenya, Lilliana, Jolanda, Ian, Latonya, David, Antwuan, Vasya, Eyobe, Macary, Perryne, and Stephanie, as well as Michon of Shared Demands, thank you for your commitment to me and to building an institution. To my longtime friend, Wayne Abbott, thank you for inspiring a generation of black engineers to become entrepreneurs, and thank you to the Abbott family. To my close friend and business partner, Lawrence Hibbert, thank you for your brotherhood, for your feedback on this book, and for allowing me the space to write it. To my brother and friend, Dr. Jeffrey Robinson of New York University, thank you for your expert feedback as a professor of entrepreneurship, and for the love and support you and your family have shown me since our years at Rutgers. To my late father, Leslie Pinkett, thank you for continuing to watch over me, in ways seen and unseen. To my brother, Daniel Pinkett, thank you for inspiring me to follow in your positive footsteps. To my mother, Elizabeth Pinkett, thank you for being a constant source of strength, showing me the power of faith, and raising me to always "do it right or don't do it at all." To the Elliott, Pinkett, Wadud, and Daniels families, including my mother-in-law, Safiyah Wadud, and my father-in-law, Rufus Daniels, thank you for your love and support of Zahara and me. To my wife, Zahara Wadud-Pinkett, thank you for always standing by me, and for your ongoing love and commitment to me. And last, but certainly not least, I must thank God with whom *all things* are possible.

—Randal Pinkett
www.randalpinkett.com

Contents

About the Author

Randal Pinkett is an accomplished entrepreneur, speaker, scholar, and author who firmly believes that "for those to whom much is given, much is expected." He is the chairman and CEO of BCT Partners (*www.bctpartners.com*), a multimillion-dollar management, technology, and policy consulting services firm based in Newark, New Jersey. BCT specializes in the areas of housing, community development, economic development, health care, human services, and education. As the Season 4 winner of NBC's *The Apprentice*, Randal served as an executive with Trump Entertainment Resorts in Atlantic City. Randal holds five academic degrees: a BS in electrical engineering from Rutgers as a championship track and field athlete; an MS in computer science from Oxford as a Rhodes Scholar; and an MS in electrical engineering, MBA, and PhD from MIT as a NSF Graduate Fellow and Lucent Cooperative Research Fellow. Randal has received numerous recognitions, including the Next Generation Leadership Fellowship, Leadership New Jersey Fellowship, and the National Society of Black Engineers–Member of the Year Award. He has been featured on nationally televised programs such as *Today*, *Live with Regis and Kelly*, and on CNN. A sought-after public speaker for public, private, and nonprofit organizations, Randal serves on the board of directors for the New Jersey Public Policy Research Institute and the Nonprofit Technology Enterprise Network. He is a spokesperson for Autism Speaks, the National Black MBA Association, New Jersey Reads, and Junior Achievement of New York. Randal is a proud member of First Baptist Church in Somerset, New Jersey, where he is happily married to his wife Zahara. Learn more at *www.randalpinkett.com*.

Introduction
New-School Thinking—
The Entrepreneur's Mindset

Who says you have to wait until after graduation to earn a decent living or to launch the business of your dreams? Wouldn't it be great if you could have your fantasy job *now*, while you're in school, and not years from now when you're out in the "real world"? Believe it or not, you can have an enviable career *immediately*—not at some distant point in the future—just by starting your own business while you're still a student. This applies to all students, from the gifted 14-year-old preparing for high school to the 55-year-old seasoned executive returning to graduate school for an MBA. Student entrepreneurship can change your world for the better. I know, because I'm living proof of how being a "Campus CEO" can be a springboard to a richer, more rewarding life—personally and professionally.

■ BOOK SMARTS + BUSINESS SAVVY = *APPRENTICE* VICTORY

Many of you may know me as the winner of the fourth season of NBC's hit reality show, *The Apprentice.* More than a million people tried out to become Donald Trump's handpicked protégé. Ultimately, only 18 of us were chosen for the TV show, and I ended up outlasting the 17 other job candidates to hear Trump say "You're hired!" As you might suspect, being selected by "The Donald" to work for Trump Entertainment Resorts in Atlantic City, New Jersey, meant newfound fame, exciting career opportunities, and a hefty six-figure salary. What most viewers didn't know, however, was that I already owned my own multimillion-dollar business—a venture I started with a couple of college classmates while I was a student at Rutgers University in New Jersey. My company, BCT Partners, specializes in management consulting, technology consulting, and policy research for government agencies, Fortune 500 companies, and philanthropic organizations. We've provided strategic planning, information technology, and organizational development solutions for federal, state, and local government agencies such as the U.S. Small Business Administration and the U.S. Department of Housing and Urban Development; global corporations such as General Motors, Johnson & Johnson, and Citigroup; and large foundations such as the Ford Foundation, the Rockefeller Foundation, and the Annie E. Casey Foundation.

While launching my first venture on campus at Rutgers, I maintained a 3.9 grade point average, was captain of the track-and-field team, and was named an NCAA Academic All-American. During my collegiate tenure, I also became a Rhodes scholar, earned a total of five degrees—including an MBA and a PhD— and managed to complete all my studies completely debt-free. Read that last sentence again. It wasn't a misprint. I said that even after earning five degrees and studying at some of top schools in the world, including Rutgers, Oxford, and MIT, I graduated without one red cent in student loans or credit card debt. That's no small feat, especially since the average undergraduate today leaves school saddled with $20,000 in student loans and roughly $3,000 on his or her credit cards. Thankfully, I won't have to pledge my firstborn to Visa or spend 15 to 20 years paying off the folks at Sallie Mae.

■ THE BENEFITS OF STUDENT ENTREPRENEURSHIP

What has been the secret to my success? A big part of it was becoming a student entrepreneur. I launched no less than five businesses during my years on various campuses, and these experiences gave me equal doses of academic training and business savvy. I say this not to brag but to let you know that you don't have to wait until *after* graduation to find a career, make money, and begin doing what you love. Instead, you can blaze a pathway to success and generate income now by starting your own business while on campus. In doing so, you'll take advantage of that unique period in your life—while you're a student—when a range of once-in-a-lifetime perks, advantages, and resources are available to you. As a student entrepreneur, you'll have access to a number of free resources, from office equipment and computer hardware to graphic design services and office space. You'll enjoy a wealth of information and tools right at your fingertips, courtesy of your library, business school, career center, and other campus resource centers. You'll have virtually unrestricted, one-on-one contact with some of the best "consultants" money can buy—and you don't have to pay these consultants a dime for their expertise because they happen to be the very same professors and teachers you're learning from every day. You'll also be eligible to enter business competition plans, meet influential and connected alumni, and rub shoulders with venture capitalists looking to finance promising start-ups originating on campuses just like yours. The list of benefits for student entrepreneurs goes on and on. I'll tell you about all of them throughout *Campus CEO*.

■ NO "OLD-SCHOOL" THINKING HERE

If you're a student and you've already launched a company—or are currently mulling over an idea—the notion of creating a business while you're hitting the books may seem like a no-brainer. But to others, the idea of becoming a student entrepreneur might appear to be a radical concept. For generations, parents, educators, and others have repeated the message that the chief reason to get an education is to land a job. The thinking was to finish high school and then go on to college. With a degree in hand, you'd be more attractive to prospective employers and you'd set yourself apart from those who didn't have a college education. But in the past decade or so, changes have occurred that completely turned that "old-school" thinking on its head:

- *College costs rose dramatically.* Any student today knows that the financial pressures of college can sometimes be more taxing than the academic rigors of campus life. It's easy to see why that's the case: The average annual price tag to attend a four-year public school in America now tops $12,000, according to the College Board. It's more than double that amount—roughly $29,000 a year—if you're at a private school.
- *Student loans escalated.* To help pay for rising college costs, many people are taking on unprecedented levels of student loans. Nellie Mae reports that the median student loan debt is $20,000 for those who've attended four-year colleges; the median debt load is $52,000 for people who've finished grad school.
- *Credit card debt among college students skyrocketed.* Widespread credit use has become the American way. The typical student in the United States owes nearly $3,000 on credit cards.
- *The job market became a lot tougher.* Although government figures put the unemployment rate at around 5 percent, it can be difficult (even for college grads) to snag a good-paying job and keep it. Many of you know family members who worked for companies that have been downsized.

■ The Student Entrepreneurship Movement

According to a census of entrepreneurship education by the Ewing Marion Kauffman Foundation, more than 80 percent of two-year and four-year colleges currently offer courses and/or programs in entrepreneurship. And the interest is not just among business students.

The graph that follows shows data from the Kauffman Foundation concerning the percentage of graduate students who have any plans of ever "working independently" or "starting their own business." As you can see, it is greater than 50 percent across all areas of study.

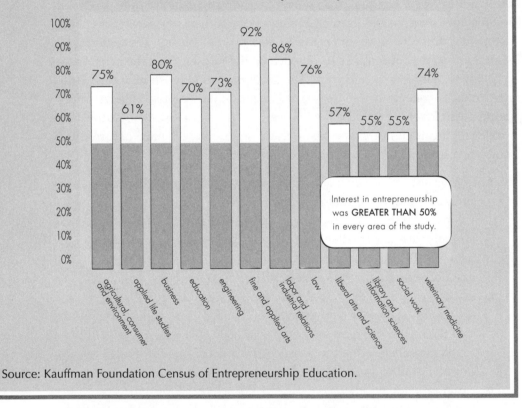

Student Interest in Entrepreneurship

Interest in entrepreneurship was **GREATER THAN 50%** in every area of the study.

Source: Kauffman Foundation Census of Entrepreneurship Education.

Depending on your age, it's possible that you, too, may have received a pink slip.

■ *Entrepreneurship exploded on college campuses and among youth in general.* Back in 1970, only 16 business schools in the United States offered classes in entrepreneurship. Today, more than 825 schools have entrepreneurship courses. Entrepreneurship is also a hot trend among high school and middle school students. Survey results from the Young Entrepreneur Foundation survey found that 90 percent of teachers and guidance counselors say their students are interested in becoming entrepreneurs. However, 75 percent of them say their students have no idea where to turn. *Campus CEO* offers these students a road map.

■ NEW-SCHOOL THINKING: THE ENTREPRENEUR'S MINDSET

In the 21st century, entrepreneurship isn't just a goal or a mission, it's an empowering mindset. People often think of entrepreneurship as simply owning a business, but really the art of being entrepreneurial is about adopting a mindset and belief system that there's always a way to use creativity, passion, and inspired vision to create value in the world—or to take something that already exists and make it better. You can easily spot a person with the heart and mindset of a true entrepreneur. Beyond possessing seemingly boundless passion, entrepreneurs have the following characteristics:

- *Creativity*—possessing an inventive or clever approach to situations
- *Resourcefulness*—subscribing to the notion that he or she can turn nothing into something
- *Courage*—taking calculated risks while maintaining a trailblazer's mentality and the belief that he or she can achieve anything
- *Vision*—seeing and seeking opportunity where others don't
- *Perseverance*—maintaining a healthy acceptance of failure as a way to learn and strengthen oneself

Throughout *Campus CEO,* I'll share with you how you can develop the "entrepreneur's mindset"—or deepen it if you already possess these traits. Adopting the entrepreneur's mindset can help you achieve exponentially greater success in life—personally and professionally—regardless of whether you ever start a business. Indeed, one of the key messages I hope you'll derive from this book is that entrepreneurship is not exclusively about owning a business: it's about using your talents to make a positive impact in your areas of influence, and leveraging all the resources at your disposal to create value for the greatest number of people you can reach. As a result, the person who creates a nonprofit to help cancer patients, the individual who dedicates himself

■ Seven Student Myths about Entrepreneurship

Here's what I've heard some (misguided) college students say about becoming entrepreneurs:

Myth #1: Being an entrepreneur is very risky.
Fact: Going into business for yourself these days is really no more risky than taking a corporate job, where you could get laid off at any time, have your benefits slashed, or be forced to work overtime without being compensated for those extra hours. Furthermore, if you are a student living on campus, you are likely avoiding certain potentially significant expenses, such as a mortgage or a family to support.

Myth #2: I'm too young to own my own business.
Fact: Youth can work to your advantage. Leverage your passion, energy, and enthusiasm for your work and your age doesn't have to be a hindrance at all. In fact, being young can work in your favor from a work-productivity standpoint. How many 60-year-old guys do you know who are able to toil away for 14 hours straight, day in and day out? Not that you want to maintain that kind of schedule all the time, but in some cases that kind of intense work is necessary when you're an entrepreneur. Many experts believe that the best innovators are, in fact, young people.

Myth #3: I'm too inexperienced.
Fact: You may not have the same corporate experience as a more seasoned workplace employee, or even of someone who's been running his or her own show for a few years, but your so-called "inexperience" means you can approach problems with a fresh set of eyes and a unique perspective, and you won't be bogged down by the "We've always done it that way" type of thinking that trips up other "more experienced" people. Also, running a business is an incredible way to gain valuable work experience in the same way you might pursue a part-time job or internship.

Myth #4: It's not the right time.
Fact: There's probably never been a better time to become an entrepreneur. As a student, you have a flexible schedule and flexible hours, in addition to large blocks of time during semester breaks to cultivate your business. Plus, you have access to campus resources that are immediately at your fingertips.

Myth #5: If I start a business, my grades will definitely suffer.
Fact: Many campus CEOs report the exact opposite phenomena. Running a business requires discipline and organization, which will spill over into other areas of your life. In my own case, I graduated with a 3.9 GPA, so running my campus business definitely didn't hurt me academically.

Myth #6: Student businesses are only small-time enterprises or mom-and-pop–type operations.
Fact: The reality is that a significant number of campus ventures have mushroomed into major, global brands. Think Google, Dell,

(continued)

■ Seven Student Myths about Entrepreneurship

and Microsoft, to name a few. Moreover, many student businesses have the very real potential to be extremely high-growth operations that last well past your graduation date.

Myth #7: I need a lot of money to start a business.

While a lack of financial capital is often cited as one of the greatest challenges to starting a business, most businesses are typically launched with modest amounts of money and little or no investment capital. This was indeed the case for my partners and me as we started

with almost nothing. So don't take yourself out of the game just because you don't have a lot of money.

If you're scared to take the plunge, or if you have a bunch of naysayers or unsupportive people around you, it may be hard to see the truth about these myths—at least until much later when you're further along in your career. But believe me when I say that these misconceptions can be dream killers, stopping you from starting a business based on misinformation or ignorance. You're smarter than that.

to preserving the environment, and the performance artist who tirelessly brings her craft to underprivileged youth are no less entrepreneurial than the founder of a pet store or even the corporate receptionist who figures out a way to answer customer phone calls in a more efficient manner. In pursuing their respective interests, each one exhibits the entrepreneur's mindset. And regardless of what you're studying in school, so can you.

■ WHO NEEDS COLLEGE ANYWAY?

Let me say that I'm very much aware of the raging debate going on right now among entrepreneurially minded students across the United States, and indeed across the globe. Many question the need for a higher education. They say that dropping out of college is actually a good thing because it will get you started and focused on your business ventures that much sooner. For those of you who might be contemplating leaving school because you're itching to make your mark in the business world, let me first say that I applaud your enthusiasm and passion. And to be honest, even though I happen to hold five degrees, I do not believe that having a degree is mandatory to be successful in life.

Nevertheless, for the budding entrepreneur, college often offers a support-ive training ground as well as an ideal launchpad for a new enterprise. Even if you ultimately decide not to pursue the life of a business owner, I encour-age you to experience the richness of college life. The academic environment opens up a host of social avenues and professional connections that are tough to match anyplace else. Additionally, your years of higher education should help you grow and mature as an individual as you tackle a variety of intellectual challenges, civic pursuits, community activities, and personal endeavors.

If you detest the thought of relying heavily on credit cards and student loans, wasting away at a meaningless part-time job, or living on whatever money your parents can afford to send you to survive, don't despair. Money problems shouldn't force you to skip meals, become roommates with half a dozen other students, or take dead-end jobs that have no relevance to your college program or career goals. You also shouldn't have to work full-time for someone else if you don't want to. There's a better way—a far better way to navigate the aca-demic world. This book offers a plan to help you not just survive but also to thrive during your college years.

■ HOW TO USE THIS BOOK

I've written *Campus CEO* as a step-by-step guide that any student can use to launch a moneymaking business. I also want this book to be valuable and practical to all students because that is what entrepreneurially minded students want. I realize that you are already getting plenty of theory in the classroom. Therefore, *Campus CEO* is also loaded with lots of specific real-life informa-tion, proven strategies, business concepts, and little-known tips to develop your thinking about entrepreneurship in general. After all, being more creative and innovative in life can help you in immeasurable ways, regardless of whether you ever launch your own business.

While much of the guidance in this book is aimed specifically at under-graduate and graduate students, even high school and middle school students can benefit from this book's advice. I believe in cultivating the entrepreneurial spirit at an early age. Even the federal government now recognizes the need to encourage young people to consider becoming business owners. That's why the House of Representatives passed legislation establishing National Entre-preneurship Week (*www.entrepreneurshipweekusa.com*), for which I am a proud national spokesperson. Every year you can expect to see numerous activities and events all designed to cultivate the entrepreneurial spirit among young people between the ages of 15 and 25.

Campus CEO is broken down into four sections, following the cycle of starting and growing a business.

Part One, "Starting Your Business," will explain everything you need to know about starting your business, from figuring the best time to launch (does it matter if you launch in the spring or fall?) to gaining any necessary approvals from the campus administration (what should you do if your business idea gets a thumbs-down?) to the kinds of businesses typically started by students. College-bound students will want to pay particularly close attention to Chapter 1, "All Campuses Are Not Created Equal." This chapter will help you evaluate how strong a given campus is when it comes to teaching entrepreneurship, as well as providing the critical support, tools, and connections that developing entrepreneurs need. By the way, if you're already on a college campus, you're probably wishing you had this book before you picked a school. But don't sweat it. Even current college students will learn smart strategies for making the most of your campus environment, particularly by leveraging your school's unique strengths and bolstering those areas where your campus may be weak on the entrepreneurship front. I will also explain how you can gain the technology edge—particularly by leveraging the awesome and free tools available to students—that will give your business a leg up over the competition.

Part Two, "Financing Your Business," explains the ins and outs of finding lenders, investors, and others who supply cash to campus-based start-ups, even at state schools and two-year colleges, not just at top-ranked campuses such as Harvard, Yale, or Stanford. You'll also learn the basics of creating financial statements; advice about how to manage cash flow; and safeguards to protect your business from disruptions, disaster, or financial ruin.

Part Three, "Balancing Business and Education," offers a wealth of ideas that will help you balance your work, social, and academic life; maintain top grades; and graduate on time. You'll discover how to integrate academics and entrepreneurship by profiting from your professors and mentors, using your studies and research projects as the foundation for business ventures, and leveraging your student status to take advantage of myriad on-campus and off-campus free or low-cost resources.

In the final section, Part Four, "Growing Your Business," you'll learn how to use the campus media, local news, Internet, and other outlets to market and promote your business on campus; and how to expand beyond your own campus, perhaps spreading your business to other schools, across country or even across the world. The final chapter of the book details the top ten mistakes that Campus CEOs make—and tells you how to avoid or fix those blunders. And trust me, you will mess up at some point along the way. I certainly did. Throughout this book, I'll also share with you where I went awry, and what I did to put myself back on the path to success. Once you're done reading, you'll be able to find additional information and resources by visiting the book's Web site, CampusCEO.com (*www.campusceo.com*), where you can also tell me your story!

■ WHY "FAILURE" IS OK WITH THE ENTREPRENEUR'S MINDSET

There is a great saying that "Failure is not falling down, but staying down." If you're serious about being an entrepreneur, you should learn as soon as possible that some degree of failure is not only likely, it's a *necessary* part of building your business. So if at any point you get knocked down—maybe a bank turns down your loan application, you choke during your elevator pitch to an important angel investor, or a business you were sure would be a winner turns out to be a loser—the key is to get right back up again, dust yourself off, and figure out where you went wrong. In business, it's not how many times you fall down, it's how many times you get back up. If you possess the emotional wherewithal to do that, or at least have the capacity to develop that kind of internal fortitude, you've already won half the battle. It's only through your failures that you'll truly learn some of the best lessons that life—including the business world—has to offer.

■ JOINING THE RANKS OF THE RICH AND FAMOUS

Based on what you know so far, do you think you have the guts to become a Campus CEO? If you answered "Yes," please know that you'll be joining some pretty elite company in starting a business as a student. Across the country, tens of thousands of other bright, ambitious students have done the same thing. In fact, nearly two-thirds of college students intend to become entrepreneurs at some point in their careers, according to the U.S. Small Business Administration. You'll read about dozens of enterprising young entrepreneurs throughout *Campus CEO.* You may not instantly recognize them or their businesses, but don't be surprised if one day they become household names. In fact, if you follow the advice in this book, you may become a household name too! It's not a farfetched possibility, especially considering the legacy of a number of other very well-known Campus CEOs, all of whom first made their mark while in school. Among the names you'll certainly know are:

■ **Companies Started by Campus CEOs**	
Microsoft	Napster
Dell	Tripod
Facebook	TheGlobe.com
Google	Plaxo
Kinko's	Student Advantage
Yahoo!	Netscape
Federal Express	Pizza Hut

- *Sean "Diddy" Combs.* If you're a music lover, chances are you're hip to the fact that this music, fashion, and entertainment mogul founded Bad Boy Records and launched his own clothing line. But did you know that Diddy got his start selling tickets to parties and music events while he was a student at Howard University in the late 1980s?
- *Larry Page and Sergey Brin.* Before these two Internet billionaires founded Google, they developed a new system of Internet search engines in their college dorms at Stanford.
- *Bill Gates.* As the founder of Microsoft, Gates is the richest man on the planet. But guess where he cut his teeth in the software world? That's right: in school. Gates honed his programming skills on the minicomputer of his Seattle high school, Lakeside School. He then developed his software skills at Harvard, which he attended before dropping out in his junior year to focus his efforts on software development.
- *Michael Dell.* Another billionaire, Dell started a computer company called PC's Limited from his room in Jester Hall while an 18-year-old student at the University of Texas at Austin. A year later, Dell dropped out of college to devote himself to running the business full-time, and in 1987 he officially changed the name of his enterprise to Dell Computer Corporation. In 2006, *Forbes* magazine named Dell one of the world's richest people, putting his net worth at an estimated $16 billion.
- *Frederick Smith.* The founder of Federal Express dreamed up the idea for this global transportation and delivery company while he was a student. Smith wrote a paper on the idea of FedEx before receiving his bachelor's degree in economics from Yale in 1966. Some believed such a venture would fail, but FedEx later became the world's first overnight express delivery company.

You may or may not long to be rich and famous like these people, but if that is your goal, it sure won't hurt you to become entrepreneurially minded. Doing so has definitely opened doors for me. I'm proud to say that I count myself among a growing breed of Campus CEOs—those talented individuals who recognize the importance of combining both educational knowledge and business smarts. What I've done thus far in my life may be remarkable in the eyes of some people, but it's also totally achievable for you, too. Any would-be entrepreneur can do it. In fact, it's my hope that the information I share with you in *Campus CEO* will equip you to duplicate—and even surpass—my success.

Regardless of your major, background, or area of interest, *Campus CEO* will show you how to turn your academic and professional dreams into reality. If your idea of the "Big Woman on Campus" or the "Big Man on Campus" is the popular athlete that scored the winning goal or basket in last week's game, get ready to change your thinking. In today's environment, the Big Woman or Big Man on Campus is the Campus CEO—you know, the one who's running his or her own company, living it up, and getting paid! If you're ready to join the ranks of other ambitious, successful Campus CEOs, turn the page and let's get down to business!

■ PART 1

Starting Your Business

All Campuses
Are Not Created Equal—
Weighing Your Options

During my career, I would estimate that I've addressed hundreds of thousands of students at speaking engagements at more than 100 different schools in the United States and overseas. It's always a thrill for me to meet students from all ages, backgrounds, interests, and abilities. One of the benefits of maintaining a busy speaking calendar is that it allows me to hear firsthand from entrepreneurially minded students about the strengths and weaknesses of their campuses as they pertain to supporting student entrepreneurship. Based on these interactions, I can tell you unequivocally that all campuses are not created equal when it comes to helping you become a first-rate Campus CEO.

So let me do a little Monday-morning quarterbacking here and tell you all the things I wish I'd known when I was a high school student picking a college campus—one that would have bolstered my college business activities to the fullest. Some of you may not have adult mentors or role models to push you toward owning your own business. Even if entrepreneurship runs in your family, I'm going to give you a heads-up on what you should be thinking about as you approach or attend college, and evaluate various campuses as starting grounds for entrepreneurs. The goal of this chapter is to help you assess any college's potential as a business headquarters before you even set foot on campus.

What about if you're already on campus? You're still going to learn plenty about how to make the most of any campus environment. Furthermore, I'll warn you now: after you analyze the good, the bad, and the ugly at your college, some of you are going to wind up thinking: My campus could do a lot better when it comes to helping young entrepreneurs! Well, before you start to organize a massive student protest, or rush over to the registrar's office to demand a full refund of your tuition, take a moment to think about this: Maybe it's true that your college has much to be desired when compared to other hotbeds of entrepreneurial activity. But maybe it's time somebody (hint: you) did something to shake things up. Who says you can't be the one to start a club for would-be business owners? Why can't you get busy putting your college on the map when it comes to student entrepreneurship? After all, isn't that part of being a CEO—bringing new ideas, products, and services to the public? Aren't you ready to create something new that didn't exist before? Well, this may be your chance to really get in on the ground floor of a new venture and put your unique stamp on things—by starting an entrepreneurial revolution on campus.

■ BUT I HAVEN'T EVEN DECLARED MY MAJOR YET!

At this point, if you have any doubts about whether you've got what it takes to make it as an entrepreneur, don't throw in the towel just yet. You might be totally clueless about a possible college major, or uncertain about what potential business you could launch. If that's the case, relax. Some of you are probably even thinking: I still don't even know what the heck I want to do with the rest of my life! Again, put those anxieties aside for now. If you even have a tiny little inkling in the back of your mind that you *might* want to own your own business someday, this chapter is going to aid you tremendously. It's going to help you see the possibilities and resources available at certain campuses—and within college life in general. At the very least, by the time you're finished reading this chapter, you'll have a much better idea of the type of campus you'd want to attend (and the type of schools you'd like to avoid) if entrepreneurship is in your future.

■ TEN WAYS TO EVALUATE CAMPUS ENTREPRENEURSHIP

There are ten ways to evaluate a potential school if you're interested in student entrepreneurship. Actually, there are probably dozens of ways to do so, but you *do* have tests to prepare for, papers to write, and, not to mention, a business to get off the ground, right? So we'll stay with the most important criteria you should be looking at when assessing potential campuses or your current college. The ten critical areas are:

1. National entrepreneurship rankings
2. Faculty
3. Courses and overall focus on entrepreneurship
4. Specialty offerings
5. Business plan competitions
6. Investor activities
7. Awards and grants
8. Campus-specific considerations
9. Incubator programs
10. Alumni resources

Let's take a look at each of these areas in much more depth. As we continue, remember to be brutally honest about how your own campus (or potential campus) stacks up in each of these areas.

1. National Entrepreneurship Rankings—Or What's Your Campus's Business Rep?

Whenever you visit a college campus, you can expect the campus administration, staff, and faculty to put their collective best foot forward and try to present the school in the best possible light. Well, it's one thing for a college to boast about how great it is at helping student entrepreneurs, but it's another matter entirely for an independent third party to give a school props. And a variety of national magazines do just that by ranking hundreds of college campuses as entrepreneurial destinations. For instance, *FORTUNE Small Business*, Forbes.com, *Entrepreneur* magazine, and *U.S. News & World Report*, all weigh in on who they think makes the grade. In a *FORTUNE Small Business* article from March 8, 2006, writer Patricia B. Gray selected "10 Cool Colleges for Entrepreneurs." Among one of the stellar schools that made the cut: the University of Rochester, for integrating entrepreneurship courses in virtually every department on campus—even in music, religion, and engineering. Also in 2006, *Entrepreneur* magazine highlighted Columbia, DePaul, and Ohio State University as standout campuses, along with a host of other notable schools. Meanwhile, *U.S. News & World Report* chimed in too with its own listing, citing Babson College as number one, an enviable reputation the campus has earned among nearly every national ranking of entrepreneur programs.

■ Entrepoint's Top Colleges for Entrepreneurship

Beyond the magazine listings, there's another ranking source you might want to consider. TechKnowledgePoint Corporation partnered with *Entrepreneur* magazine in 2006 to produce "the most in-depth rankings in entrepreneurship" called Entrepoint (*www.entrepoint. com*). Although these in-depth rankings aren't free (as of this writing they cost students $19), they are perhaps the most comprehensive information source available profiling the entrepreneurship programs at hundreds of colleges and universities in the United States. For example, when you buy the Entrepoint college rankings, you also get access to Entrepoint's detailed school directory that is loaded with 14 pages of statistics for each school, interactive tools, and articles about entrepreneurship. The rankings tell you everything about a school: from the size of its endowment to the number of corporate sponsors it has to the total number of business-related centers available on campus and more. All in all, not a bad way to spend $19.

But clearly, rankings are just one way to measure a school. In fact, relying on rankings exclusively may be the lazy way—or at least just a quick-and-dirty way to get an overview of what other people think. But what do *you* think based on what you're looking for in a school? Read on, because the criteria that follows may give you more insights than a who's who listing of business schools or entrepreneurship programs found in a ranking report.

2. Faculty

You should definitely check out the faculty carefully at any college you attend or plan to attend. Start by asking how many professors teach entrepreneurship on campus. The answer to this question will be an eye-opener. If you hear an answer like "one" or "two," you know right off the bat that this school probably isn't an entrepreneurship powerhouse. That's not to say, however, that the college may not have other strong areas of appeal or interest for the aspiring entrepreneur. But believe me, it helps to have a supportive, knowledgeable faculty to teach you a thing or two. The next thing you should try to determine is how good the faculty is—whether it's 2 professors, 25, or more who are teaching entrepreneurship. Needless to say, the term *good* might be a bit speculative. By *good,* I mean, how experienced they are. Have any of them been entrepreneurs in the past? Have they dealt with the real-life issues that business owners face? Can they relate firsthand to the hassles associated with launching a start-up? Again, if you have professors who can share some "in the trenches" wisdom, you're golden. If not, you may have to look elsewhere for serious mentorship and advice. It's also worth asking about their connections. Do they have lots of friends or associates in the business world? If so, you may ask them to facilitate an introduction. Thereafter, it's your responsibility to make sure your professor's friend or associate gets to know you. Of course, you should take time to get to know your professors and I'll provide some specific tips on how to do this in Chapter 12.

3. Courses and Overall Focus on Entrepreneurship

Some campuses truly stress entrepreneurship as an integral part of student life, while others provide only minimal—if any—support and resources for the aspiring business owner. In 1970, a national survey of business schools found only 16 courses offered in entrepreneurship. Today, more than 2,000 colleges and universities around the country either teach entrepreneurship or offer some form of entrepreneurship training, according to the Ewing Marion Kauffman Foundation. Your overall objective when looking at the coursework offered at a school should be to size up the campus's commitment to an entrepreneurship program. This can range from introductory courses such as "Introduction to Entrepreneurship" and "Writing a Business Plan" to more advanced topics such as "Technology Transfer" and "Legal Issues for Entrepreneurs."

Depending on whether you're an undergraduate or graduate student—or maybe even a high school or middle school student—the entrepreneurship coursework and curriculum offered could run the gamut from intense to virtually nonexistent. Take Harvard University, in Cambridge, Massachusetts, for example. Harvard has 17 endowed chairs in entrepreneurship. All the school's MBA students are required to take an entrepreneurship course during their first semester. To teach students the art of starting their own businesses, Harvard relies heavily on "case studies." But the school has updated its approach by bringing in CEOs of the companies under discussion. This adds a modern-day component and a real-life element to the coursework, especially since recent visitors have hailed from fields as varied as the airline industry (David Neeleman, CEO of JetBlue) and fashion design (Kate Spade, CEO of Kate Spade).

Entrepreneurship centers. Another indicator of your school's over-all focus on entrepreneurship is the presence of an entrepreneurship center. According to the *Journal of Small Business Management*, in "An Examination of Entrepreneurship Centers in the United States: A National Survey," this means "having a Center for Entrepreneurship which may use titles such as 'Free Enterprise,' 'Family Business,' or 'Innovation Center,' academic curriculum in entrepreneurship, external outreach activities, and faculty that perform research in the field of entrepreneurship." Entrepreneurship centers can provide a range of resources, including:

- Undergraduate and graduate courses
- Connections to business mentors and alumni
- Technology commercialization
- Internships
- Venture capital
- Journals and newsletters
- Student organizations
- Business plan competitions
- Guest speakers, special workshops, and seminars
- Conferences
- General advice and counseling

For example, the Institute for Entrepreneurial Studies (IES) is the entrepreneurship center at the University of Illinois at Chicago. There, students can explore a range of entrepreneurship classes, attend annual symposia on entrepreneurship, consult with entrepreneurship faculty, and compete in the IES business plan competition. IES also offers a certificate in business administration for practicing entrepreneurs and sponsors the Chicago Area Entrepreneurship Hall of Fame.

Student entrepreneurship organizations. Also look for student organizations focused on entrepreneurship. There may be a campus-specific student group such as the Entrepreneurship Association at the University of Wisconsin–Madison, or you may find an affiliate of a national or international organization such as the following:

- Collegiate Entrepreneurs' Organization (*www.c-e-o.org*)—CEO is a global entrepreneurship network serving more than 500 colleges and universities that is housed at the aforementioned IES. CEO's mission is to inform, support, and inspire college students to be entrepreneurial. CEO also has an elevator-pitch competition of interest to young entrepreneurs.

- Students In Free Enterprise (*www.sife.org*)—SIFE is a global nonprofit organization active in 47 countries and territories. Working in partnership with scores of businesses and higher education institutions from around the world, SIFE establishes student teams on university campuses. Faculty advisors lead the teams and students are challenged to develop community outreach projects that touch on one of SIFE's four educational topics: market economics, entrepreneurship, personal financial success skills, and business ethics.

- Future Business Leaders of America (*www.fbla.org*)—FBLA's operates chapters at middle schools and high schools, and on college and university campuses through its Phi Beta Lambda (FBLA-PBL) association. FBLA-PBL's mission is to bring business and education together in a positive working relationship through innovative leadership and career development programs.

- Delta Epsilon Chi (*www.deltaepsilonchi.org*)—Delta Epsilon Chi is an international organization (U.S. and Canada) for college students with an emphasis on business-related areas including marketing, management, and entrepreneurship. Student chapters organize activities to promote leadership, networking, experiential learning, career and professional development, community service, and recognition.

- Business Professionals of America (*www.bpa.org*)—BPA's mission is to contribute to the preparation of a world-class workforce through the advancement of leadership, citizenship, academic, and technological skills. BPA local chapters are organized in certain member states, according to middle school, secondary school, post-secondary, and associate divisions.

Small business development centers. Small business development centers (SBDCs) may also reflect your school's interest in entrepreneurship. SBDCs offer assistance to small business owners through training, seminars, loans, counseling, newsletters, publications, and various forms of technical assistance. A number of SBDCs are located on college campuses in partnership with the U.S. Small Business Administration. Given their focus on small business owners, which is not exclusive to the university population, some SBDCs work more closely with students than do others. Regardless, their presence alone can be of potential benefit to you. You can find out whether there is an SBDC near your current or prospective institution by visiting the America's Small Business Development Center Network's Web site (*www.asbdc-us.org*).

In summary, you should be able to tell by the academic environment how focused the campus is on entrepreneurial pursuits. If you track down an enterprise center, a department devoted to entrepreneurship, an entrepreneurship club, a small business development office, and so on, these types of resources suggest that entrepreneurship is an important part of the program at your school.

■ National Consortium of Entrepreneurship Centers

Beyond determining how serious your campus is when it comes to entrepreneurship curriculum, you should find out if your school belongs to the National Consortium of Entrepreneurship Centers (NCEC) (*www.nationalconsortium.org*). This group was founded in 1996 through the efforts of the University of Maryland and the Kauffman Foundation. The organization's goal is to provide a forum through which participating members can collaborate and communicate about the specific issues and challenges facing university-based entrepreneurship centers. The administrative home of the NCEC is the Johnson Center for Entrepreneurship & Innovation in the Kelley School of Business at Indiana University–Bloomington. The NCEC boasts 150 members whose college-based entrepreneurship centers span from up-and-coming players to well-established and nationally ranked programs.

---

4. Specialty Offerings

I truly believe that all campuses have something to offer. If you're smart and creative enough, you can leverage almost any asset at a college and make it work for you. Maybe you're interested in a college that is known to cater to older students, and you happen to fit that category. By all means, seek out what resources are available to you there. Or perhaps you are a female, a member of a minority group, or you have certain special interests; then you would do well to think about campuses that have specialty programs with strong appeal in these areas.

Here is just a sampling of how a few schools are developing special-interest programs:

- University of Texas–El Paso offers an up-and-coming Center for Hispanic Entrepreneurship.

- Florida International University in Miami has the largest minority enrollment of any institution in the United States and offers courses on international trade that promote starting ventures to facilitate trade with South and Central America and in the Caribbean.
- Howard University, in Washington, D.C., requires every incoming student to take part in what's called "Entrepreneur's Boot Camp" during orientation. This is an eight-hour course that highlights the history of entrepreneurship in the African-American community.
- Simmons College in Boston is the only women's business school in the United States and has launched an innovative, six-month entrepreneurship program tailored specifically to women. Applicants must have an MBA; most already have a decade of work experience.
- Sitting Bull College of Fort Yates, North Dakota, one of the first tribal colleges in America, has created a unique and much-needed program that teaches entrepreneurship to Native Americans and encourages them to create jobs on the Standing Rock Reservation, where the unemployment rate is an alarming 76 percent. At Sitting Bull, educators model some of their activities after the Amish in an attempt to duplicate the Amish tradition of remaining economically and culturally independent.
- The University of Colorado at Boulder offers a specialty "green" entrepreneurship program, encouraging students to create ecofriendly and socially responsible businesses. The school is aided by an active group of supportive, like-minded business leaders in the city's organic and natural-products industry.

5. Business Plan Competitions

Is there a business plan competition offered at your school? You can find a useful list of business plan competitions at *www.smallbusinessnotes.com/planning/competitions.html.* These types of competition allow you to present your business idea to a host of people: either faculty judges, student panelists, members of the corporate community, alumni, and sometimes venture capitalists looking to fund new ideas. Business plan competitions have become quite popular among active student entrepreneurs, mainly because they promise big dollars for those who win these very competitive contests. No matter where you are in the country, chances are there's a business plan competition offered within striking distance. While you do have to be either a full-time or part-time student to enter these competitions, in most cases you don't have to be enrolled at the particular school hosting the competition. In some cases you do, but even then you can usually team up with a student from that campus to be eligible to participate. Does it sound too good to be true? Check out some prominent business plan competitions worth knowing about:

- One of the best-known business plan competitions in the country, which I participated in during my years there, is the **MIT $100K Entrepreneurship Competition** (*www.mit100k.org*). At the MIT competition, six awards are given out. Two winners are chosen in two contests: the Venture Competition and the Entrepreneurship for Development Competition. Each winner banks a grand prize of $30,000. Then two runners-up are chosen in each contest, for a total of four runners-up, who each take home a $10,000 prize. That's enough cash to launch many an enterprise.

- New York University's Stern School of Business boasts one of the largest business plan competitions, currently valued at $150,000. Open to the greater NYU community, the **NYU Stern's Business Plan Competition** has a traditional track and a social entrepreneurship track and offers two first prize winners access to NYU's Berkley Center for Entrepreneurial Studies.

- Purdue University's Burton D. Morgan Center for Entrepreneurship offers the **Purdue University Life Sciences Business Plan Competition** in which $134,000 in prize money is up for grabs "for innovative products and services in the life sciences industry."

- Are you a graduate student with a million-dollar idea and the ultimate elevator pitch? Then you might want to toss your hat in the ring for **Wake Forest University's Elevator Competition** for MBA candidates. In 2006, $65,000 in money was handed out to student start-ups. The grand prize winner received $5,000 in cash, another $40,000 in professional services, and a meeting with a venture capitalist. Moreover, 20 semifinalist teams also received $1,000 cash each.

- If you happen to go to school in the Boston or New England section of the country, check into the resources available from **The Entrepreneurial Management Institute (EMI)** at Boston University. There you'll find a host of regional resources for student entrepreneurs, including business plan competitions around the country. The Web site (find it at *www.bu.edu/ entrepreneurship/resources.htm*) also offers a newsletter. EMI hosts Business Plan BootCamp, where entrepreneurs of all ages learn from successful venture capitalists. BU also holds two mini BootCamps per year designed to offer students a crash course in business plan preparation. As might be expected, some participants in the 30-hour BootCamp have indeed gone on to compete in the Institute's $30K Business Plan Competition.

■ For West Coast students, there's **San Diego State University's Venture Challenge,** where students present business plans for the chance to win up to $15,000 each. Check out *http://sdsu.theitpros.net* for more information.

6. Investor Activities

Say the word *investor* to any entrepreneur and you're likely to see his or her eyes light up. Investors can hold the keys to the kingdom for some entrepreneurs who really need funding. I actually bootstrapped all of my college businesses. Like the majority of entrepreneurs, I grew each venture without any outside investors, but rather by reinvesting whatever profits I could generate back into the companies. But depending on how capital-intensive your needs are, at one point or another you may find yourself in need of an "angel" investor or "private equity" investor or funding from a "venture capitalist" or VC (I'll talk more about these financing options in Chapter 6). If your school has ties to an established group of investors, you're one or two steps ahead of the competition. Some schools have faculty members who even sit on the board of certain investment firms. Other campuses, such as the University of North Carolina at Chapel Hill, work really hard to hook up students with local investors. Whatever the case, make it a point to find out how connected your campus is to prospective sources of funding. Start by asking professors or the director of the entrepreneurship center on your campus whether there are structured opportunities and arranged events in which students can meet with investors.

■ Youth Venture

Not all competitions, contests, and available prize money are earmarked for the college crowd. Younger students can take advantage of several programs, too. Youth Venture, for instance, is aimed at empowering young people ages 12 to 20 by providing them with all the tools necessary to create civic-minded organizations, clubs, or businesses. Youth Venture (*www.youthventure.org*) gives young people access to mentors, media opportunities, as well as funding up to $1,000 in seed capital to launch their organizations.

7. Awards and Grants

Investigate whether any students at your school (or potential school) have won big awards and whether the faculty there routinely apply for entrepreneurship-related grants and awards. Here are a few to take a look at:

- **Global Student Entrepreneur Awards** (*www.gsea.org*)—A well-recognized program from the John Cook School of Business at Saint Louis University. Since 1998, GSEA has honored outstanding undergraduates and now awards more than $80,000 to college entrepreneurs each year. The program's mission is "to inspire students to adopt entrepreneurial endeavors by bringing global visibility to undergraduate business owners whose companies adhere to high ethical standards and are innovative, profitable, and socially responsible." As of January of 2006, The Entrepreneurs' Organization (*www.eonetwork.org*), a global community of business owners, all of whom run companies with revenues in excess of $1 million, became the facilitator of the GSEA program.

- **The BRICK Awards** (*www.dosomething.org*)—An awards program organized by the nonprofit Do Something that recognizes young social entrepreneurs, outstanding leaders under the age of 25 who are making a difference in their local communities. BRICK awards are given for accomplishments in the areas of community building, health, or the environment. Winners in the "18 and under" category receive a $5,000 scholarship for higher education and a $5,000 community grant, while winners in the "19 to 25" category receive a $10,000 community grant.

- **Students In Free Enterprise** (*www.sife.org*)—SIFE, mentioned earlier, also recognizes individuals and student teams for their community outreach. Through regional and national competitions, SIFE presents awards in its core areas of market economics, entrepreneurship, personal financial success skills, and business ethics.

And just to show you how these awards are serious business, consider the case of Adam Blake, who as a junior at Texas Christian University became the $10,000 first-place winner in the 2005 GSEA competition. Blake owns two real estate and property management businesses, B&B Acquisitions and Blake Venture Corporation. Blake started B&B Acquisitions his freshman year by buying and renting property to college students. He's since expanded the business tremendously, getting into commercial real estate and amassing a real estate portfolio valued at nearly $1 million. Now that's a Campus CEO!

If your school hasn't applied for grant money, consider advising faculty of three places to turn to for such funds:

- **The Ewing Marion Kauffman Foundation** (*www.kauffman.org*)—In 2003, the foundation launched its Kauffman Campuses initiative, a $25 million grant program that awarded multimillion-dollar grants to eight colleges and universities, based on their proposed five-year plans to "inject entrepreneurship into the fabric of the university." The chosen schools: The University of Rochester in New York, Wake Forest University in Winston-Salem, Howard University in Washington D.C., Florida International University in Miami, University of Texas at El Paso, Washington University in St. Louis, University of Illinois at Urbana-Champaign, and the University of North Carolina at Chapel Hill.

- **The Coleman Foundation** (*www.colemanfoundation.org*)—Coleman's Entrepreneurship Excellence in Teaching Colleges is a national program recognizing and supporting entrepreneurship education in colleges and universities with 4,500 students or fewer. These competitively awarded grants go to schools with existing entrepreneurship programs that have strong plans for program expansion, cross-campus outreach, and/or community involvement.

- **National Collegiate Inventors & Innovators Alliance** (*www.nciia. org*)—NCIIA awards course and program grants ranging from $2,000 to $50,000 to institutions to strengthen existing curricular programs or build new programs in invention, innovation, and entrepreneurship.

So far, money from the Kauffman Foundation, the Coleman Foundation, and others has paid off. For example, before the Kauffman grants, in the 2002–2003 academic school year, 1,521 undergraduates were enrolled in entrepreneurship courses at these schools. In 2005, that figure nearly tripled to 4,109 students. Now that figure is more than 7,000.

8. Campus-specific Considerations

Obviously, every college campus is different. Some are in urban environments, while others are in small town settings. Some focus on younger students and the 18- to 21-year-old crowd, while certain campuses cater to graduate students and older students who have returned to school. All these factors, and more, can impact the success of a campus business.

Geographically, the location of your school will influence your opportunities to

- meet young entrepreneurs at other schools;
- take advantage of program resources at nearby colleges, universities, government agencies (i.e., U.S. Small Business Administration office) and nonprofit organizations (i.e., Small Business Development Center);
- connect with and possibly work for start-up ventures in the area; and
- network with local entrepreneurs and investors and thus lead to internships and mentoring.

■ Mind Your Own Biz

In 2005, the Small Business Administration announced a partnership with Junior Achievement Worldwide to launch a small-business portal for teen entrepreneurs. You can find out more about the initiative at *www.mindyourownbiz.org*.

In addition to geographic considerations, the savvy Campus CEO also needs to take demographic considerations into account. Think about your college for a moment. Is your campus known as an academically stringent university or a "party school"? What's the balance of female versus male students? What are the most commonly selected academic majors at this particular educational institution? How many students receive financial aid? And does your campus offer convenient access to business retailers such as Kinko's, Staples or Office Depot? Some campuses are all-inclusive, such as Stanford, which has every business service available to students who don't ever have to leave the relatively secluded Palo Alto, California, campus. Consider whether that is potentially critical to your business. For those considering Web-based businesses, location may be less important than other factors, such as marketing and technology.

Naturally, a number of other factors govern your decision of where to go to school and, in some cases, you may not have complete control over the decision. Regardless, the more you are able to evaluate an institution using these considerations, the better you will be able to take full advantage of what it has to offer.

9. Incubator Programs

An incubator is a facility or company designed to promote entrepreneurship and help start-up companies, usually by providing the shared use of resources, management expertise, and intellectual capital. I can tell you firsthand that it really pays to have an incubator program on campus that allows you access to everything from office space and technology to supplies and supportive advisors.

As I mentioned previously, my company, BCT Partners, has its roots at Rutgers University. We subsequently used the nearby technology business incubator facilities at the New Jersey Institute of Technology (NJIT) Enterprise Development Center (EDC) (*www.njit-edc.org*), and still maintain an office there to this day. According to its Web site, EDC accelerates the successful development of entrepreneurial companies through an array of business support resources and services developed or orchestrated by EDC management and offered both in the incubator and through its network of contacts. EDC works with companies in the areas of chemistry, biomedicine, software, engineering, education, Internet services, and retail. It has been invaluable to our growth at BCT Partners, providing below-market rent, free legal assistance in partnership with the Rutgers Community Law Clinic, seed investment grants, meeting space, available rooms for expansion, and connections with other EDC companies, plus a host of other benefits. As a result of utilizing EDC's resources, it has been a much easier road for us to travel as entrepreneurs.

The University of Texas at Austin is also a prime example of a really good incubator program. To accelerate the creation of new start-ups, UT offers students at its business incubator a variety of support services. Apparently, the program is so good that out of the 62 companies that have been launched to date, four are listed on Nasdaq. I should mention that UT is also known for hosting MOOT CORP.®, a prestigious international business plan competition with a huge payout: $183,500, which makes it the largest prize of any such contest.

Georgia Tech's Advanced Technology Development Center (ATDC) is a nationally recognized business incubator focused on science and technology. With the tagline "Helping Georgia entrepreneurs build great technology companies," ATDC works with entrepreneurs throughout the state of Georgia to provide a wide range of assistance from the campus research laboratory to the general marketplace. ATDC has produced more than 100 companies, including publicly traded firms such as MindSpring Enterprises, now part of EarthLink.

These are just a few examples of what a business incubator on your campus may have to offer. In Chapter 10, I'll elaborate on the importance of business incubators, the potential benefits of incubators to your company, and how to find out if there is one located near you.

10. Alumni Resources

Universities are always looking for ways to support students after they graduate, and their entrepreneurial pursuits are no exception. Two of the best starting points to find out about alumni resources for entrepreneurs are the career services department and the alumni relations department. Postgraduation benefits may include discounts on certain courses such as a "refresher course" or "boot camp," the ability to attend special events such as seminars, symposia, or conferences, ongoing assistance from faculty, exclusive access to networking functions, and the opportunity to mentor up-and-coming student entrepreneurs.

A representative from these departments can also tell you about successful alumni business owners. I've heard of a lot of students launching businesses on campus, and obviously that's very impressive. But in my opinion, it's even more awe-inspiring when students manage to keep those ventures going long after they've left the campus halls. Find out how many student businesses that launched are still up and running a year, two years, or five years later. Obviously, the answer you want to hear is that there are a great number of postcollege success stories. Hopefully, their stories will inspire you, too, to keep up your business when you graduate.

■ TAKE YOUR CAMPUS TO THE NEXT LEVEL

Hopefully, you recognize a few strengths in some of these ten areas for a school you may be considering, or are already attending. But what if that's not the case? Don't feel like all is lost. Here are three ways you can enhance your campus's profile and help turn it into a prime spot for campus entrepreneurship:

1. *Tap into hot spots for the latest information about student entrepreneurship.* A favorite resource of mine is the Collegiate Entrepreneurship section of the previously mentioned Ewing Marion Kauffman Foundation. It lists plenty of resources for and about college entrepreneurs. Check it out at *www.kauffman.org/entrepreneurship.cfm/college_entrepreneurship.*
2. *Read magazines and Web sites.* Magazines and Web sites are great, inexpensive, current, and topical. *YOUNG MONEY* is a terrific publication (*www.youngmoney.com*), as is the "Biz U" column of *Entrepreneur* magazine, the "Teen Startups" section of *Entrepreneur.com* (*www.entrepreneur.com/tsu/*), or

the collegiate entrepreneurship blog network, Mindpetals (*www.mindpetals.com*). Gather ideas from these sources about what other Campus CEOs are doing and determine what's worthy of emulating on your campus.

3. *Align with student-run entrepreneurship organizations.* Get involved with local chapters of national and international student-run entrepreneurship organizations and look to attend their conferences. This includes organizations such as those mentioned earlier like CEO, SIFE, FBLA-PBL, Delta Epsilon Chi, and BPA. Beyond affiliating with these national and global networks, also consider creating your own association that operates locally. At Yale, for example, there's the Yale Entrepreneurial Society, which is a nonprofit group that works to promote entrepreneurship in the greater Yale community.

Now that you've got a very good sense about what to look for in a campus—or how to boost the level of entrepreneurship at your school—let's move on to the next area you'll need to tackle: figuring out exactly what business you'll create, and honing in on the optimal time to launch that business to give yourself the best possible start for success.

CAMPUS CEO CHECKLIST

After you finish Chapter 1, take these steps to start on your path to entrepreneurship:

☐ Find out how your campus ranks when it comes to teaching entrepreneurship.

☐ Discover which teachers or professors at your school have ever run their own businesses.

☐ Collect applications for business plan competitions of interest to you.

☐ Visit *www.gsea.org* and request information on the Global Student Entrepreneur Awards.

☐ Inquire about whether an incubator facility exists on campus or someplace nearby.

☐ Ask a career services counselor or alumni relations officer about postcollege success stories of entrepreneurs.

☐ Join Collegiate Entrepreneurs' Organization (*www.c-e-o.org*) and Students In Free Enterprise (*www.sife.org*).

PROFILE OF A CAMPUS CEO

■ **Name:** Rishi Kacker and Matt Pauker

■ **Business:** Voltage Security

■ **Web site:** *www.voltage.com*

■ **Founded:** 2002

■ **Their Story:** Voltage makes security software that allows users to encrypt documents, files, and e-mail simply by pressing a button. The cofounders of the company, Rishi Kacker and Matt Pauker, created the technology as a summer research project while attending Stanford University. The duo worked tirelessly day and night, tinkering for a year in the basement office of their campus's engineering building, hoping to create their breakthrough technology—and hoping to experience a business breakthrough as well. Kacker and Pauker entered Stanford's highly competitive business plan competition and won. That victory brought venture capitalists coming. It also gave Voltage's founders the right to get free legal advice for a year from one of the Silicon Valley's top law firms. With help from these key legal advisors and others, Voltage has since mushroomed into a leading privacy management company with 75 employees and scores of big-name customers. Using identity-based encryption, Voltage now provides solutions for secure communication and data at rest to leading financial services, health care, government, and pharmaceutical companies. Voltage defines data "at rest" as files, PC disks, and stored data, as opposed to data "in use," such as Web services and application security, or data "in motion," which refers to file transfers, messaging, VoIP, and the like.

■ **Advice to Student Entrepreneurs:** "No matter how good your idea is, the success of your business is all about the team. A new venture has so many challenges that if there isn't absolute integrity and trust with the core team the venture doesn't stand a chance. Choose wisely—how will this person respond when the going gets tough? After that, be humble, embrace what you don't know, and surround yourself with excellent people. Best of luck and enjoy the ride."

—**Rishi Kacker,** *Fortune* (November 28, 2005)

What Business Should You Launch— And When?

" *Everyone's on the verge of the same idea at the same time, and that's when someone should start a company.* **"**

—Marc Andreessen, Cofounder of Netscape (with Jim Clark) in a speech for the MIT $50K Business Plan Competition in MIT's *The Tech* (November 18, 1996)

2

Two questions every student entrepreneur must ultimately ask are: What kind of business do I want to start, and when is the best time to launch it?

I'll help you answer both questions in this chapter, and use my own story of serial entrepreneurship as an example. I'm going to give you some ideas about the various types of businesses you might create, including certain companies you may not have ever considered. I'll also explain how to evaluate the campus environment, your abilities, limitations, and other factors to determine the best possible time to launch a business.

■ ANSWERING THE "WHEN" QUESTION

Let's tackle the timing question first. The best overall advice I can give you about timing the launch of your business is this: "Practice what you preach as early and as often as possible." If you aspire to become an entrepreneur, then you can never start too soon, even if it means taking small steps at first. If art is your passion, then visit every museum and art house in your area (and beyond) and see what you can learn from the curators and staff. If you love tinkering with computers, ask a local company or school whether it discards old equipment. Taking apart and rebuilding those old computers may spark a creative idea or stroke of genius within you. A big part of being an entrepreneur means seeing the possibilities in almost every circumstance. So many times, however, students mistakenly think that "being" an entrepreneur refers solely to the unique act of running one's own business. I would argue, though, that if you've adopted the entrepreneurial mindset, there's always a way for you to be in an entrepreneurial mode, regardless of whether or not that constitutes the full-fledged running of a business. For instance, you can work alongside an entrepreneur, you can take entrepreneurship classes, or you can intern at a type of business in the industry in which you one day hope to have your own company. You can also work to solve social problems in society, or to apply lessons that you've learned in the classroom to real-world situations.

The timing of starting a new business will be affected by more than your own personal timeline, however. You probably already know that in certain instances, the outcome of launching a new product or service is often tied to when that new offering is put into the marketplace. Some new campus ventures must be seized immediately, especially when customer demand is high and no competition exists. In other cases, the success or failure of a new college-based business depends on a variety of other issues, which have nothing to do with timing. I don't want you to become overly obsessed with your official start date. Nevertheless, you clearly want to start a new operation at the optimal time.

But when exactly is that? Well, for starters, you'd be wise to avoid rushing your business to market prematurely, before you've conducted any market research whatsoever. You also obviously want to avoid launching new concepts at inappropriate and potentially disastrous times. Finals week—when everyone is pulling all-nighters studying—probably isn't the ideal time to get your colleagues interested in your new video-game business. You should also consider the question of "when" to start a business in terms of when it's best to generate sales, from an economic point of view taking into account environmental and seasonal factors. If you're in Florida and your business would appeal to sun worshippers coming for spring break, then you'd better make sure you've kicked into high gear by early March. Launching that business in May or June—or worse, in the fall—means you've missed the boat that school year.

Most critical, though, is to launch when things are personally most opportune for you, the entrepreneur. Don't open your doors for business when you're having major personal problems, the week you know that you have three killer papers due, or the month you're scheduled to have surgery on a bad knee. If you move quickly—getting to market as soon as possible while still exercising good judgment and some proper planning—you'll be fine with regards to the timing of your business launch.

■ THE "WHAT" AND "WHEN" OF MY FIRST BUSINESS

My first entrepreneurial endeavor was a lemonade stand when I was eight years old. I stood in a bad location with cars racing by for hours and hours. And for all my efforts, I sold two cups of lemonade. Fortunately, though, I never gave up. I held flea markets where I would sell my old toys to other kids. That venture was successful until my mom shut me down: she wanted me to hand down my toys to my cousins. Later in grade school, I would make custom notebooks, similar to a popular brand known as Trapper Keepers, that I would sell to classmates.

Despite these early ventures, my entrepreneurial activities were pretty much dormant throughout high school, mostly because I was so involved with sports, academic clubs, and various student groups. College, though, was a major turning point for me in terms of seeing myself as an entrepreneur and moving forward in the business world.

A friend of mine, Wayne Abbott, grew up with me and was responsible for planting the seeds of campus entrepreneurship in my mind. Though he was two years older, Wayne and I became very close childhood friends. His family moved into the same area of East Windsor, New Jersey, around the same time as mine did; we attended the same public schools from kindergarten to high school; and our families were two of approximately ten African-American families in the neighborhood who formed a group called "Our Kids" that organized social events and cultural activities for the young people. He graduated from our high school, Hightstown High School, in 1987, and went on to Rutgers University, majoring in electrical engineering. Two years later I followed in his footsteps.

In college, Wayne was the president of the Rutgers Chapter of the National Society of Black Engineers (NSBE) and he subsequently made sure I was actively involved in the organization during my first year. At NSBE meetings on campus, Wayne would always drive home the message that corporate America was not the only path for us to follow.

To demonstrate that point, Wayne started his own company, called AIP, which stood for AWARE Information Products. It was an on-campus retailer of primarily Afrocentric T-shirts, apparel, and other cultural items, which were increasingly popular among students at the time. Among the black engineers at Rutgers, there was a strong spirit of social consciousness and entrepreneurship; so much, in fact, that of my cohorts, about a half dozen or so of us started our own businesses—largely based on what we saw Wayne doing. We all wanted to do something that we were passionate about.

Finding My Passion

During the summer before my senior year, I conceived of a company that I originally called Mind, Body & Soul Enterprises. It was started with two divisions:

1. A retail sales division, primarily focused on selling compact discs, records, and tapes out of my dorm room, and
2. An educational services division, which offered workshops, seminars, and lectures for students as a community service, teaching the importance of obtaining a good education as well as other topics relating to leadership and professional development.

Similarly, the name of the company conveyed two messages—"Music for the mind, body, and soul," as well as educational services fostering "Mental, physical, and spiritual development." Because I wanted to combine my social activism with my business pursuits, I used the money I would make from the sales of music products toward paying for trips and educational presentations at various high schools and colleges. I grew up in a very spiritual, church-centered family and had always been involved in different community-service activities. So the idea of giving back and being concerned for others was always a natural part of anything I did. I liked the notion of using my business endeavors to help out the community.

Starting the Business

In my junior year I launched my first business, because Wayne had convinced me (and many of my peers) that it was something we should seriously consider. My cofounders for Mind, Body & Soul Enterprises were also two of my roommates: Jeffrey "JR" Robinson and Aldwyn Porter—each of us with complementary skill sets. JR was already an entrepreneur with a related business and somewhat similar interests. Jeff started NIA Educational Services, doing outreach to high school students, so it made sense for him to lead the educational services division. Aldwyn was very popular and quite knowledgeable about music and entertainment. Because of that, I convinced him to head up the retail sales division. We already knew that there was no music store on campus. We just had to figure out how we could bring really good music on campus—and sell it for a profit. We began by hunting down music distributors (called "One Stops") in the northeast part of the country. We researched and found two: Universal One Stop in Philadelphia, Pennsylvania, and Northeast One Stop in Latham, New York.

After we registered our business with the New Jersey Division of Revenue, we got our tax identification number and our sales tax certificate. With those documents in hand, we were authorized to order wholesale music product. We went with Northeast One Stop as our primary distributor because we learned, much to our surprise, that upon placing our order the company would ship product the next day. Universal One Stop served as our secondary distributor when needed. By the fall, all the pieces of the puzzle were in place. We could get huge volume discounts from the One Stops as long as we placed a minimum order of ten items. Ultimately, they would both come to know us by name because we would check their catalogs on a daily basis to browse their new music titles. Both of their catalogs were as thick as phone books. As expected, when we saw what they were charging, the prices were a lot less than what we were paying in stores. They charged anywhere from $4 to $9 for a CD. When we sold these CDs on campus, we charged our customers $12 apiece. In fact, the older the item, the cheaper it cost and the more money we made off of it.

To market the company, we printed one-sheet flyers and postcards with lists of new releases and singles, and descriptions of the types of songs and different music that we could get. Then, to spread the word across campus, we said: "Just tell us what you want, and we can get it." We sold the music out of our dorm room, would bring the music list or product to the dining halls, and even set up tables at campus events. MBS was fairly popular with students, and I did, in fact, start using some of the money I earned to hold student seminars encouraging young people to go to college. We designed curriculum and lesson plans, and we particularly encouraged minorities to consider engineering and science majors. After melding these two areas—the music retailing business and the educational seminar operation—we quickly realized the enormous demand for out educational offerings. Up until that point, our efforts had been purely community-service–oriented. But the strong demand showed us that people were willing to pay for educational seminars and workshops, and our activities in this arena didn't have to be completely philanthropic. So we started thinking: How can we do well and do good? To this day, a lot of my ventures have had that social entrepreneurial spin.

■ The National Foundation for Teaching Entrepreneurship

NFTE (*www.nfte.com*) programs are located throughout the world to teach entrepreneurship to young people from low-income communities and to enhance their economic productivity by improving their business, academic, and life skills. NFTE also offers BizCamp™, a two-week intensive summer program for students ages 13–18. At the end of the program, students compete for cash awards to fund their businesses.

Our First Big Break

In my senior year, I was fortunate enough to win a Rhodes scholarship and was invited to speak at a private school in New Jersey called Montclair Kimberley Academy. At MKA, as the school is known, there was a young lady in the audience named Helen Walter. Her mother happened to be the director of scholarship programs at the National Action Council for Minorities in Engineering (NACME). Helen told her mother about me and what I'd been doing. Helen's mom, Aileen Walter, later called me and asked for assistance in organizing a weekend of workshops and seminars around professional development for students who had received scholarships from Fortune 500 companies and who would later perform internships for those same companies. Aileen invited us to submit a proposal to facilitate an entire conference, which included workshops focused on career planning, résumé writing, interviewing skills, maximizing the internship experience, leadership, and team building. Keep in mind that we were college seniors at the time. We would be helping to train college sophomores. So we were only two or three years older than the students in the program, but I think that's what Ms. Walter liked. Our proposal for an entire weekend of services was $4,573. I know now that we *completely* underpriced ourselves, but at the time it felt like a lot of money to ask for. That day, right after we gave them a minipresentation of our proposal, they said: "You've got it. It's yours."

To get a "Yes" just like that was mind-blowing! We left that meeting feeling like we'd won the lottery! We immediately enlisted the help of three additional students, Lawrence Hibbert, Dallas Grundy, and Shawn Wallace. Lawrence and Dallas would become partners in the company shortly thereafter, while Shawn maintained a long-standing relationship working with us. The experience also convinced us to change the name of the company to MBS Educational Services & Training. Music retailing on a campus was one thing. But the educational seminar business looked far more promising—and it was. That initial contract wound up being the first of many that took us on an entirely new trajectory for the next seven years. We continued to incubate MBS to the point where the company was earning, at its peak, just shy of $400,000 a year while I was still a student. The MBS business model ended up largely centered on charging corporate, educational, and nonprofit clients to provide workshops and seminars at conferences, universities, and corporate training events.

Our client list read like a who's who of corporate America. Sometimes, I still don't know how we pulled this off, but we managed to get an enviable roster of clients, including General Motors, Exxon, AT&T, Merck & Co., Lucent Technologies, PNC Bank, Citigroup, NACME, the United Negro College Fund, and the Thurgood Marshall Scholarship Fund, to name a few. Our initial target audience was students and young professionals. Then we evolved and started offering seminars for both emerging and seasoned professionals, too. We wound up operating in three primary markets; the first was high school and college students. Our seminars were largely based on helping them think about and plan for getting to the next phase of their lives, whether that meant attending college, landing an internship, getting a first job, going to graduate school, or the like. The second market we served focused on transitioning new hires into the corporate workplace and mentoring programs for new hires. The third and most lucrative market segment for MBS Educational Services & Training was working with corporations to enhance their summer internship programs. In this capacity, we developed workshops and seminars built around everything from public speaking and presentation skills to communication and interviewing techniques.

As you can see, it was my passion for music that first financed my civic pursuits, which themselves turned into a viable business helping students and others. If you want to launch a great campus start-up, you'll need to find something you're passionate about, too, which takes us to the heart of this chapter. Throughout the remainder of the book I will share some of the lessons I've learned from growing MBS Educational Services & Training into a six-figure company, which then allowed me to grow BCT Partners into a seven-figure company.

■ ANSWERING THE "WHAT" QUESTION

Now let's address the meatier topic at hand—namely, what type of business should *you* start?

Choosing a Business Idea

When choosing a business, consider the four steps outlined in Figure 2.1, which speak to your interests, goals, capacity, and evaluation of different ideas. I'll walk you through each step but keep in mind that while the steps are presented sequentially, it is best to think of them as part of an iterative process. After examining your interests, goals, and capacity, you will generate prospec-

FIGURE 2.1 Choosing a Business Idea

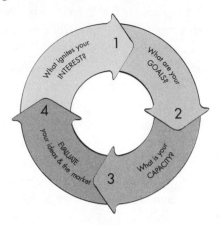

tive business ideas and, based on these considerations, evaluate your ability to pursue them. But, as new and different concepts come to mind, you may change your perspective on your interests, adjust your goals, or think differently about your capacity to undertake those ideas. That's when the cycle starts all over again, leading up to what is hopefully an idea worth investigating more deeply.

Step #1: What ignites your INTEREST? First, consider your hobbies, interests, and passions. What really fires you up and gets you motivated? You should do some soul-searching here to think about what areas not only interest you today, but those that are likely to be of interest to you one year, five years, or perhaps ten years or more from now. In other words, choose areas where you probably will have *sustained* interest, not just a passing fancy about something. In my case, Mind, Body & Soul Enterprises was focused on music and education/community service, all of which I was passionate about, and remain so to this day. If you haven't already, you should ask yourself the following questions to help reveal what you are passionate about:

> *What interest, passion, or desire are you most afraid of admitting to yourself and others?*
> *What would you do if you knew you could not fail?*
> *What would you do if money was not a concern in your life?*
> *What one thing do you dream about doing that you've never told anyone?*
> *What do you fantasize about doing while driving your car or taking a shower?*

> *Who do you know that's doing something you'd like to do?*
> *Describe yourself doing it.*
> *List five things that you want. List five things that you're good at.*
> *When you were young, what did you know you would do when you grew up?*
> *What would you regret not having done if your life was ending?*
>
> Source: Taken in part from *Life Makeovers* by Cheryl Richardson

Students and experts say the following all rank as hot areas of interest on many campuses for budding entrepreneurs:

- Information technology
- Life sciences
- Social entrepreneurship

Information technology. The rise of information technology–oriented companies among student-based businesses isn't surprising, given that the 25-and-under crowd is the first generation to grow up with the Internet. And when I say technology-oriented companies, I don't mean businesses that are purely in the information technology field; I mean companies that take advantage of technology in smart ways. (Chapter 5 will give you more tips about leveraging technology.) This includes everything from companies that actually develop software and Web applications to companies that are actually powered by software and Web applications such as social networking sites and online retailers. By taking full advantage of technology, your campus business can save you plenty of time from an operational standpoint, better serve customers, and earn you a lot more money. Although the dot-com era has come and gone, information technology continues to pique the interests of student entrepreneurs.

Life sciences. The life sciences are any of the several branches of science, such as biology, medicine, ecosystems, or anthropology, that deal with living organisms and their origins, as well as their relationships to each other and their environment. Businesses geared toward the life sciences may develop new tools for cell research or new approaches for caring for animals or plants. Other areas may be related to maintaining the general health and well-being of humans. Certain entrepreneurial opportunities lie in the health care profession, providing goods and services to health care facilities, hospitals, assisted-living communities, mental health institutions, pharmacies, or neighborhood health clinics.

Starting a business focused on the life sciences could ultimately aid in a better understanding of the natural world we live in and in a more defined way for us to address issues of personal well-being and worldwide concern such as global warming, threats to human health such as the Ebola and HIV viruses, and maintaining viable and abundant food supplies. These are hot areas, and opportunities in these fields will continue to be plentiful.

Social entrepreneurship. Social entrepreneurship is an area receiving tremendous attention from students. My friend and first business partner, Dr. Jeffrey Robinson, is now a professor of entrepreneurship at New York University. He defines social entrepreneurship as "the process of using entrepreneurial and business skills to create innovative approaches to social problems." Social entrepreneurs seek out business opportunities that create wealth, but also improve society or make a positive impact in communities. I consider myself a social entrepreneur to the extent that all my ventures, beginning with MBS, have focused on the double bottom line: financial returns (doing well) and social returns (doing good). A triple bottom line social venture would also deliver healthy environmental returns.

The importance of giving back has been instilled in me since I was young and it continues to be reflected in my business endeavors today. BCT Partners is a for-profit consulting firm specializing in information technology, strategic planning, and organizational development. However, our focus areas—housing, community development, economic development, human services, health care, and education—are all very socially oriented. Furthermore, we've conducted a considerable number of projects in low-income and underserved communities. Dr. Robinson adds, "The challenge with social ventures is to maintain both a financial and a social bottom line. On the financial side, you have to strive for sustainability and profitability to stay in business. On the social side, you have to measure and ensure that you're having a positive impact. The good news is that there are more funding sources looking for double bottom line and triple bottom line companies than ever before" (see the list of social venture funds in Chapter 6).

Some students are actually surprised to find out that they can run a business and address a social issue. As you contemplate what ignites your interest, I strongly encourage you to consider the possibilities of not just being an entrepreneur, but being social entrepreneur and channeling your creativity and energy into making a profit *and* making a difference. Social ventures are undoubtedly one of the hottest areas in youth entrepreneurship.

■ The Emerging Entrepreneurs Network

The Emerging Entrepreneurs Network ("Eonfire") is a student-driven network for aspiring social entrepreneurs, socially responsible businesspeople, and civil-sector leaders. With a growing number of chapters on college campuses, Eonfire combines theory and practice, reflection and action, and thinking with doing. It organizes discussions, workshops, seminars, and speakers' series, while also supporting and encouraging its members to launch social ventures. Learn more by visiting its Web site at *www.eonfire.org*.

Step #2: What are your GOALS? In this step you should consider several long-range objectives for you and your company and wrestle with where you see yourself after graduation, particularly in relationship to a business.

Generally speaking, the range of student businesses can be broadly classified into four categories—*campus-based, campus-incubated, campus-centered,* and *campus-enterprise*—as shown in Figure 2.2. They are not mutually exclusive, and, at times, different businesses may overlap into multiple categories, but it's still a useful way of thinking about your goals.

- The left axis captures the focus of your company, either campus-focused or market-focused:
- A *campus-focused company* provides products and services that are geared primarily, if not exclusively, toward students and/or college and university campuses.
- A *market-focused company* is one that offers products and services to the general marketplace. The target market for these businesses is not limited to students, colleges, or university campuses.

The bottom axis describes the growth potential of your company.

- A *lifestyle company* is a small to medium-size venture designed for income replacement or to fit the owner's lifestyle. The growth potential of a lifestyle company is limited either by design (i.e., personal choices made by the founders as they have no desire to expand) or by circumstance (i.e., limited opportunities for expansion because of the business model, insufficient funding, or a mature/declining market). After graduation, students may choose to disband their lifestyle company, or maintain their involvement as a full-time endeavor or part-time activity that provides supplemental income.

FIGURE 2.2 Types of Campus Businesses

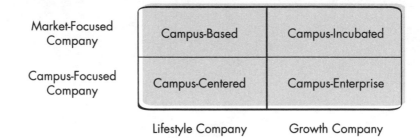

- A *growth company* is a firm with the potential to reach a significant size and scale. The promise of growth companies can lead the principals to forgo or defer their education. It can also lead them to pursue outside investors as a means to take full advantage of the window of opportunity presented by the venture.

Based on these axes, the following is a description of the four types of campus businesses:

- **Campus-based** (market-focused, lifestyle company): Businesses in traditional or mature industries that are simply operated on a campus (i.e., out of a dormitory). General examples include catering, Web site design, music retail, graphic design/desktop publishing, consulting, etc. Specific examples include Dream On Information Technology, a Web site and software design company founded by two students at the University of Central Florida, and MnC Events, an event management company founded by Megan and Cedar Watson (twin sisters), also at the University of Central Florida.
- **Campus-incubated** (market-focused, growth company) businesses are those that are somehow incubated by the campus environment. Their origins are found in a college or university laboratory, research project, class project, grant-funded initiative, or even as the brainchild of student(s) with the discretionary time to conceive the venture. Campus-incubated firms can also generate intellectual property or other potential revenue-generating assets that are then commercialized by way of a formal venture. General examples include certain biotechnology, life sciences, and information technology firms. Specific examples include Google, Yahoo!, Netscape, and Facebook. This may involve a patent or

licensing arrangement with the university, possibly through a technology licensing office. For example, MIT has an entire office dedicated to technology licensing: *http://web.mit.edu/tlo/www/industry/inquiries.html.*

- **Campus-centered** (campus-focused, lifestyle company) businesses that uniquely cater to campuses and/or students, sometimes with the potential to expand their customer base to nonstudents. General examples include reselling textbooks, transcription services, food delivery, editing/proofreading, and tutoring. Specific examples include AllDorm. com, a collegiate marketing company founded by four students at Santa Clara University; and DCSnacks.com, a late-night delivery service in Washington, D.C. (formerly known as CampusSnacks.com), and Store-4Summer.com, a dormitory moving and storage company (formerly known as CampusBoxes.com), both founded by George Washington University student Matthew Mandell.

- **Campus-enterprise** (campus-focused, growth company) businesses represent ventures that are either focused on a single college or university campus (or a cluster of schools) and then expand to other campuses, or launch across multiple campuses at their inception and maintain a focus on campuses. General examples are nearly identical to campus-centered businesses; the only difference is that campus-enterprises span multiple campuses such as a campus food delivery chain or a campus textbook reseller network. Specific examples include Student Advantage, a student discount program honored on college and university campuses across the country, and Cluck-U-Chicken, a restaurant chain established in 1985 at Rutgers University that serves unique and diverse chicken recipes. One of Cluck-U's goals is to locate one of its restaurants near every college campus across the country.

In addition to helping you think about the kinds of campus businesses that might pique your interest, the four categories in Figure 2.2 are equally helpful in clarifying exactly what your ultimate goal is. Consider the following questions:

- *Do you envision a company that is campus-focused or one that is market-focused?* If you launch a campus-focused business that involves tutoring college freshman, for instance, can you see yourself doing the same thing—or even wanting to—five years after you receive your degree? MBS was originally a campus-based enterprise with our retail sales division selling CDs on campus. Once we decided to abandon this division and focus exclusively on the educational services division providing workshops, lectures, and seminars, we shifted from a campus-focused company to a market-focused company.

■ *Do you see yourself pursuing a lifestyle company or a growth company?* You might consider a lifestyle company if your ultimate goal is to run a business, but you're not necessarily looking to grow it to scale (or it doesn't have the potential to grow to scale). For example, whether you like it or not, a single pizza parlor has limited growth potential. On the other hand, a company that manufactures a product based on an advanced technological innovation could have unlimited growth potential.

The point is: Consider what best suits your tastes and desires as well as the realities of the venture you are pursuing. Your choice—whether it is made by you or the market—has implications for the long-term viability of the company. Our original goal for MBS was that of a lifestyle company, one that would generate some extra money for each of the partners. However, once we saw the market potential for educational services and training, our goal became that of a growth company and that orientation has continued with BCT Partners.

Step #3: What is your CAPACITY? When evaluating your capacity or ability to pursue a new venture, a useful concept to consider is *capital*. Capital is best understood as anything that can be possessed or accumulated. You should determine the extent to which you (or your team) possess or have accumulated five forms of capital when evaluating your capacity to pursue a new venture. Those five forms of capital are:

1. *Human capital* refers to the knowledge, experience, training, and skill set that you, your employees, partners, or others bring to your venture individually. Often, this is immensely valuable.
2. *Intellectual capital* is the knowledge, experience, and skills resulting from your team's collective efforts or synergy. Here, the whole is greater than the sum of its parts as your team is able to generate ideas and accomplish tasks together that could not be accomplished apart.
3. *Social capital* leverages the relationships, contacts, and network of friends, family members, and other affiliates that a person may be able to bring to the table. In many instances, a person with strong social ties is considerably valuable to an enterprise because often "It's not what you know, it's who you know."

4. *Cultural capital* is knowledge and intuition of certain cultural norms, standards, and preferences. For example, as a student you are in a great position to understand the wants and needs of other students. This gives you a certain measure of cultural capital that might be more difficult for a nonstudent to possess. The same may be true for your knowledge and intuition of other demographic groups, geographic locations, communities, market segments, organizations, and more.

5. *Financial capital* is either a direct contribution of money or assets to the company, or providing the company with access to money or assets as needed. This is often the most difficult form of capital to acquire, but don't worry; the next section of the book is dedicated entirely to ways you can finance your business.

There is also a sixth consideration, which has to do with the amount of *time and effort* you are willing to put into the venture. This is commonly referred to as *sweat equity:*

■ *Sweat equity* is a catchall for the time, effort, and hard work that are often expended to ensure the success of the business. Sweat equity is a proxy for "Doing whatever you have to do to get the job done," which includes everything from consecutive all-nighters to meet an important deadline, to answering your cell phone at 5 AM because a customer needs something addressed immediately, to your relentless pursuit of a meeting with the key decision maker at a company who could become a major client.

My experience has shown me everyone—including students—can bring a valuable and varying mix of human, intellectual, social, cultural, and financial capital to the table, and certainly a high measure of sweat equity. All five forms of capital are valuable and all are interrelated (as shown in Figure 2.3). Most important, when properly coordinated with a good dose of sweat equity, all can contribute to a company's success.

Obviously, these forms of capital are not without limits. So you must honestly assess your own parameters and confines. In other words, do you currently have any money (financial capital) or at least solid access to people or organizations that could supply you with funding? On the social capital front, do you have relationships you can leverage that would benefit a business? As far as human capital goes, do you possess certain skills that are closely aligned or perhaps even perfectly matched for the venture you might be considering? Or will you have to "get up to speed" on the knowledge front just to learn the

FIGURE 2.3 The Five Forms of Capital and Sweat Equity

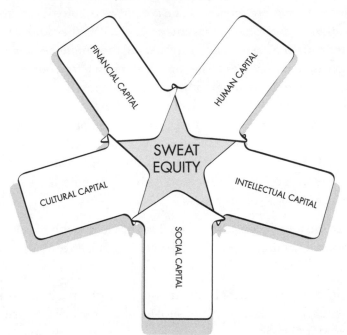

basics? With respect to intellectual capital, what problems can your team confidently solve by working together? What new possibilities are created? Lastly, in the area of cultural capital: Are there markets where you and your team have unique insight? How can this be leveraged? Your capacity or wherewithal to pursue a new venture along all of these lines matters greatly.

In my case, MBS was established at a time when I had the greatest capacity—during the summer before my final year in college. My knowledge and skills (human capital) were at an all-time high based on my previous years on campus, and I had developed a number of valuable relationships (social capital) through my leadership roles on campus, as well as from my heavy involvement with the National Society of Black Engineers. In bringing JR and Aldwyn on board, I had the beginnings of a great team (intellectual capital) and, as a student looking to sell music to other students, I had a good degree of insight to the market (cultural capital). Like many students, I lacked money (financial capital). However, I had the greatest amount of discretionary time and could put forth great effort (sweat equity) because I had already met most of my engineering requirements and I had completed my four years of eligibility on the track-and-field team. In short, my capacity to pursue the venture was quite high overall.

Step #4: EVALUATE your ideas and the market. To evaluate your ideas, first take a hard look at your answers to the three previous questions and then start brainstorming some potential business ideas. The range of companies student entrepreneurs have created over the years is both vast and impressive. In fact, take a look at the following spectrum of companies. According to *Quintessential Careers,* this is just a sampling of the types of businesses started by college entrepreneurs. As you can see, the possibilities are limitless:

- Aquarium service
- Coffee shop
- College marketing, promotions, and consulting firm
- Computer sales and repairs
- Custom cookie business
- Detailing service (automobiles, aircrafts)
- Disc jockey business
- Dorm design and dorm accessories
- Genealogy software company
- Glow-in-the-dark bicycle technology
- Greeting card company
- Landscaping company
- Motivational speaking company
- Music business
- Online investment newsletter
- PDA communications computer consulting
- Real estate developer
- Rehabilitation software company
- Replica hockey jersey company
- Residential and commercial painting company
- Retail clothing store
- Sign manufacturer
- Summer storage service for college students
- Web-hosting company
- Web sites where students can list and exchange textbooks
- Web/graphic design
- Window-cleaning service
- Workout facility/gym

Source: Quintcareers.com

■ Looking for Business Ideas?

Two good sources of information about ideas for a business are:

■ **Business Owners' Idea Café** (*www.businessownersideacafe.com/ business_people/index.php*)— A list of potential business ideas including insight and advice from experts in specific industries.

■ **Entrepreneur.com's "Getting Ideas" Section** (*www.entrepreneur.com/Your_Business/YB_Node/0,4507,110,00. html*)—A list of articles, tools, and tips for finding the perfect business idea.

When evaluating the market, you really have to apply your most objective analytical skills, because your interests, goals, capacity, and ideas alone don't count for much if there's not a market need for your business. Just think, if I were the only one who was really into music, I wouldn't have experienced anywhere near the success I did with MBS if my peers didn't share an interest in the music products I was selling.

To evaluate what opportunities exist that best meet or coincide with your own interests, goals, capacities, and ideas, you can objectively analyze the needs of the marketplace in two ways: *market research* and *competitive analysis*. Market research could entail any of the following approaches:

■ *Ground your knowledge of your industry.* Obtain books, articles, and other publications that describe the inner workings of your industry. The Internet is also an excellent resource for researching an industry, including trends, latest developments, historical perspectives, and the major players. If possible, it may also be useful to obtain a copy of a real (or fictitious) business plan. Often these can be obtained from entities such as your campus entrepreneurship center, the local Small Business Administration office, Small Business Development Center, Service Corps of Retired Executives office, chamber of commerce, and the like. You want to become as much of an expert as possible concerning your industry.

■ *Survey fellow students.* Distribute surveys and questionnaires to fellow students or other potential customers, or host focus groups right on campus. This will give you a sense of whether your anticipated product or service has a true audience just waiting for your business to come along.

■ *Benchmark similar business activity on other campuses.* Talk to friends at other schools and find out what's happening on their campuses. If businesses similar to yours exist there, then find out what they're doing that is working well, or what is not working well that your business could improve upon.

- *Interview professors, mentors, or other experts in the field.* Your professors and mentors will certainly possess in-depth knowledge about particular industries. They can also be an excellent bridge to relevant research, reports, publications, and other experts in areas outside their expertise.

■ Small Business Assistance Organizations

You can turn to a number of small business assistance organizations for help. They offer some combination of training and technical assistance, counseling, awards and recognition, newsletters, workshops, seminars, conferences, and assistance with financing, accounting, contracts, grants, and disaster recovery. Some of the more prominent entities are listed in Figure 2.4; there is likely one or more on or near your campus.

- *Obtain access to industry or trade databases, associations, publications, and reports.* For almost every industry, periodicals, databases, organizations, and other resources can provide valuable market intelligence. Chapter 3 identifies some specific sources of information; also be sure to consult the business librarian at your school.

Competitive analysis determines how well your product or service rates when compared to other companies in the market. It's important to understand your competition at a very detailed level so you ensure that you're filling a real gap in the market, not duplicating existing products or services, and offering something with a distinct advantage. Some questions to consider include the following:

- Are there existing companies that offer the same (or similar) product or service?
- What are their strengths and weaknesses?
- How is your product or service different or distinct from theirs?
- How do they compare in terms of location? Price? Quality? Reputation?
- What can you learn from what they do well? What could you improve upon?

Some tips on performing competitive analysis include the following:

- *Utilize a competitor's product or service. Buy your competitor's product or try out its service.* Experience firsthand how it markets and sells to the public. Also consider working for one of your competitors to learn the business and the industry.

FIGURE 2.4 Small Business Assistance Organizations

Organization	Description	Location(s)
U.S. Small Business Administration (SBA) *www.sba.gov*	National, federal agency responsible for working with small businesses	Headquartered in Washington, DC. Field offices in every state
Service Corps of Retired Executives (SCORE) *www.score.org*	Source of free and confidential counseling, workshops, and advice to entrepreneurs. Also offers "Ask SCORE" for online advice	Headquartered in Washington, D.C., with 389 chapters nationwide
Small Business Development Center (SBDCs) *www.sba.gov/sbdc/*	Operated on college campuses with support by private sector, federal, state, and local government agencies	1,110 centers nationwide
Women's Business Centers (WBCs) *www.sba.gov/womenin business/welcome.html*	Centers providing small business assistance to women entrepreneurs. Typically operated by nonprofit women's business assistance organizations	80 centers nationwide
Chambers of Commerce *www.uschamber.com*	Local and state organizations representing the interests of business owners	Headquartered in Washington, D.C., with 1,000+ local chambers of commerce
National Minority Supplier Development Council (NMSDC) *www.nmsdcus.org/*	Regional organizations forging ties between minority-owned businesses and corporate America. Also offers certification	Headquartered in New York, with 39 regional councils
Women's Business Enterprise National Council *www.wbenc.org*	National organization fostering connections between women-owned businesses and large corporations	Headquartered in Washington, D.C.

- *Visit a competitor.* Go to your competitor's office, talk to its employees, and perhaps arrange an information interview with a manager. Collect brochures, pamphlets, business cards, and other marketing materials.
- *Go online.* Visit your competitor's Web site, search for articles or postings written about it, or advertisements and marketing information. If possible, also research the background of the founders and key management.

- *Interview customers.* Go out and talk to actual customers of your competitor, including family, friends, and other students that have used its products and services, or have considered using its products and services.
- *Identify industry and trade databases, associations, publications, and reports.* Using the same or similar sources for market research, seek out industry resources to learn more about your competitors and competitive space.

Many of these are free or certainly very low-cost ways for you to get feedback on a business idea. I'll revisit both market research and competitive analysis in Chapter 3, which covers creating a powerful business plan.

Also take the time to examine your own campus environment for unmet or unfulfilled needs. Sure, there may be the traditional wants and needs that college students have—for everything from music, books, and food to convenience items and academic assistance. But what about things that may be missing: if you can find a need and fill it, you'll probably have the genesis of a successful enterprise. Necessity is indeed the mother of invention. Lastly, consider whether there are up-and-coming or niche opportunities that you can help create. During the dot-com era, students from different universities did everything from trading books and swapping college paraphernalia to creating social interaction and online dating services using the Web. New opportunities are being introduced every day, so never limit your sense of possibilities.

■ FINAL STEP—MAKE THE CALL: "GO" OR "NO GO"?

The input you receive from evaluating your ideas and conducting market research and competitive analysis, along with some creative brainstorming and iterative evaluation on your part should give you a healthy amount of information from which to make a more informed go-no-go decision. When it comes to making the final decision on whether to pursue an idea, you're really generating your own system for evaluating a business venture without knowing with 100 percent certainty how viable that venture may turn out to be. That's one of the differences between entrepreneurs who decide to take on the risk of embarking on a new business idea and someone else who decides to go work for an established company. The start-up business owner is operating on his or her belief that there exists in the marketplace a need for that person's product or service, and that customers will, in fact, buy them from the business owner. By contrast, the employee—someone, for instance, who goes to work for a big bank—rarely even questions whether there's a need for the bank or if customers will walk in the door. It's simply assumed that people need banks and reach out to these financial institutions for services. As a result, you can bet that many a parent will encourage their children to "get a job" rather than become an entrepreneur and "make a job." If you ever encounter moments of doubt once you reach the go-no-go decision, it is during these moments I encourage you to remember the entrepreneur's mindset of ingenuity, imagination, determination, and, most important, courage and vision. Whether you aspire to become an entrepreneur or not, the mindset can empower you to follow your dreams and look past those who might seek to discourage you.

By all means you should do your homework. By "homework," I am referring to evaluating your interests, goals, capacity, ideas, and the market carefully, along the lines of what was presented in this chapter. You should also perform thorough due diligence and strategic research about the business you're considering launching, along the lines of what is presented in the following chapters: What is your business model? Who's your competition? What's your target market? How much revenue do you expect to generate? When do you foresee your business turning a profit? What kind of marketing and sales strategies will best help you achieve success? Which mentors and advisors can assist you and so forth. We will explore all these considerations next because they are vital in your quest to become a Campus CEO.

MBS was conceived and developed over the course of the summer prior to my senior year in college. Our interests were aligned with the venture. Our goals were clear. Our capacity was commensurate with what was needed to get the company off the ground. We conducted market research by soliciting feedback from friends in terms of whether they would support the venture. And based on a careful evaluation of this information, we decided it was a go. Try not to fall victim of "paralysis by analysis" or allow any of the seven myths of entrepreneurship to prevent you from making it a "go" for your venture too!

CAMPUS CEO CHECKLIST

After reading Chapter 2, take these next steps to starting your business:

☐ Launch your company at a time that is good for you personally and an opportune time in the marketplace.

☐ Explore *what ignites your interests* by examining your hobbies, interests and passions.

☐ Determine *what are your goals* for yourself and your company (campus-focused vs. market-focused company, and lifestyle vs. growth company).

☐ Evaluate *what is your capacity* to pursue a business according to the five forms of capital and sweat equity.

☐ Choose and *evaluate your ideas* for a potential business.

☐ Conduct research to *evaluate the market* on your proposed venture.

☐ Analyze your business competitors.

☐ Make a "go" or "no go" call to move forward with your business.

PROFILE OF A CAMPUS CEO

■ **Name:** Ryan Allis

■ **Business:** Virante

■ **Web site:** *www.virante.com*

■ **Founded:** 1990s

■ **His Story:** Ryan Allis is the CEO of Virante, Inc., a Web-marketing and search engine optimization firm with 2006 sales of more than $2 million. An economics major and a senior on leave from the University of North Carolina at Chapel Hill, where he is a Blanchard Scholar, Allis has also founded several other businesses. He is also the CEO of Broadwick Corporation, a provider of the permission-based e-mail marketing software known as IntelliContact. And he's written a popular book, *Zero to One Million,* a guide to building a company from nothing to $1 million in sales. A highly accomplished Campus CEO, Allis is known as a leader in the world of collegiate entrepreneurship. In addition to being CEO of Broadwick and Virante, Ryan is chairman of the Carolina Entrepreneurship Club at UNC– Chapel Hill, founder of The Anti-Poverty Campaign, founder of The Entrepreneurs' Coalition, a nonprofit organization dedicated to encouraging entrepreneurship in developing countries, the founder of *www.zeromillion.com,* an online community of and resource for entrepreneurs and businesspeople, a member of YEO Raleigh-Durham, and a volunteer with Junior Achievement of Eastern North Carolina. He's received numerous accolades for his efforts, including being named one of *BusinessWeek*'s Top 25 entrepreneurs under the age of 25.

■ **Advice for Student Entrepreneurs:** "Have a vision and communicate it. Make sure you clearly communicate your vision for the company. No one follows a leader who cannot communicate the way in which the company will succeed. Each employee's future is tied closely to the success of your company. Make sure they believe in your company, what it stands for, and its products and services, and make sure they know that the hard work they are putting in now will pay off."

—**Ryan Allis,** posted on his ZeroMillion.com Web site

Put It on Paper—
Creating a Powerful Business Plan

3

If you've ever applied for a job or internship, you've probably heard it said that a strong résumé is a good way to "get a foot in the door" of a prospective employer. For entrepreneurs, a strong business plan is the critical document that's going to help you get a foot in the door of a potential investor or lender. The business plan, like your résumé, has to represent you accurately, favorably, and completely. It's your shot at telling someone everything he or she would want to know about your business. It should make that individual confident about supporting your enterprise. A powerful, compelling business plan not only attracts investor interest, it can also act as the magnet you may need to convince others to join your team. In short, a finely tuned business plan is your way of demonstrating to the world that you've thoroughly assessed the viability of your venture and that you are uniquely qualified to successfully market your product or service.

■ DEVELOPING YOUR BUSINESS MODEL

Something to consider before developing your company's business plan is your *business model*. Stated simply, your business model describes the way your company will make money. A more formal definition is that the business model converts *technical inputs* such as your product or service into *economic outputs*

FIGURE 3.1 The Business Model

such as value your company delivers or the profits it's able to generate. In "The Role of the Business Model in Capturing Value from Innovation" (*Industrial and Corporate Change*, June, 2002), professors Henry Chesbrough and Richard S. Rosenbloom depict the role of a business model as shown in Figure 3.1.

When compared to a business plan, which is best developed in a written form with pictures added later, I believe business models are often best developed as a picture, with words added later. For example, a picture of our business model at Mind, Body & Soul Enterprises, including inputs and outputs, is shown in Figure 3.2.

This picture is easily understood and self-explanatory. The words we used to describe it are as follows: Our basic business model at Mind, Body & Soul Enterprises was to purchase compact discs from a distributor at wholesale prices, and advertise and promote the company such that students would hear about us from these efforts or word of mouth. This would lead them to visit our store and purchase our CDs at retail prices, which generated a profit for the company. The combination of pictures and words ensures clarity on your business model and makes it that much easier to articulate it to potential investors or partners. As I'll discuss in Chapter 5, in certain instances financiers aren't necessarily investing in your company, they are investing in your business model.

Some closely related concepts to the business model are the *value proposition*, *value chain*, and *value network*. A *value proposition* is a clear, specific, and succinct statement about the benefits of your product and service, as well as how it is distinguished from other products and services. Our value proposition at Mind, Body & Soul Enterprises was to provide compact discs for students who love music. Unlike other retailers, our CDs were affordable and conveniently sold on campus, while there was no other competing retailer in the vicinity. A *value chain* is the sequence of activities needed to produce your product or deliver your service. For example, the value chain for Mind, Body & Soul Enterprises involved ordering wholesale compact discs, inventorying, marketing, and sell-

FIGURE 3.2 The MBS Business Model

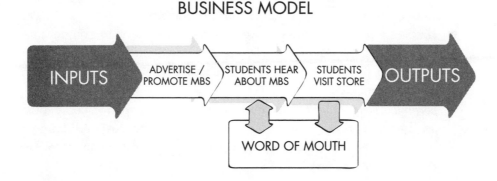

ing each item, and providing customer support for delivery, sales, and returns. Our position in the overall value chain for CDs was clearly toward the end of the chain. Other companies were positioned further up the chain, performing activities such as writing and producing the music, manufacturing and packaging the discs, and shipping the finished CDs to wholesalers. Lastly, the *value network* is the system of competitors, partners, and other complementary entities that can be utilized to deliver more value to your customers. For example, Mind, Body & Soul Enterprises' value network included other local retailers, student organizations that invited us to set up vendor tables at their events on campus, and the campus publications in which we advertised our products. By donating a portion of our proceeds to student organizations at their events, we were able to deliver more value to our customers by enabling them to support their own organizations.

Chesbrough and Rosenbloom identify six areas you should address in developing your business model:

- *Articulate your value proposition.* What is the problem being faced by your customer? How does your product or service address the problem? What value does the customer gain as a result?
- *Define your market segment(s).* Who are the customers being targeted for your product or service? Are there different needs for different types of customers? If so, how will you meet those needs?
- *Identify your position in the value chain.* Where does your company fit into the value-chain structure? How will your company enhance or add value to the chain?

- *Determine your revenue-generating mechanisms.* What is your cost structure? How is revenue generated (sales, subscription, leasing, membership, commission, etc.)? What is your profit margin?
- *Describe your position in the value network.* Who are your competitors? How is your product or service differentiated from theirs? Are there companies or organizations you can partner with to add more value to your customers?
- *Formulate your competitive strategy.* What is your company's competitive advantage? On what basis will this be accomplished (cost or differentiation such as quality, location, etc.)? How will your company maintain this advantage?

Why is it so important to develop a business model? A well-crafted business model can mean the difference between modest achievement and unparalleled success. In fact, sometimes a company's innovation is not in its product or service, but rather, in its business model. For example, Luke Skurman conceived of College Prowler when he was a junior at Carnegie Mellon in Pittsburgh. A class he was taking required him to develop a business plan. So Skurman—who was a business major with an emphasis in entrepreneurship—fleshed out his plan with a professor. As it turns out, that professor provided some critical input to Skurman's business model. Skurman originally thought he would have an advertising-based business model for CollegeProwler.com, which is a publisher of books and guides about more than 250 college campuses nationwide. Fortunately, though, Skurman's professor suggested that Skurman generate sales by actually offering a tangible product for sale—like the book itself. That one simple—but vitally important—change in Skurman's business model likely accounted for hundreds of thousands of dollars in revenues and profitability. Skurman officially founded the company in 2002, upon his graduation. In 2006, College Prowler expects its sales to top more than ten times what they were in 2004. To aid in thinking about your business model, I recommend *Open Business Models: How to Thrive in the New Innovation Landscape* by Henry Chesbrough.

■ CREATING A POWERFUL BUSINESS PLAN

Once you've settled on a business concept and a business model, the logical next step is to write a business plan. So how do you go about creating the best one possible? And is it really necessary to create one before you officially launch your venture? The advantages of putting together a business plan are many. It will help you:

- Better understand the industry in which you operate
- Gather vital information about your competitors and the overall marketplace
- Anticipate potential problems, weaknesses, and threats to your business
- Identify business opportunities, your core strengths, and areas of differentiation
- Reflect about what your company's mission, vision, and values entail
- Demonstrate your overall strategy and financial projections to banks, private investors, and others
- Avoid costly mistakes such as pursuing the wrong target audience

If you're like many entrepreneurs, you may feel like you don't want to "get bogged down" with paperwork or feasibility studies or anything that will prevent you from actually "doing" whatever it is you do. I understand your enthusiasm to jump right in, because I know it can feel like you're moving in slow motion if you have to stop and analyze a lot of information and think through a ton of "what-if" scenarios. So yes, it's possible to start a business without creating a business plan. But you're far more likely to be successful if you go ahead and complete the business planning process.

Know the Audience for Your Business Plan

Before you begin writing, ask yourself: Who is the primary audience for my business plan? The answer to this question can affect the way you write it as well as the areas where you may pay greater attention. Some of the potential target audiences for a business plan include the following:

- *You and Your Partners.* Here the *process* of writing the plan is just as important as the *product.* In other words, the process or act of writing the plan will help to solidify your understanding of the opportunities and challenges facing your business. In gathering data, conducting marketing research, analyzing competition, and the like, you will reach a level of understanding you could not achieve otherwise. Once the product or plan itself is completed, it can serve as an ongoing reference concerning your strategic and tactical direction.

FIGURE 3.3 Keys to Knowing the Audience for Your Business Plan

Audience	Emphasis
You and your partners	Strategic and tactical considerations
Investors	Return on investment
Banks	Ability to repay debt
Advisors	Soliciting feedback

- *Investors.* Investors read business plans with an eye toward ensuring a return on their investment. So they may look closely at your company's intellectual property or proprietary assets, business model, and financial projections. Naturally, they are interested in the entire contents of the plan, but to the extent that your plan demonstrates a long-term competitive advantage and a solid approach to generating profits, it will be more attractive to investors. Because investors typically provide equity financing, they will also want your plan to substantiate the market opportunity, as well as your ability to penetrate the market and grow.

- *Lenders.* Lenders, such as banks, provide debt financing. As a result, a business plan targeted at a lender should emphasize the stability of the market as well as how the business will pay back the debt. The biggest concern in the mind of a bank loan officer will be whether or not the venture is a risky one. While equity investors may believe "high risk, high reward," a lender's mantra is likely "high risk, high worries." Business plans for lenders tend to be as concise as possible to demonstrate sustainable cash flow over the period of the loan.

- *Advisors.* You may consider writing a draft of your business plan and submitting it to advisors such as your professors. Here, it would be permissible to flag areas of uncertainty or areas that could benefit from feedback. Unlike other types of business plans, you can also include sections that aren't completely polished with the hopes of finishing them once you've received their input.

Figure 3.3 summarizes the keys to knowing the audience for your business plan.

Even if you do not aim to secure start-up capital or loans for your business, it's still a terrific idea to create a detailed business plan—if only for yourself. Having this document can be a black-and-white reminder of such things as your overall mission and values. It may help you to make better business decisions that are in keeping with your broad objectives. And a well-crafted business plan also helps you set goals for your business. But a business plan is not meant to be set in stone; on the contrary, it can be a living and breathing document that changes over time as your business evolves, matures, and grows.

Business Plan Outline

While there is no magic formula you must follow, there are a dozen or so key sections you should include to produce a winning business plan.

The 14 crucial elements of a strong business plan follow.

Table of Contents. Although the *Table of Contents* will come in the beginning of your business plan, you will actually create this document last. You'll first need to construct all the other elements of your business plan, number your pages appropriately, and then draw up your Table of Contents. This will serve as a quick guide for any reader of your business plan. If an investor or lender wants to jump right to the section on your Management Team, for instance, he or she will know exactly where to turn by using your Table of Contents.

Executive Summary. After the Table of Contents, every good business plan begins with an *Executive Summary*. Like the Table of Contents, you are also certain to write this document last. The Executive Summary is typically a one-page overview (two pages maximum) of the highlights of your business plan. The various subsections may include overviews of the following:

- Business Description
- Competitive Advantages
- Products and Services (including any intellectual property)
- Market Research and Analysis
- Competitive Analysis
- Marketing Plan
- Management Team (including brief biographies)
- Financial Plan

Here is where you will succinctly convey all the relevant parts of your business in a way that anyone reading your business plan will immediately understand your business concept, know what you're selling, and see your competitive advantage. Highlight the value of your product or service, marketing approach, competition, your management team's expertise, your funding requirements, and the possible return on investment for interested lenders or investors. Think of your Executive Summary as an enhanced, more detailed version of your "elevator pitch" about your company and what you do.

Business Description. The *Business Description* section provides a complete description of your company, and your products and services.

Company Overview. Describe your company history, location, and legal structure, how long you've been in business, and exactly what your company does. You should describe what distinguishes your company in the marketplace. Identify the market conditions, market opportunity, and the key factors leading to success in the marketplace. Here you may also include your company's mission, vision, and values. This will give the reader a sense of the company's purpose, what it is striving to become, and what it stands for. Also indicate whether there are any existing clients, contracts, leases, or other relevant agreements pertaining to the operation of the business.

Product/Service Overview. Clearly explain your products and/or services. You should precisely describe what you are selling, including relevant information about any features, functionality, packages, or programs being offered. If you have multiple products or a variety of services, be sure to describe them all. Be sure to clearly define true *benefits* to clients (i.e., they'll save time or money), rather than merely reciting the *features* of your products or services. Illustrate the problem being addressed, the needs being met, or the opportunity being seized by your products and/or services. You should also state whether or not you have copyrights, patents, or trademarks protecting your products or services. Although intellectual property and other proprietary information should be highlighted here, it should not be provided with significant detail. If sensitive information is mission-critical to your operations, it perhaps should not be disclosed in the business plan. Investors and lenders will want to know how customers will use your products or services, and what the benefit to the customer will be.

Industry Overview. In putting together the *Industry Overview* section of your business plan, this is your chance to really shine as a student entrepreneur. You'll want to summon all the research and writing skills you have to make this section as clear and transparent as possible. And with all the available resources to you on your school's campus and elsewhere, you should have little or no problem demonstrating your absolute command of what's going on within your industry. To do so, make sure you offer commentary about economic, political, or social trends affecting your industry. Discuss whether there are relatively high or low barriers to entry, as well as how easy or difficult it is to exit a business in your industry. Describe whether or not economies of scale exist or could be better exploited. In some cases, a bit of history about your industry may also be relevant. After reading this section, an investor or lender should feel like he or she has a firm grasp of the industry in which you operate. This is crucial because you're far more likely to get funding from a source if he or she understands your business—and the industry in which it operates.

Market Research and Analysis. In the *Market Research and Analysis* portion of your business plan you need to demonstrate that you have a firm grasp of the marketplace and that you know precisely who your intended customers are and why they want or need what you're offering. It is not enough, however, to simply show that a profitable market exists. You also need to demonstrate exactly why customers will buy from you, rather than from a competitor. You can illustrate customer demand by using testimonials, letters from customers, focus-group information, or anything else that shows there is an interested body of buyers just waiting to buy (or repurchase) whatever it is you're selling.

Customers. Describe the target customers and customer segments, and how their needs may vary. What are their preferences? Who are the decision makers? What governs their spending decisions?

Market Size and Trends. This section provides intelligence, figures, data, and other evidence that a market exists for your product and service. Define the approximate size of the market and any anticipated trends or patterns moving forward. Particularly here, but certainly throughout the business plan, you should identify your sources of information as well as the assumptions underlying any projections. Usually, the more reputable the source and the more realistic your assumptions, the more compelling your case.

Competition. Use this section to thoroughly describe your competition and to explain your company's key points of differentiation. Provide neutral, third-party information on each competitor's market share, products, services, and strategies. In discussing your competition, you should point out each company's strengths and weaknesses. Don't make the mistake of hyping your company and bashing the competition. Point out what they're doing right as well as what

■ Market Research Resources

In addition to the market research approaches shared in the previous chapter, explore the sampling of market research information sources that follow. All of these are likely to be available at your campus library, some of which have a business librarian specifically focused on providing such assistance.

■ Industry Reports
  - Hoover's
  - Dun & Bradstreet/Gale Group Industry Handbook

■ Databases
  - LexisNexis® Statistical
  - Standard & Poor's NetAdvantage
  - Dun & Bradstreet Million Dollar Database

■ Government Sources
  - U.S. Census Bureau Current Industrial Reports (CIR) (*www.census.gov/cir/www/*)
  - U.S. Department of Commerce, STAT-USA/Internet (*www.stat-usa.gov*)
  - Federal Interagency Council on Statistical Policy (*www.fedstats.gov*)

■ Business and Trade Publications
  - ABI/Inform on ProQuest Direct
  - Encyclopedia of Business Information Sources
  - Factiva by Dow Jones and Reuters

■ Trade Associations Information
  - Encyclopedia of Associations
  - ASAE and The Center for Association Leadership Member Directory (*www.asaecenter.org*)

they're doing wrong. But if there are audiences the competition isn't reaching, marketing strategies they're not utilizing, or operating efficiencies they're not capturing, be sure to say so—and then back up your claims with hard data.

Competitive Analysis. Benchmark your company against the competition. State how you plan to gain a competitive edge in the market and what sets your business apart from the competition in the eyes of your customers. This is often called your "unique selling proposition." You should also discuss how you plan to meet various goals and objectives in the face of existing competition, and how you would handle new players who might enter the field.

Marketing Plan. The *Marketing Plan* describes how you will enter the market, build awareness of your product or service, sell to customers, and grow the company to achieve greater market share or expand into new markets. It should closely consider the following six Ps of marketing:

- *Product.* What is the product or service you are marketing? Do you plan on expanding your product line or suite of services?
- *Price.* What is the cost to the customer and what is the value he or she will derive from your product or service?
- *Place.* How and/or where will you distribute, deliver, or provide access to your product or service?
- *Promotion.* What incentives will you offer? What types of advertising activities will you sponsor? What communications and public relations activities will you organize?
- *Positioning.* How is your product or service positioned in the marketplace? How is it branded? What are the points of differentiation? What are your competitive advantages?
- *People.* How will you ensure excellent customer service? How will you create a memorable customer experience?

Marketing is how to gain the attention of your customers, establish and build credibility, motivate them to purchase your products or services, deliver customer service, and retain them as long-term customers. Sales is the implementation of marketing so that a transaction is actually completed. In laying out your Marketing Plan, you should also describe the methods by which you will sell to your target clients. For instance, will you sell directly to them, face-to-face, over the Internet, through sales agents, using direct mail, or by some other method? A good Marketing Plan addresses both your *marketing strategy* for making customers aware of your company and your *sales tactics* for how you will convince customers to purchase your products or services.

Entry and Growth Strategy. Your entry and growth strategy describes exactly how you plan to establish your presence in the marketplace and, once that is accomplished, how you plan to grow your company thereafter. Here you should address questions such as the following: How will you initially acquire customers? How will you gain market share? What are the tactics you will use to grow the company? Will you solicit investors to fund your growth? Will you look to partner with or acquire other companies? The key factors leading to success in the company's marketplace should also be identified. Lastly, be sure to describe any plans to expand into new markets.

Economics of the Business. Earlier in the chapter, we introduced the concept of the business model. The *Economics of the Business* section describes various economic and financial characteristics of your business model. These include the following (many are discussed in greater detail in Chapter 7):

- *Gross Margin.* A measure of your company's efficiency
- *Operating Margin.* A measure of your company's profitability before interest and taxes
- *Profit Margin.* A measure of your company's profitability after interest and taxes
- *Fixed and Variable Costs.* Fixed costs do not change with increases in sales or business activity, while variable costs do. The details on these figures provide insight to what drives the cost structure of your company.
- *Breakeven Analysis.* An analysis of the amount of time needed for the company to recoup any initial investments. This is useful for understanding when the company becomes profitable.
- *Cash flow Analysis.* An analysis of the amount of time needed for the company to become cash flow positive. This is useful for understanding when the company begins generating cash.

These figures paint an overall picture for your company's economic and financial durability, while the Financial Plan (described later in this chapter) provides additional, more detailed information.

Design and Development Plan. The *Design and Development Plan* describes the activities that must take place to bring your product or service to the marketplace. This includes any technical requirements, costs, design considerations, development tasks, pending product enhancements or improvements, and the current status of these activities. If there are any proprietary issues, or anticipated difficulties or risks involved in completing the plan, they should also be described here.

Operations Plan. The purpose of an *Operations Plan* is to flesh out critical details of exactly how your company will function. This includes how you will manufacture your product, retail your goods, or furnish human resources in the delivery of services. Where appropriate, it also describes the following:

- Supply chain (network of manufacturers, distributors, suppliers, and sales channels)
- Geographic location of suppliers in relation to your location
- Arrangements for shipping, handling, and logistics
- Regulatory issues

- Uses of equipment
- Seasonal considerations
- Legal concerns

Lastly, the Operations Plan should provide a schedule and timeline depicting key milestones that must be reached.

Management and Staffing Plan. Here you will provide detailed information about the founders and main principals in your business, such as majority investors and members of the board of directors and the advisory board. For each of the founders, owners, and members of the management team you should provide a biography. Their biographies should provide a few key points of information:

- Name and title
- Professional and work experience (highlighting relevant experience)
- Roles and responsibilities (i.e., research and development, finance, operations, etc.)
- Education and credentials
- Honors and awards
- Equity ownership (percentage) and compensation (i.e., salary, bonus, commission, etc.)

Your goal is to show that your company has the right people organized in the right way to ensure the ongoing viability of the company. Be aware that investors are certain to be looking for managers with relevant experience. For this reason, emphasize professional experience and past successes more than your team's academic credentials.

Also identify any vacant positions that may be needed to complete your team, as well as how you plan on recruiting and hiring the necessary talent. Depending on how many key individuals make up your overall team, it may also make sense to include an organizational chart. If you have incentives in place to keep key personnel, be sure to point that out too.

Opportunities and Risks. The *Opportunities and Risks* section of your business plan will convey best-case and worst-case scenarios associated with various circumstances your business may face. It's vitally important that you be realistic in this section. Be circumspect in your analyses, and present as accurately as possible the upside benefits and the downside risks for anyone who decides to invest in your business or loan your company money. Outline the

■ Business Plan Books, Videos, and Software

Some helpful tools that will help you create the best possible business plan include the following:

■ *Business Plans That Work* by Jeffry A. Timmons, Andrew Zacharakis, and Stephen Spinelli. Timmons, Zacharakis, and Spinelli are all colleagues at Babson College, one of the leading institutions for entrepreneurship. In fact, Spinelli founded Jiffy Lube shortly after graduating from McDaniel College.

■ *Hurdle: The Book on Business Planning* by Tim Berry. Written by the creator of Business Plan Pro, a veteran business planner who has more than 20 years' experience and a Stanford MBA degree.

■ "How to Write a Great Business Plan" by William Sahlman in the *Harvard Business Review* (available for PDF download).

■ *The Business Plan—Your Roadmap to Success* Video. Order at the *Small Business Administration Answer Desk* (1-800-827-5722).

■ *Palo Alto's Business Plan Pro* (*www. paloalto.com/ps/bp/*). The best-rated business plan software on the market.

■ *Palo Alto's Business Plan Pro: Social Enterprise Edition*. A special edition of Business Plan Pro developed with the Social Enterprise Alliance (*www.paloalto. com/ps/se/*).

basic market, technology, and competition risks your company faces, and then explain what steps you will take to counter them Also describe the opportunities you could leverage by expanding your capital base, along with the risks your venture could face if you don't secure necessary funding or generate anticipated revenues. Some students may worry that showing a worst-case scenario is self-defeating or presents their company in a bad light. In truth, it makes you look like a more seasoned business professional, because it shows that you have taken the time to think through every possible scenario—whether good or bad. Investors and lenders know that an entrepreneur who can spot potential threats is more likely to be successful in business because that individual will have the foresight to take the appropriate steps to ward off those threats.

Financing Requirements. If you're seeking funding from a lender or investor, it's a good idea to include a section describing your *Financing Requirements* in your business plan. But if you're developing a business plan solely to help you manage your operations and develop proper strategies, you can omit this section. In this part of the business plan, you will state the amount of money you're seeking, indicate the purpose of the investment or loan, and describe how an investor will generate an attractive return on his or her money or how a lender will be repaid. Obviously, the financial statements you've submitted in your business plan must show that your company will have the ability to repay an investor or lender to attract serious interest from these funding sources.

Financial Plan. The *Financial Plan* section of your business plan is another area where you must be rigorous in your details. Here you will provide everything from your existing revenue-and-profit scenario to your projected profit (or loss) over given time periods. You should also include actual or expected cash flow tables, a financial breakeven analysis demonstrating when the company will recoup any initial investments, and an exit strategy to show the point at which investors in your business might recoup their money. This isn't the place for wishful thinking or unfounded predictions about anticipated revenues or profits. Try to back up your projections with hard data that support your underlying assumptions. Chapter 7 provides detailed information about the following financial statements that should be in your business plan:

- Income statement
- Cash flow statement
- Balance sheet

You should include annual summary versions of each statement for up to five years, and quarterly detailed versions of each statement for up to three years from commencing operations.

Appendixes. In this final section of your business plan, the *Appendixes*, you'll include important supporting documentation that will help substantiate any assumptions, claims, or statements you've made that might raise questions. For instance, if you talked about a growing trend in your industry, you could include articles on advertisements that bolster your claims. Other materials to include in the appendixes are leases, purchase agreements, and letters of intent from suppliers, vendors, or other partners. Additionally, you should also include the résumés of all the principals in your business in the Appendix of your business plan. Don't overload the Appendix section; it shouldn't feel like a dissertation that is full of annotations, references, and page after page of citations. But you do want to offer sufficient backup materials to demonstrate that your conclusions and the information you are presenting is all based on solid, verifiable data—and that you aren't just shooting from the hip.

Writing a Mini–Business Plan

There's no question that writing a business plan is a lot of work. For some students, it can take six months or more to write a fully developed plan. But what about those of you who aren't seeking funding, or who perhaps don't want to construct a full-fledged business plan? While I urge you to go through the process of creating a business plan, because it will prove highly instructive and beneficial for you, there is a less laborious way to create a "mini–business plan" that will also provide important insights into your business and industry. This mini–business plan is called a Preliminary Venture Analysis, or PVA, or Business Opportunity Summary. A PVA can give you the information you need to make a fairly quick decision on the feasibility of launching a new company or creating a new product line. Sometimes you can even receive funding from investors based exclusively on the information in your PVA. A PVA is similar to the executive summary of a full-blown business plan. The major difference is that you would spend less time researching and gathering information for the PVA, so it doesn't reflect the same level of depth as does an executive summary.

> ### ■ Business Plan Web Sites
>
> For more information about business plans, check out the following Web sites:
>
> ■ **Business.gov.** The business link to the U.S. government (*www.business.gov*)
>
> ■ **BPlan.com.** The largest single collection of *free* sample business plans online (*www.bplan.com*)

For example, you can take a PVA to organizations such as the Investors' Circle (*www.investorscircle.net*) and if your business profile meets its criteria, it will circulate your funding application to potential angel investors. Investors' Circle has offices in Brookline, Massachusetts, and San Francisco, California, and it helps socially responsible entrepreneurs find financing up to $5 million. Once, in seeking funding via Investors' Circle, I submitted a two-page application for financing that was akin to a PVA. My application provided a description of my business and the market in which it operated. It also highlighted the financial investments my partners and I had already made, and specified the amount of funding we were seeking ($1 million). Lastly, our application contained condensed financial statements and assumptions, a brief summary of the experience and background of the principals in our firm, and a statement pertaining to the social and environmental impact of our business. Again, all of this in just two pages!

At college campuses across the country, in classes, or in business plan competitions, you can also create PVAs that can get you either funding or important feedback. As you can see, the process of completing a PVA-style mini–business plan is far less taxing that constructing a traditional, full-blown business plan.

The Importance of Sharing Your Business Plan

Some students are reluctant to share their business ideas with others. They fear someone stealing their ideas, or going to market with their concepts first. It's possible that such theft could happen. But within the context of your studies and your entrepreneurial pursuits, you want to be sure you're soliciting feedback and insights from professors, other students, business experts, and others when you explain your idea for your venture. These people may be able to recommend alternative strategies or point out important business considerations that you overlooked. The way to protect yourself from idea theft is to ask reviewers of your business plan to sign a *nondisclosure agreement* (NDA). An NDA is a legal contract through which the second party agrees not to disclose information contained in your business plan to a third party. However, be aware that some investors may not sign NDAs given the number of business plans they review; and even some professors may not sign NDAs for reasons stemming from their professional ethics. The takeaway is this: IF a trade secret, patentable technique, or other piece of sensitive information is that critical to your business, it probably shouldn't be in the business plan at a level of detail to be fully disclosed anyway. NDA templates are available on the Internet; however, in instances where you want to ensure full protection, you should consult with an experienced business attorney.

Final Tips

Here are a few tips when preparing the business plan:

- Before you submit a business plan to prospective investors or bankers, add a clean, simple cover sheet, preferably one that includes your company logo or emblem.
- Near the top of the cover sheet, type out: "A Business Plan For" and underneath that statement put your business name, address, telephone number, fax, and Web site.
- Lastly, list yourself—or the pertinent contact person—at the bottom of the cover sheet.

My final piece of advice is not to adhere too strictly to the outline I've presented. If there are sections you must add or remove to best describe your business concept, then by all means do so. Powerful business plans come in all shapes, sizes, and colors. It's not a cookie-cutter process. When all is said and done, *the best business plan is one that accurately reflects your plan for the business.*

CAMPUS CEO CHECKLIST

To get started creating your own business plan:

☐ Develop your business model in pictures and words.

☐ Determine the audiences for your business plan: you and your partners, investors, lenders, or advisors.

☐ Gather the required documentation and compile the basic elements needed to create your overall business plan.

☐ Write a brief description about your business and what it does (or will do).

☐ View sample business plans online.

☐ Identify two or three individuals who can provide valuable feedback on your business plan.

PROFILE OF A CAMPUS CEO

■ **Name:** Shayla Price

■ **Business:** The Scholarship Tutoring Program

■ **Web site:** *www.shaylaprice.com*

■ **Founded:** 2005

■ **Her Story:** Like many high school students planning to enter college, Shayla Price worried about whether or not she could afford the cost of attending an institution of higher learning. But instead of just fretting about it, Price created a plan to assure that she could attend college—without taxing her family's finances or going into debt. Price, who wound up being one of the class valedictorians when she graduated from Thibodaux High School in 2004, embarked upon a massive scholarship search campaign that culminated with her winning more than $100,000 in scholarship funds. On the heels of her success, she wrote *The Scholarship Search: A Guide to Winning Free Money for College and More*. Price also launched The Scholarship Tutoring program, a business designed to help students with résumés and essay writing, gathering recommendations from teachers, and applying for college applications and scholarships.

She's received great response to both her book and her business—so much so that she now has to plan her school schedule around her scholarship counseling activities. Upon graduation, Price plans to either pursue a law degree or work within the nonprofit sector. One of her career goals is to establish a nonprofit organization that will teach young people how to fund their college education.

■ **Advice for Student Entrepreneurs:** "Stay focused. Some people stray or get distracted by other things in life. But if you really want something, you have to stay as focused as possible—and that goes for getting scholarships or starting a business."

—Shayla Price

Structure Supports Success—
Laying a Strong Foundation

Disorganization can be a business killer. Too many times, beginning entrepreneurs run chaotic operations because they focus too much on day-to-day activities and fail to properly organize their businesses. This chapter will examine the crucial aspects of your organizational foundation both conceptually and practically. Actually, you need to be concerned with four different types of structure: *legal structure, organizational structure, physical structure,* and *virtual structure.* But first I would like to discuss choosing the all-important name for your company.

■ IT'S ALL IN A NAME

Take care in choosing a proper name for your company. This may sound like basic advice, but your name, in many ways, will be part of your brand, your reputation, and, perhaps, ultimately what you're known for. Think about the name Google. It's synonymous with Internet search engines. And the name Xerox immediately conjures up images of copying, right? Xerox has built up such a brand reputation that its name alone occupies a certain space in the minds of many consumers. Don't try to be too cute with a name, but don't feel that you have to have something so business-oriented that it does not reflect you, your company's mission, and what you stand for. Obviously, from a tactical standpoint you'll be better off choosing a name that isn't taken and one for which you can acquire a Web domain (i.e., *http://www.yourcompanynamegoeshere.com*). You can check the availability of a domain name by going to either Network Solutions (*www.networksolutions.com*) or Register.com (*www.register.com*). In the best of both worlds, your name and your domain are one in the same. For example, 1-800-FLOWERS is also the Web site: *www.1-800-FLOWERS.com.* Now that's easy to remember!

Registering a Name with the Local, State, and Federal Government

In addition to registering your business domain name, you'll want to get your business properly registered with local, state, and federal agencies, too. Doing so offers you a measure of protection by preventing somebody else from using the identical business name. Imagine the confusion in the marketplace that could be caused by two companies having the same name. You certainly wouldn't want customers who are seeking your product and services to go to another business—especially a competitor—just because that company has the exact name or business listing that you do. Thus, to avoid such confusion, a smart business owner will register the company's name as quickly as possible after the name has been selected.

In certain instances, it's not just a choice of whether or not you want to register your business name; it may be mandated by law. Whenever you create a business name that isn't your own name or doesn't have the name of the entity that owns the business, you must meet legal requirements set down for fictitious or assumed business names. In most cases, this means you'll have to register your business with your county clerk's office and possibly with the state and federal government as well. Let's say you've launched a hand car wash service. At the local level, when you register your business, as an individual you will be deemed to be "Doing Business As" some legal entity. Your "DBA" form, therefore, will say something to the effect of: "Joe Jones, Doing Business As: Clean Car Care Services." If your business is an LLC, a limited partnership, or a corporation (all described in greater detail later in this chapter), in most states your business name is automatically registered once you file your articles of organization, statement of limited partnership, or articles of incorporation, respectively, with your state filing office. Again, by registering your name first, no other entity will be able to use the same name. You'll also need to register your business name to show proof that you are a legitimate company to a bank where you would want to open a business checking or savings account. Although most registrations

■ Choosing a Catchy Tagline

It can be helpful in business to also have a tagline. Choose one carefully, because it will be like an elevator speech describing what your company is all about. For example, at MBS, we changed from our initial tagline of "Workshops, Lectures, and Seminars for Students, by Students" and jazzed it up a bit to "Catalyst of Change, One Person at a Time." We felt the latter stated directly that we sought to facilitate positive change among every single customer who attended our workshops, lectures, and seminars.

At BCT Partners, our tagline is "Your Partner in Solutions That Matter." We believe it does a great job of conveying two messages. The first message is the way we work with our customers as their "partner," working alongside them to identify "solutions" to problems. As a consulting firm, we provide strategic planning, organizational development, and information technology solutions. In doing so, our customer's goals become our goals. The second message is the kinds of project we undertake. As a socially responsible consulting firm, the solutions that "matter" to us, and our customers, are those that address issues relating to housing, community development, economic development, health care, and education.

When it comes to picking a good tagline, consider one that (popular examples included):

■ Describes a characteristic or memorable feature of your product or service
  - Kellogg's Rice Krispies: *"Snap, Crackle, and Pop"*
  - Federal Express: *"When it absolutely, positively has to be there overnight"*

  - Prudential Financial: *"Growing and protecting your wealth"*

■ Captures the feeling or emotion you hope to elicit from customers
  - McDonald's: *"I'm Lovin' It"*
  - Kentucky Fried Chicken: *"Finger Lickin' Good!"*
  - Maxwell House Coffee: *"Good to the Last Drop"*

■ Suggests an action or offers a directive
  - Apple: *"Think Different"*
  - American Express: *"Don't Leave Home Without It"*
  - Nike: *"Just Do It"*
  - Sprite: *"Obey Your Thirst"*

■ Says something profound or thought-provoking
  - The United Negro College Fund: *"A Mind is a Terrible Thing to Waste"*
  - U.S. Department of Transportation: *"Friends Don't Let Friends Drive Drunk"*

■ Conveys quality or excellence
  - General Electric: *"We Bring Good Things to Life"*
  - Lexus: *"The Relentless Pursuit of Perfection"*

■ Poses a question
  - California Milk Processing Board: *"Got Milk?"*
  - Verizon: *"Can You Hear Me Now? . . . Good"*
  - UPS: *"What Can Brown Do for You?"*

Whatever you choose, just make sure you pick a company name and a tagline that conveys how you want to be known and perceived in the marketplace.

for small businesses take place at the county level, some states require you to register your fictitious business name with the secretary of state or another state agency. Just call the county clerk's office and inquire about the proper procedure in your region. Naturally, you should be prepared to pay a nominal fee (usually around $10 to $50) to get your business properly registered through one or more agencies. Lastly, certain states also require you to publish your fictitious name in a local newspaper and then submit an affidavit known as a "proof of publication" to the county clerk or state agency to illustrate that you have fulfilled the publication requirement. Your local newspaper can assist you with this if it's required in your state.

Most small businesses and start-ups won't need to register their company names with federal authorities. However, for those of you who intend to market your service or product in more than one state—or perhaps internationally— you'd be wise to apply for federal trademark protection as well. When you register your business name with the U.S. Patent and Trademark Office (USPTO), you signal to every other entrepreneur in the country that your business name is already taken. It also gives you a leg up, legally speaking, if you should ever have to defend your name in court against anyone who has infringed upon your business name. To find out whether your name qualifies for trademark protection and to learn how to register it as a trademark, visit the USPTO at *www.uspto.gov.*

■ LEGAL STRUCTURE

When it comes to the legal structure of your business, you have four main forms to choose from:

- *Sole proprietorship*
- *Partnership*
- *Corporation*
- *Limited liability company (LLC)*

Note that the first three—*sole proprietorship, partnership,* and *corporation*—are legal *entities,* while the *limited liability company* represents a legal *status.* I will describe each of these structures, as well as discuss the pros and cons of different legal structures. However, to ensure the best decision for your needs, you should consult with an experienced business attorney, a certified public accountant (CPA), and a business insurance company representative. Please bear with me as I walk you through the various legal and structural considerations.

Sole Proprietorship

A *sole proprietorship* is the simplest of the three forms, where nothing is needed to set up the legal structure. A sole proprietorship is legally the same entity as its owner; in that regard there is no limitation of liability. If the company is sued, the owner is sued. Similarly, the company's profits (and debts) are considered the owner's who must then pay personal income taxes on any profits. However, sole proprietors do avoid being taxed twice, whereas corporations are taxed twice. A sole proprietorship has only one owner. There are no partners. Consequently, it cannot issue shares and, therefore, cannot accept investors. As a sole proprietor you can register to "do business as" an alternate trade name, which can also enable you to do banking under that name. We were initially established as a sole proprietorship under my name, but doing business as "Mind, Body & Soul Enterprises." Although it wasn't necessary, we did apply for an employer iden-tification number, or EIN (the equivalent of a Social Security number for a busi-ness), so that in the event that we changed the legal structure of the company, where an EIN is required, it would already be assigned to the entity.

Partnership

A *partnership* is an agreement between two or more individuals to engage in business activity for profit. Under the partnership umbrella exists *general part-nerships, limited partnerships,* and *limited liability partnerships.* For *general partner-ships,* all partners bear unlimited liability and are personally liable for profits and debts. For *limited partnerships,* there are both general partners and limited partners. Furthermore, partners may be held responsible for the actions of fel-low partners. General partners have management responsibility and unlimited liability, while limited partners have no management responsibility and no liability. *Limited liability partnerships* provide limited liability protections for all partners (in many states, however, less protection than corporations and LLCs), while partners also typically play an active role in the management of the com-pany. Typically, in all three cases, a partnership agreement is drafted to define how profits are distributed. Based on the distribution figures, each partner is then responsible for paying personal income taxes on his or her share of the profits. The partnership agreement also defines each partner's role in the man-agement and control of the company, as well as identifies what to do with a partner's ownership shares in the event of departure, disability, death, or bankruptcy. Generally speaking, partnerships are not utilized very often. They are most prevalent among medical practices, law firms, architectural firms, and in other professions where professional liability for the individual partners buffers them from any liability deficiencies of a partnership arrangement. Lastly, also note that a *joint venture* is a general partnership that is formed to undertake a specific project or opportunity, such as real estate.

Corporation

A *corporation* is a legal entity separate from its members. Shareholders bear no personal liability for the debts or other obligations of the corporation. As the corporation grows, the owners can continue to profit whether or not they remain involved with the company. And unlike sole proprietorships and partnerships, which dissolve upon departure, disability, or death, or bankruptcy of the owner(s), corporations can exist forever. Corporations require greater administration than do the other forms. There is more recordkeeping, more paperwork, the need to establish and maintain a board of directors, and an annual shareholders meeting requirement (in most states). At tax time, corporations require the assistance of a business lawyer and tax accountant. Under the corporation umbrella exist both Subchapter C corporations (or C-Corps) and Subchapter S corporations (or S-Corps). C-Corps can have an unlimited number of shareholders, foreign or domestic, but also suffer from "double taxation." For C-Corps, both the corporation's profits and the shareholder's dividends are taxed. By contrast, S-Corps are limited to 75 or 100 investors (U.S. residents only) yet are only taxed once—profits are assigned to shareholders only, who then pay personal income tax on their earnings. Small businesses often opt for the S-Corp when there are a limited number of investors and they are all U.S. residents, so as to minimize the company's tax burden.

Limited Liability Company

Finally, a *limited liability company* or *LLC* can combine the single taxation of a sole proprietorship or partnership with the limited liability of a corporation. However, the LLC is a legal *status* as opposed to a legal *entity,* so there is some flexibility in how you structure an LLC. To be specific, when forming an LLC, you must decide whether to be taxed as a sole proprietorship, a partnership, an S corporation, or a C corporation. This choice must be made at the time you file your first taxes (note: that choice will remain until or unless you file paperwork requesting a change). In this regard, the company and its owners (or "members") can avoid double taxation as long as the choice is made to be taxed as a sole proprietorship, a partnership, or an S corporation. LLCs are often preferred over LLPs because in many states LLPs provide a reduced form of limited liability. LLCs are often best suited for small business owners, while the decision of whether to be taxed as a sole proprietorship, partnership, or corporation varies, depending on the size, needs, and wherewithal of the company.

The good news is that you're generally not locked into whatever choices you make. While it is not trivial, you can change your legal structure as your company grows. In growing from a five-figure company, as Mind, Body & Soul Enterprises, to a six-figure company as MBS Educational Services & Training, we evolved from a sole proprietorship to an LLC that was taxed as a partnership. In growing from a six-figure company as MBS Educational Services & Training to a multimillion-dollar firm as BCT Partners, we evolved again from an LLC that was taxed as a partnership to an LLC that was taxed as an S-Corp.

A synopsis of the highlights, advantages, and disadvantages of each legal structure and status is shown in Figure 4.1.

In light of all these choices, you should consult with an experienced business attorney, a certified public accountant (CPA), and a business insurance company to find the best fit. Also consider soliciting advice from business school and law school professors.

For many student businesses considering their legal structure, it's probably best to keep it as simple as possible and scale accordingly. Your objective should be to marry the form of the company to the size, the needs, and the wherewithal of the business. Obviously, certain structures—such as being incorporated—require more rigor, more accounting, and more paperwork than other structures do. But no matter what you do, you're going to need some level of accountability concerning your business to keep it running efficiently.

Legal, Accounting, and Tax Advice—"Get a Good Lawyer and a Good Accountant"

A common piece of advice for new business owners is to "get a good lawyer and a good accountant." I couldn't agree more. Sifting through these legal structure options is just the tip of the iceberg concerning various other considerations for which good legal and financial advice will help tremendously. If you

FIGURE 4.1 Highlights, Pros, and Cons of Legal Structures

Entity	Highlights	Pros	Cons
Sole proprietorship	■ One owner ■ Owner and company are same entity	■ Simple to create and administer ■ Single taxation	■ Unlimited liability ■ Cannot accept investors
General partnership	■ Two or more individuals bound by an agreement ■ General partners have management responsibility and unlimited liability	■ Simple to create and administer ■ Single taxation	■ Unlimited liability (all partners) ■ Cannot accept investors ■ Partners liable for other partners
Limited partnership	■ Two or more individuals bound by an agreement ■ Limited partners have no management responsibility and no liability	■ Simple to create and administer ■ Single taxation	■ Unlimited liability (general partners only) ■ Cannot accept investors ■ Partners liable for other partners
Limited liability partnership	■ Two or more individuals bound by an agreement ■ Partners have limited liability	■ Single taxation ■ Limited liability	■ Limited liability provides less protection than corporation or LLC
S corporation	■ Separate legal entity from shareholders	■ Limited liability ■ Up to 75 shareholders ■ Single taxation ■ Exists forever	■ Requires greater administration
C corporation	■ Separate legal entity from shareholders	■ Limited liability ■ Unlimited shareholders ■ Exists forever	■ Double taxation ■ Requires greater administration
Status	**Highlights**	**Pros**	**Cons**
Limited liability company	■ Combines liability benefits of corporation while avoiding double taxation	■ Limited liability	■ Must decide legal entity status for tax purposes

don't have the money to hire a business lawyer or an accountant, consider the following options:

- Solicit advice from business school and law school professors.
- Invite a specialist in the legal field or accounting profession to join your advisory board (described later in this chapter).
- Find out if there is a legal clinic or assistance center on campus. For example, Rutgers University has a community law clinic that offers free legal assistance to the campus community.
- Reach out to nonprofit legal-aid and small-business assistance organizations where experts offer their services, sometimes pro bono.
- Consider using one of the accounting packages referenced in Chapter 5. Just be sure to have a tax accountant review your recordkeeping when you set it up, as well as review your financial records when it's tax time.

While you can probably do without a lawyer if you're simply setting up a sole proprietorship, you definitely should consult a lawyer under any of the following circumstances:

- You need help understanding or protecting your legal rights in any business matter.
- You're entering into a complex business deal or a legal transaction that's over your head.
- You have a corporate legal problem of any kind.

By the way, if you do hire professional accountants or lawyers, make sure you know what you're getting, because you'll likely need a bookkeeping accountant, a tax accountant, and a lawyer with expertise that is specific to your industry. A bookkeeper will help you with payroll, keep good accounting records for you, and let you know when accounts payable are due. But a tax accountant is—or at least should be—more strategic, and will be able to help you minimize your tax burden. For example, in addition to your state and federal personal income tax return (i.e., Form 1040, 1040A, or 1040EZ), you may also need to file one or more of the following forms with the Internal Revenue Service: Schedule SE (self-employment tax), Schedule C (profit or loss from business), Form W-2 (employee wage and tax statement), Form 1099 (independent contractor payments), or Form ST-100 (quarterly taxes) with your state/local government. While it is no substitute for professional tax expertise, you can also contact the IRS directly to request forms or receive assistance:

IRS Web Site:	*www.irs.gov/businesses/*
IRS Toll-free Assistance (for individuals):	1-800-928-1040
IRS Toll-free Assistance (for businesses):	1-800-829-4933

If you retain a lawyer, he or she should have experience with businesses in your industry. We once learned this the hard way. Our company found a lawyer who worked a full-time job and moonlit on the side. We had been working with him for years until we were awarded a large government subcontract. A friend of ours, who happened to work for the prime contractor who awarded us the subcontract, called us up and said, "You need to get a lawyer who knows government contracting to represent you." Apparently, our lawyer was in meetings with these people asking questions about basic terms and concepts and saying, "What does this mean?" "Can you explain this?" Needless to say, we let him go. When looking for legal, accounting, and tax assistance, here are a few suggestions based on this experience:

- Ask your professor or someone from the university's legal or accounting department for a referral.
- Interview candidates to understand their prior, relevant experience.
- Request references and check them thoroughly.
- Avoid long-term contractual agreements in the event the person does not work out.

These simple tips alone will help you to avoid the mistakes we made.

■ Business Incorporation Online

There are resources online that can walk you through the entire process of business registration and formation. For a fee, they will complete the necessary paperwork and, pending your signature, submit it to the appropriate government agencies for approval. Following is a list of sites you may consider.

- MyCorporation (*www.mycorporation.com*)
- The Company Corporation (*www.corporate.com*)

- Inc. File (*www.incfile.com*)
- Legal Zoom (*www.legalzoom.com*)
- BizFilings (*www.bizfilings.com*)

In addition to helping you create a corporation, nonprofit corporation, LLC, or partnership, they also provide some combination of related services to assist with annual reports, copyrights, trademarks, and patents. Most offer a free quote for their services online.

■ ORGANIZATIONAL STRUCTURE

Organizational structure speaks to a number of considerations. This includes determining your *organization's foundation,* which includes your mission, vision, and values. It also entails designing your *organization chart.* These items should be captured in your business plan, as discussed in Chapter 3. And, finally, it involves deciding what to *make, buy, or borrow;* that is, deciding what activities should be "insourced" or performed directly by you and your team; what activities should be "outsourced" or performed by consultants, contract staff, or temporary hires; and what should be "borrowed" or acquired via in-kind contributions, barter, volunteerism, and other creative means. This is a strategic consideration for organizing your company's resources optimally.

Organizational Foundation

In *The Fifth Discipline,* author Peter Senge describes the relationships between great organizations and their mission, vision, and values—concepts he refers to as "governing ideas." According to Senge, vision is the "What?"—the picture of the future you seek to create; mission or purpose is the "Why?"—the organization's answer to the question, "Why do we exist?"; and values are the "How?"—they answer the question, "How do we want to act, consistent with our mission, along the path toward achieving our vision?" Senge argues that great organizations have a larger sense of purpose and seek to contribute to the world in some unique way, to add a distinctive source of value. Along the same lines, I see mission, vision, and values as representing the very foundation of great companies, as shown in Figure 4.2.

Right off the bat, you should know that if you want to become a "big dog" in your industry, you've got to have a big-dog mission, vision, and values. They must reflect the kind of organization you ultimately would like to create, the place you want to occupy in the consumer's mind, and the philosophy you want to stand for—perhaps for decades and beyond. That's what building a long-lasting institution is all about, as opposed to just creating a company that will only survive during your campus years.

At MBS, the six founding partners—JR, Aldwyn, Larry, Dallas, Raqiba, and me—dedicated an entire weekend on campus to establishing a mission statement for the company that captured our purpose.

FIGURE 4.2 Organizational Foundation and Governing Ideas

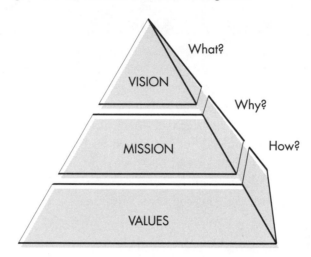

MBS Misson

To empower men and women to fulfill their individual and collective purpose through mental (Mind), physical (Body), and spiritual (Soul) development.

To guide our overall business strategy, our long-term vision was as follows:

MBS Vision

To create an institution that will:

- *Be a catalyst of positive change;*
- *Empower others to reach their highest potential;*
- *Inspire and encourage people to strive for excellence;*
- *Educate the broadest possible audience through innovative technology, intriguing content, and interactive learning;*
- *Facilitate an awareness of technology and its role in society.*

Lastly, we chose a set of values that represented the company's day-to-day guiding principles. The following seven values were meant to permeate all our interactions with each other as well as with our customers:

MBS Values

Integrity, excellence, balance, synergy, community, growth, and innovation.

I think we did pretty well for our first mission, vision, and values. You'll see in Chapter 9 that these were later modified and improved when we launched BCT Partners.

When it comes to your company's mission, vision, and values, it's not necessary to come up with something long-winded, technical, or overly complicated. Just summarize what feels right to you in describing the "What?", "Why?", and "How?" for your organization. However, do take the exercise seriously and challenge yourself (and your business partners) to answer these fundamental questions because these governing ideas represent the foundation for your enterprise. And while they can be modified and tweaked later, they will speak volumes to yourself, your colleagues, and your customers about exactly what your company believes in. Start out with governing ideas that reflect where you want to be in 5, 10, or 20 years, so you can increase the likelihood of getting there. This is what it means, as Stephen Covey says in the *7 Habits of Highly Effective People*, to "begin with the end in mind."

Organization Chart

An organization chart is more than just a visual depiction of the reporting structure of your company. An organization chart reflects the priorities of your company, the balance of responsibility, and the allocation of resources. A well-designed organization chart makes certain that your customers' needs are being met in an efficient and effective manner. It also ensures that the appropriate people are communicating with one another, and that members of your team are sufficiently empowered. Think about it: even if you are a team of two, it's still necessary to define what you will do and what your teammate will do.

Two ways of thinking about the design of your organization chart are to organize either by *market* (or customer segment) or to organize by *function*. Each of these considerations has to do with how you organize those individuals whom you designate to lead key areas of your company. Take a campus bookstore operating out of a dormitory as an example. The owners determined through market research that there are three primary areas of interest among students on their campus, namely, textbooks, fiction, and nonfiction. Each of the three primary leads could be focused on one of these areas, as shown in Figure 4.3.

The advantage of organizing by market is that you can directly meet the needs of your customers. Another way of organizing by market would be to assign these three leads to certain geographic designations (i.e., each could be

FIGURE 4.3 Organization Chart by Market

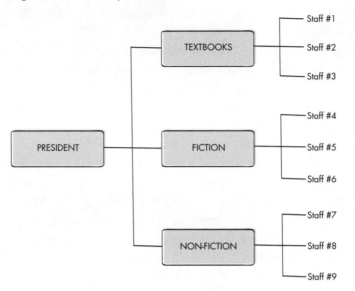

assigned to a different campus or a cluster of dormitories). The disadvantage is that each of the three leads is now responsible for overlapping functions, such as marketing, advertising, ordering, and sales, which can lead to inefficiencies. The alternative way of organizing, by function, would designate leads for specific functional areas, such as marketing and advertising, operations, and sales, as shown in Figure 4.4.

The advantage of organizing in this manner is it focuses on the skill set required for each lead. You can assign someone who is majoring in business to lead your marketing and advertising on campus, someone who is majoring in communications or loves interacting with people to lead your sales efforts, and your most organized friend to take charge of operations. The disadvantage is that, depending on the nature of your business, you could easily find that one of your leads is shouldering a much heavier load than the other leads or, conversely, you could have areas without sufficient resources to function effectively. For example, if your company's success is ultimately driven by sales, then you may need to dedicate more people to sales than marketing, advertising, or operations.

The following are additional pieces of advice concerning your organization chart:

FIGURE 4.4 Organization Chart by Function

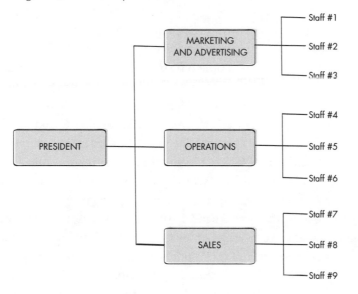

- When assigning responsibility, always play to people's strengths.
- Look to assign multiple, complementary responsibilities to a single position, especially when you're small (for example, you might assign marketing, advertising, and sales to one person).
- Try to minimize the number of levels in your organization chart to avoid unnecessary hierarchy, which can lead to inefficiency.
- Hold meetings on a regular basis, especially between and across different areas.
- Encourage everyone in your company to see themselves as part of a team, especially when you are small; consider organizing simple team-building activities such as social events.

To find an organization chart that works for you, consider the areas requiring the greatest attention within your company, and consider the particular needs of your customers. Once you've done that, experiment with different arrangements by trying to strike an appropriate balance between the two. The charts presented here are more traditional and hierarchical, so don't be afraid to get creative and research alternative structures such as a flat or matrix organization chart. Keep working at it until you find something you're comfortable with and don't be afraid to tweak it when necessary.

Advisory Board

To ground your business in reality, and to help prepare it for success, you should integrate into your organizational structure a way to systematically and routinely receive input from people who don't work on your business in a day-to-day capacity. The best way I know to do this is to identify mentors who can serve as advisors to your enterprise. Honestly, we didn't do a good enough job of identifying potential mentors. We were a little cavalier thinking we could do it all ourselves. We should've established an advisory board of specialists who possessed skills and knowledge in a number of different areas. No campus-based business today should be without such a team of advisors—comprised of faculty members, local entrepreneurs, and experts in your field (I'll discuss specific ways to identify mentors in Chapter 12). Although we had pretty good political contacts and solid social contacts, we were challenged in finding other entrepreneurs as mentors and role models. I think having such a person or persons would've made a big difference for us. I don't care if you only know the owner of a corner store—develop a relationship with that business owner and ask him or her about the challenges of being an entrepreneur. I guarantee you'll learn some valuable lessons.

Make, Buy, or Borrow

To run an efficient business, you will also need to make critical decisions about how you will get a number of inevitable and ongoing functions routinely completed within your organization. I call this the "make, buy, or borrow" decision process. Essentially, you need to think about what activities you (or your partners, employees, or interns) should make or do internally within your company, and which ones you should not. For example, let's take an area that every entrepreneur must tackle: administration. If we think about something as basic as answering your phone or fielding customer phone calls, you'll see that your decision is threefold. You may decide to answer the phone lines directly (or make an employee do it); you may opt to purchase a dedicated phone mail system to handle the calls (thus buying this service), or you might choose to route your calls through a campus incubator or shared office center to use the telephone receptionist who already works there. In this instance, you're borrowing her administrative support.

Beyond administration, of course, there are myriad tasks that must be regularly completed to keep your business progressing. Here is a partial list of categories for these tasks:

- Administration
- Operations
- Resource Management
- Project Management
- Accounting
- Finance
- Human Resources
- Public Relations
- Marketing and Sales
- Legal
- Manufacturing
- Supply Chain
- Business Development
- Client-Relationship Management
- Partner-Relationship Management
- Information Technology

Again, it will not be possible or necessary for you to make or do all these functions. And even if you had all the capital your heart desired, neither would it be prudent to buy all these services. It may be feasible to borrow some things, but not others. So spend some time thinking about what will be most realistic for you. Because you'll be looking at this area with an entrepreneurial mindset, don't be afraid to get creative. Some of the best entrepreneurs out there are, in fact, so very successful because they are experts at being resourceful without being resource full, and they don't feel the need to throw money at every single problem or issue they face.

In many ways, the make, buy, or borrow decision might be best summarized in these terms:

- *Make what is mission-critical to your business.* Consider some of the mission-critical activities that are absolutely necessary for your business to succeed. Ideally, these are the things you want to make or do yourself. Certain necessary areas can be borrowed or bought, such as administrative assistance, legal assistance, and accounting assistance. In these instances, you may only need these services occasionally and it would be too costly to retain someone full-time. But then there are areas that represent the very core of what your company does. If you're running a catering business and nobody on your team knows how to prepare quality meals, then you're in trouble. Preferably, *someone that is "in-house" and on your team must possess the subject-matter expertise to know your core business activities very well.* If that is not the case, you need to fully understand how that expertise will be learned or obtained, and the importance of having an experienced professor, advisor, mentor, or partner working for you increases considerably. MBS was a training company and, fortunately, our team had basic training experience from our work in student organizations, and worked hard to learn as much as we could thereafter.

- *Borrow what you can acquire on an ad hoc basis.* Think about ways to get what you need without paying for it. Sometimes it may involve bartering, sometimes it's brainstorming or volunteering—anything you can get for your business that doesn't require a capital outlay. Early on, at MBS, we borrowed contract templates from the Web because we couldn't afford to have a lawyer draw them up. And at Rutgers, if you were a student organization and you wanted to have a speaker, you had to use a certain contract. We borrowed the university's existing contract, modifying the language as appropriate. Note: if you do borrow certain things, make sure you don't violate any copyright laws or misappropriate any individual's or institution's proprietary information and do your best to ensure you're not compromising on quality.

- *Buy what's critical that you can't do yourself.* If you don't have anyone on your team who can perform core tasks for your business *or* the task needed is indeed critical and you believe there is someone who can do it better *and* there is no way for you to borrow it from someone else while maintaining a high level of quality, then you may need to "outsource" and buy it. At MBS we eventually had no choice but to buy certain legal and accounting assistance because none of the partners brought that expertise to the table and we absolutely needed good counsel and financial assistance to grow the business.

There's a wide range of territory that business owners have to cover. This includes mission-critical tasks that you must do personally, as well as other duties that can readily be farmed out or creatively acquired—and they should be.

■ PHYSICAL AND VIRTUAL STRUCTURE

There are two ways for your team to meet and keep in contact—*physically*, that is, in person, or *virtually*, via e-mail, Internet, mobile phone, etc. Your primary physical consideration is: where should your base of operation be located, if anywhere? Your primary virtual consideration is the following: which technologies—from among the myriad of those available—are appropriate to maintain communication in a given place at a given time? Now you may be saying to yourself: the answers are obvious. Here are a few tips to make sure you cover all your bases.

Office Location

It's also important to determine where to establish your company's office and base of operation. Your five primary choices are: *on-campus dormitory*, *on-campus incubator*, *off-campus apartment*, *off-campus office*, and *virtual office*.

On-campus dormitory. Your dormitory is the most readily available facility for your office and there is no additional cost for using it as an office. It is probably in close proximity to campus and is likely to have some form of free or low-cost Internet access. The first drawback is that there may be university regulations prohibiting dorm use as an office. Second, because it is an environment where you live, it could be distracting, and you won't be able to entertain clients there. Finally, you could quickly outgrow your dorm room.

On-campus incubator. If your campus has a business incubator, it is definitely an option to consider. The potential advantages of business incubators include below-market rent, close proximity to campus, availability of supportive services, room for growth, and a professional environment where you could entertain clients. Perhaps most important, many business incubators offer a wide variety of space options, ranging from a low-cost single cubicle to large office suites. I'll talk more about the benefits of incubators in Chapter 10, but, in the context of office location, the only potential disadvantages are pricing and availability.

Off-campus apartment. An off-campus apartment shares some of the same advantages and disadvantages of an on-campus dormitory. Once again, there is no additional rent, although there will likely be a cost for Internet access, as well as an increase in the cost of utilities such as electricity, depending on your line of business. Similarly, there may also be distractions, limited room for growth, and difficulty in hosting clients there.

Off-campus office. The pros and cons of an off-campus office are distinct. The clear advantages are a professional environment that is ideal for meeting with clients and room for growth by expanding into new space, where available. The clear disadvantages are that an off-campus office is the most expensive option and may not be in close proximity to campus.

Virtual office. A virtual office allows you to rent office facilities without physically operating the business there on a day-to-day basis. Virtual offices can include receptionists, meeting space, Internet access, and office space ranging from a cubicle to a suite, and more. The benefits of virtual offices are flexibility and low cost (as low as $50/month) in a professional environment. The primary disadvantage is the lack of permanency. Two of the leading providers of virtual offices are Regus (*www.regus.com*) and Intelligent Office (*www.intelligentoffice.com*).

Figure 4.5 compares and contrasts all five options. Of course, there is always the option of operating completely virtually, which is where we ended up at some point during our experience growing MBS. Our first office was our dormitory. During semester breaks and summer vacation we used my mom's dining room. Our initial communication structure for MBS was completely physical, that is, we held most of our meetings and interactions in person and on campus. But soon after the last of our founding members graduated, we had no choice but to move to a completely virtual model. We used technology to remain in touch, as we each pursued our respective academic and career endeavors away from Rutgers. Eventually, we moved into our first "official" office in Lawrence's living room—working at his dining room table. We ended up buying a cordless phone from which we solicited customers and landed contracts. We later moved from his house into the equivalent of a garage next to a high school, at which time we transitioned again to a hybrid model of communication that combined both physical and virtual forms. While some members of the team worked from the office, several others worked remotely. This is the structure that remains today.

FIGURE 4.5 Office Location Choices

Office Space	Pros	Cons
On-campus dormitory	■ No additional rent ■ Proximity to campus resources ■ Internet access may be included	■ May conflict with college or university policies ■ May cause distractions ■ Limited room for growth ■ Difficult for meeting with clients
On-campus incubator	■ Below-market rent with flexible space (typically) ■ Proximity to campus resources ■ Supportive services ■ Good for meetings	■ Not available on certain campuses
Off-campus apartment	■ No additional rent ■ Proximity to campus resources	■ May cause distractions ■ Limited room for growth ■ Difficult for meetings
Off-campus office	■ Good for meetings ■ Room for growth (if space available)	■ Costly rent ■ Not available near certain campuses
Virtual office	■ Low-cost and flexible space in a professional environment ■ Office facilities (i.e., receptionist, Internet access)	■ Lack of permanency

Blended Structure: Combining Physical and Virtual Communication

A *blended structure*, that is, a combination of physical and virtual forms of team interaction and communication, is no longer an option nowadays, but rather it's a norm. A blended structure allows the greatest flexibility in how and when everyone meets, and that the most appropriate tool/medium can be used in any given circumstance. In doing so, a virtual structure that involves e-mail and the Internet, which are almost always readily accessible, can be fully leveraged despite its limitations. Meanwhile, a physical structure and face-to-face communication, which is typically more elusive, can be maximized to the greatest extent. Just because it's summer, spring break, or time to go home for the holidays doesn't mean business has to grind to a halt. A Campus CEO cannot afford to be away from his or her business for lengthy periods of time. Under these circumstances, the appropriate blended structure can be quite helpful.

Looking back over our experience it is now clear that MBS evolved from a purely physical, or face-to-face, structure for communication and interaction to a blended structure. After graduation from Rutgers, I went to Oxford, JR went to the Georgia Institute of Technology, and Aldwyn accepted a full-time position with Corning Incorporated in upstate New York. Fortunately, it was possible to run MBS virtually throughout the day via e-mail and the Internet and meet physically in the evenings, whereas all the seminar work was completed on the weekends—which worked perfectly for everyone's schedule.

Figure 4.6 provides a useful way of thinking about when a physical or virtual structure is most appropriate, and the associated use of different technologies.

As you can see, the top axis represents "place":

- *Physical* or nontechnological forms of communication facilitate team interaction in the *same place* or same location. A team meeting is an example of communication in the same physical place, as is a letter, by virtue of the fact that if two people read it they are accessing the same physical document.
- *Virtual* or technological forms of communication facilitate team interaction in a *different place* or different location. Examples of virtual interaction include instant messaging or e-mail, which do not require both parties to be together to communicate.

The left axis represents "time":

- *Synchronous* forms of communication facilitate team interaction at the *same time* or in real time. Face-to-face conversation is a nontechnological example of synchronous communication, while a mobile phone is a technological example—both represent live interaction.
- *Asynchronous* forms of communication facilitate team interaction at a *different time* or delayed time. From a nontechnological perspective, a memo is asynchronous because it can communicate its message from one person to another at a different time.

You'll note, as well, that using certain technologies—such as computers, Web sites, and wireless Internet access—help enable some of the other tools, and can therefore span both "same time" and "different time," depending on how they are used. As a result, they do not naturally fall into any one place on the grid. I'll discuss these "enabling technologies" in greater detail in the next chapter.

FIGURE 4.6 Blended Communication Structure

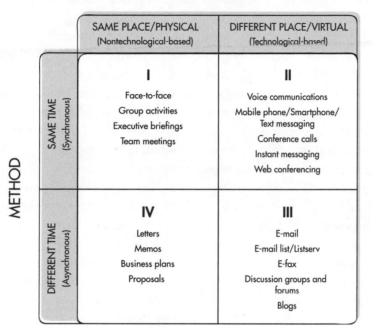

The value in this blended structure framework is that each of the four quadrants, or grid entries, can direct you to the right method of communication, in the right place, at the right time:

- *Quadrant I: Same Place, Same Time.* Includes face-to-face conversation, group activities, executive briefings, team meetings, and the like. Having your team in Quadrant I—in the same place at the same time—is usually the hardest of the four quadrant scenarios to accomplish, because of schedules, obligations, and other demands on your time and their time. Consequently, it is important to maximize this time when it is available. This is done by leveraging the approaches and tools available in the other three quadrants, so that your time together is as productive as possible.

- *Quadrant II: Same Time, Different Place.* Having your team together at the same time in a different place (Quadrant II) is second only to being in the same place at the same time (Quadrant I). These approaches are best utilized as the next best thing to being together. Voice communications, mobile phones, smartphones, instant messaging, and text messaging are ideal for person-to-person interactions such as status updates, strategic conversations, etc., while conference calls, Web conferencing, and other similar technologies are ideal for group discussion, presentations, and reporting.

- *Quadrant III: Different Place, Different Time.* Different place, different time technologies are best utilized for communicating written information quickly and easily. This includes various letters, memos, reports, and reports electronically, which can be accomplished using e-mail and e-fax. These tools can also be helpful for moderated or facilitated discussions, especially when the discussion will benefit from tracking posts and responses from users. E-mail lists, listservs, blogs, discussion groups, and forums are useful in this regard.

- *Quadrant IV: Different Time, Same Place.* Paper-based letters, memos, business plans, proposals, etc., are particularly appropriate as formal approaches of communication or to maintain a "hard copy" or paper trail for important documents. They are also ideal when confirmation is needed that an item has reached its destination. Nowadays, it's often most efficient to minimize reliance on methods in this quadrant for internal communication (i.e., when circulating a business plan or proposal among your team), while recognizing that you are more likely to have to utilize these approaches in certain instances for external communication (i.e., when submitting a final business plan to an investor, or a proposal to a prospective client).

As a case in point, let's say you are planning an important face-to-face meeting to discuss a near-final draft of your business plan for a business plan competition. Ahead of the actual in-person gathering, you could schedule a conference call (different place, same time) to identify areas that remain to be completed, assign responsibility, and clarify any questions. Then via e-mail (different place, different time) you could distribute the newly written sections and provide feedback to one another. Having completed this preparatory work, you can take full advantage of the face-to-face meeting (same place, same time) by collaboratively brainstorming ways the plan could be strengthened based on the judging criteria. Finally, once the final edits have been completed, your team can deliver a hard copy of the plan to the appropriate representative of the competition (same place, different time).

This is an example of making use of physical and virtual structures by utilizing traditional and technology-based approaches. The result is that once your team is finally together, your meeting will be much more focused and fruitful.

All the participants will have been briefed on critical information, and, thus, your in-person meeting time can be elevated by brainstorming, high-level collaboration, and discussing more strategic considerations. Using this approach, you maximize one of your most important assets—your team's time together (physical)—by leveraging technology during your team's time apart (virtual). All the technologies identified in the previous grid that can allow you to be more organized and keep your business up and running are described in Chapter 5, and more. There, I'll share with you some of the cool technology tools that can enable your company to function better and gain an edge over the competition. What's even better is that many of these technology-oriented tools are either completely free, or low-cost solutions for student entrepreneurs that will help your venture grow.

CAMPUS CEO CHECKLIST

After reading Chapter 4, take these steps toward making your business a reality:

☐ Choose a name for your business.

☐ Pick a catchy tagline for your company.

☐ Register your business locally, and if necessary with state and federal agencies.

☐ Obtain advice from an expert and select your company's legal structure.

☐ Write out the mission, vision, and values for your business to answer the questions of *what, why,* and *how.*

☐ Develop an organization chart that reflects the priorities, balance of responsibility, and allocation of resources needed to best meet your customer's needs.

☐ Create an advisory board comprised of professors, entrepreneurs, and industry experts.

☐ Implement a blended structure that combines physical and virtual forms of communication.

PROFILE OF A CAMPUS CEO

■ **Name:** Adam Witty

■ **Business:** TicketAdvantage.com

■ **Web site:** *www.TicketAdvantage.com*

■ **Founded:** 2001

■ **His Story:** Adam Witty launched TicketAdvantage.com when he was a junior at Clemson University in Clemson, South Carolina. TicketAdvantage provides safe, secure, and private transactions for ticket buyers and ticket sellers to sports and entertainment events around the world. It's been hailed as the eBay of online retailers for all sports tickets. Witty has been featured in *USA Today* for taking a team of colleagues nearly 22,000 miles across America in a 42-foot "rock star bus" tailgating at more than 45 major and minor baseball league games. The 2003 event benefited local chapters of the Make-A-Wish Foundation, and Witty created an interactive fan experience at each ball game by successfully partnering with Chevrolet, Hewlett-Packard, Louisville Slugger, and Cal Ripken Baseball among others as sponsors of the tour. These days, Witty is busy building his Advantage family of businesses, which, besides TicketAdvantage, includes Advantage Media Group, an author-owned publishing house, and Advantage Networks, a full-service sports marketing firm.

■ **Advice to Student Entrepreneurs:** "Just take action. So many students, and so many entrepreneurs study about business, they read tons of books, blogs, and magazines and they do all kinds of analysis and feasibility studies to excess because there's a sense that they need to continue to prepare. But at some point you simply have to jump in and do it. What you'll find, when you do take the leap, is that by starting your business, instead of just talking about it, you are going to attract people, mentors, and opportunities like never before. So do your homework, plan, model, and follow other successful entrepreneurs. But at the end of the day, take a leap and just do it."

—Adam Witty

High Tech and Low Cost—
Gaining the Technology Edge

5

Whether you're launching a high-tech company or a retail storefront, your business will undoubtedly benefit if you take advantage of technology. Those items vital to a student entrepreneur include everything from high-speed Internet service, sophisticated personal digital assistants (PDAs), and wireless devices to state-of-the-art computers and laptops, mobile computing technology, and access to large online databases.

I consider myself a technologist, but I recognize that some people are either unfamiliar or uncomfortable with new and emerging technologies. Keep in mind that comparatively speaking you have a huge advantage—today's youth have never known a world without technology and, consequently, are often more proficient and experienced than adults. Perhaps more than anyone else, Campus CEOs should be able to fully leverage technology both for their business as well as when exploring business opportunities.

In today's intensely competitive environment, the importance of capitalizing on cutting-edge technology cannot be overstated. Take the founders of Google, for example. They launched their search engine while on campus at Stanford. Just a few years later, they dominate the online landscape and have revolutionized how we all use the Internet to search for information. Technology continues to become more and more ingrained in our society. Every day we see a never-ending rise in the range and uses of the tools available. And not only have we witnessed the proliferation of these innovations, we have

FIGURE 5.1 Years for Various Technological Innovations to Attain 25 Percent of the Market Share. Source: Milken Institute.

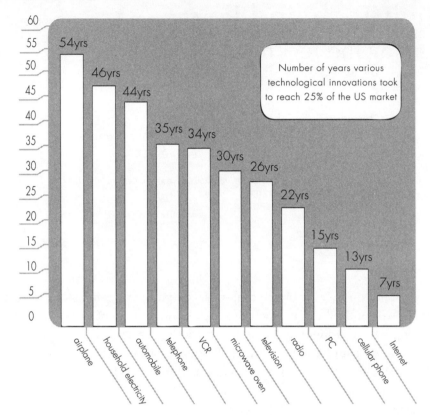

also witnessed a dramatic increase in our rate of adoption of new technologies. Figure 5.1 shows the number of years it has taken various technological innovations to reach 25 percent of the market share or 25 percent of the U.S. population. As you can see, from the airplane, which took 54 years to reach 25 percent of the market share, to the Internet, which reached the same level of penetration in a record-breaking seven years, not only have we seen changes in our day-to-day use of technology, we have also seen rapid changes in the speed at which this integration takes place. Even the person flipping burgers at a fast-food restaurant uses technology. Just look at the devices used at the drive-in or the checkout counter. That's technology, and it's here to stay.

FIGURE 5.2 The Role of Technology in Business

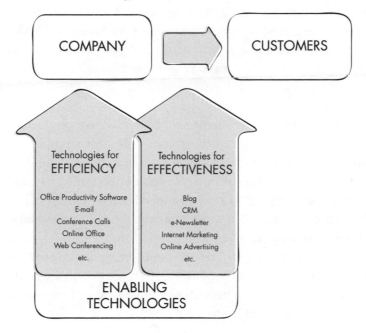

■ TECHNOLOGY'S ROLE IN YOUR BUSINESS— THE THREE "E'S"

When I think about the role of technology for a business and its customers, three things, or three "E's," come to mind as shown in Figure 5.2. The first is that technologies can be used to help your business achieve greater levels of *efficiency.* By efficiency I am referring to getting tasks accomplished, improving processes, and increasing your ability to get work completed. For example, spreadsheets were one of the first "killer applications" in business, because they made it very easy to crunch numbers. For business accountants and financial professionals, spreadsheets were a dream come true.

Second, technologies can help your company deliver products or services to customers with greater *effectiveness.* I use effectiveness to refer to better ways of providing excellent customer service, creating a memorable buying experience, and maintaining a meaningful relationship with clients. One of the more powerful ways online retailers use the Internet is to customize or tailor their Web sites to individual preferences. For example, you may visit an online bookstore that immediately recommends three new books based on your past purchases, while one of your friends would receive three different recommendations on the same site.

Third, *enabling* technologies make it possible or enhance the ability of your company to use technologies in the previous two categories. Some examples include computers, smartphones, and wired or wireless Internet services. These technologies aren't geared toward performing a specific task; rather, they "enable" the use of a variety of other technologies, such as word processing software to write a business plan or an Internet browser to search for market data.

Finally, take note that some tools aren't confined to a single purpose of efficiency, effectiveness, or enabling other technologies. For example, you could use your computer (enabling) to send a fax for internal communications (efficiency) or blast faxes to prospective customers (effectiveness). Similarly, you could use your smartphone (enabling) to e-mail your colleagues (efficiency) or to e-mail a newsletter (effectiveness). More often than not, different technologies can serve different purposes, depending on how they are utilized.

Because new technologies are constantly being introduced, consider the three "Es" of *efficient, effective,* and *enabling* technologies as a useful framework when evaluating the potential benefits not only of technologies available today, but also of those anticipated in the future.

Technologies for Greater Efficiency

As a savvy modern student, undoubtedly you know that technology can indeed help you and your business to be more efficient. More specifically, as shown in Figure 5.3, a number of tools are available to you as Campus CEO that can help you to:

- *Save time.* Posting frequently asked questions on your Web site or on a profile page on a networking site can avoid the need to respond to many e-mail or telephone inquiries from customers.
- *Save money.* Using free tools is one obvious way to save money; there are also tools such as office productivity software or Web-conferencing applications that can help you perform tasks more cost-efficiently or eliminate the need for travel.
- *Streamline communications.* By arranging conference calls, creating an e-mail list or discussion group, or utilizing an Internet phone, online office tools, or Web-conferencing tools, your team can maintain streamlined communication.

FIGURE 5.3 Technologies for Greater Efficiency

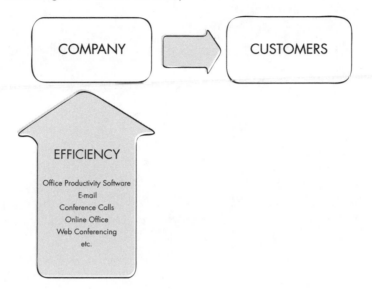

- *Centralize resources.* Online office tools can centralize all the contacts, documents, databases, and appointments related to your business, as well as provide Web-based access for your entire team.
- *Remain connected.* Tools such as e-mail, e-fax, instant messaging, and text messaging can allow you to conduct business while on the move.

By seeking out technologies for efficiency you can reduce costs, streamline operations, and improve your bottom line. I'll describe a number of these technologies in the following sections.

Technologies for Greater Effectiveness

I'm confident that you are also aware of technologies that can help your business more effectively deliver products and services to your customers. When used strategically, as depicted in Figure 5.4, these tools can greatly improve any Campus CEO's ability to:

- *Connect with customers.* Technologies such as customer-relationship management (CRM) tools allow you to manage client information and conduct targeted marketing and outreach, while Web statistics and analytic tools provide valuable feedback on the visitors and traffic to your

FIGURE 5.4 Technologies for Greater Effectiveness

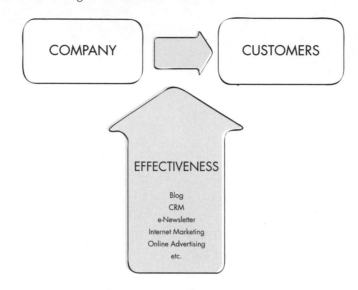

Web site so that you can better reach them. Similarly, podcasts represent a creative and exciting way to maintain regular communication and an ongoing relationship with customers.

- *Serve your clients.* Using Web conferences for product demonstrations, or online electronic commerce to directly sell products and services, or CRM tools to assist with customer service, technology can help you help your clients in the best way possible.
- *Build awareness.* Through e-newsletters, blogs, Web sites, networking site profiles, and the like, you can use technology to inform other students and the general public about your company, advertise its products and services, and provide updates on recent news or upcoming events.

By identifying the right tools to help your business become more effective, you can retain customers, expand your reach, and increase revenue. In the following section I will share some exciting tools that can help you do this.

■ CAMPUS CEO TECHNOLOGIES

The good news for Campus CEOs is that there are several completely *free* or low-cost technology tools you can utilize for your business. This includes both *proprietary* tools at a cost and *open source* or *open license* tools that are distributed at no cost. When I was a student, one of my favorite words was "free!" The categories with completely free options include operating systems, office productivity software, Web sites, blogs, domestic and international telephone calls, conference calls, e-mail, e-mail lists, e-fax, discussion groups and forums, instant messaging, and more. Furthermore, your campus probably also provides access to certain resources for free, such as state-of-the-art computer labs, software, and wired or wireless Internet service, to name a few.

Following is a categorized list of technologies of potential use to any campus business. But be aware: as I mentioned earlier, technology is evolving at quite a fast pace; you can find an up-to-date list of this information at Campus-CEO.com (*www.campusceo.com*).

Personal Computers

Personal computers (PCs) are an essential and enabling technology, which includes *desktop computers, laptop computers*, and *tablet computers*. The former is for home or office use, while the latter two are for home, office, or mobile computing purposes. PCs are run using predominant operating systems such as Microsoft Windows, Mac OS, and Linux (free and open source). PCs support a variety of applications that are critical to any business such as Web browsing, e-mail, instant messaging, office productivity applications (word processor, spreadsheet, presentation, etc.), databases, desktop publishing, and much more. Leading vendors include Apple, Dell, Hewlett-Packard, and Lenovo (formerly IBM).

Computer Equipment and Peripherals

Computer equipment and peripherals you may need to purchase include a printer, scanner, copier, and fax machine, or an all-in-one machine that combines some or all of these functions. I've found that if you need to perform any one of these functions very well, you should get a machine that is specifically dedicated to doing it. A dedicated color laser printer will almost always outperform an all-in-one device that prints, scans, copies, and faxes. However, when money is tight and you need low-cost equipment that can perform all these functions, an all-in-one device might be your most practical option.

Another tool to be aware of is *business card scanners,* which are extremely useful for organizing business cards and storing them in a database or spreadsheet. Your choices include the following products:

- Corex CardScan (*www.cardscan.com*)
- Targus Business Card Scanner (*www.targus.com*)

Once your business cards are scanned and stored by one of these tools, you can easily access your business card information and later transfer it to another software application such as an electronic newsletter engine or Internet marketing program.

Wired or Wireless Internet Access

No Campus CEO can go without another enabling technology: *wired and wireless Internet access. Wired Internet access* options include *dial-up, digital subscriber line (DSL), cable-modem, T1, T3,* and *fiber optics.* Except for dial-up, all these options represent broadband, or high-speed, Internet access.

- *Dial-up* Internet access provides modest speeds over a standard telephone line using a modem.
- *DSL* Internet access is provided over a standard telephone line using a DSL modem.
- *Cable-modem* Internet access is provided over your cable television coaxial cable using a cable modem.
- *T1* and *T3* lines are dedicated high-speed digital communications lines.

Leading vendors include Verizon, AT&T, BellSouth, EarthLink, Sprint, Time Warner, Comcast, and more.

Wireless Internet access is typically provided by taking any of the previously mentioned wired Internet arrangements and making them available wirelessly. Most new laptops have built-in wireless capabilities. For older laptop computers, you can purchase a wireless card or adapter. A second form of wireless Internet access is provided by certain mobile telephone service providers (mentioned in a later section). Here, a different wireless card or adapter, some of which connect directly to your mobile phone, is required to allow your laptop to go online, using the same connection as your mobile phone. Many students will be able to obtain wired or wireless Internet access for free from their dormitory or on campus.

Perhaps the most prevalent enabling technology is the *mobile telephone*. Nowadays, it seems as if almost everyone has one. Your options include standard *mobile telephones* as well as *smartphones* or *personal digital assistants* (PDAs) such as a Blackberry, Palm Treo, or any Pocket PC device. In addition to the ability to send and receive telephone calls from almost anywhere, your mobile telephone can support a multitude of applications, including contacts, calendaring, e-mail, Web browsing, podcasting, text messaging, and more. Leading vendors include Verizon, Sprint, Cingular, AT&T, and others.

Internet via *fiber optics*, also called *fiber to the premises* (FTTP), *fiber to the home* (FTTH), and *fiber to the neighborhood* (FTTN), involves bringing a fiber-optic cable directly to your home or office. As an enabling technology, fiber-optic services offer the "triple play" of VoIP telephone service (mentioned in a later section), very high-speed Internet access, and digital cable television, all over a single connection. Verizon is a leading vendor with its Fiber Optic Services (FiOS). AT&T offers a similar service called U-verse.

> **■ CNET's Technology Product Reviews**
>
> A great Web site for technology product reviews, comparisons, and competitive pricing is CNET (*www.cnet.com*). CNET provides up-to-date evaluations of products in several categories pertaining to home and business use, such as mobile phones, Internet phones, desktop computers, laptop computers, peripherals, Internet access, security software, Web hosting, and much more. CNET's "Editors' Choice" identifies some of the top-rated and cost-effective products in each category.

Office Productivity Software

The basic *office productivity software* applications or "office suite" includes *word processing, spreadsheet,* and *presentation* software. Options include:

- Microsoft Office (*http://office.microsoft.com*). Word, Excel, and PowerPoint.
- Lotus SmartSuite (*www.ibm.com/software/lotus/*). Word Pro, 1-2-3, and Freelance Graphics.
- OpenOffice (*www.openoffice.org*). Writer, Calc, and Impress. OpenOffice is a free and open source suite of tools.

Quite a number of templates are available online for these applications in areas such as finance, meetings, projects, legal forms, human resources, marketing, sales, and training.

Included in this category are also *accounting and finance* packages such as:

- Intuit Quicken (*http://quicken.intuit.com*) and QuickBooks (*http://quickbooks.intuit.com*)
- Microsoft Money (*www.microsoft.com/Money/*)
- Peachtree by Sage (*www.peachtree.com*)

Quicken allows you to track personal and business expenses in the same place (i.e., a sole proprietor or someone self-employed). Meanwhile, QuickBooks and Peachtree are geared specifically for businesses, and Microsoft Money offers a special edition for both personal use and business use.

Other slightly more advanced software in this category is *databases* and *desktop publishing software.* For *databases,* the leading options include:

- Microsoft Access (*http://office.microsoft.com*)
- Lotus Approach (*www.ibm.com/software/lotus/*)
- FileMaker Pro (*www.filemakerpro.com*)
- OpenOffice Base (*www.openoffice.org/product/base.html*), which is a free and open source tool.

These tools are particularly useful for building custom databases, that is, when you have specific information you need to manage and generate reports. Once again, templates are also available for typical uses such as an address book database, membership database, expense reports database, inventory database, and more. Depending on the specific kind of data you're looking to capture, off-the-shelf tools may be available that are specifically designed for these purposes such as e-mail marketing or customer relationship management tools (both described in a following section).

Desktop publishing and *graphics* software are good for custom-designing business cards, brochures, advertisements, banners, flyers, newsletters, and other collateral requiring creative design. The leading options include:

- Microsoft Publisher (*http://office.microsoft.com*)
- Adobe PageMaker (*www.adobe.com/products/pagemaker/*)
- Adobe Photoshop (*www.adobe.com/products/photoshop/*)
- QuarkXPress (*www.quark.com/products/xpress/*)
- OpenOffice Draw (*www.openoffice.org/product/draw.html*), which is a free and open source tool

E-mail

Electronic mail or *e-mail*—the ability to send and receive messages to and from electronic communications systems (i.e., desktop computers, laptop computers, smartphones, etc.)—remains *the* "killer application" on the Internet. Among the popular and free choices for *Web-based e-mail* are the following:

- MSN Hotmail (*www.hotmail.com*)
- Yahoo! Mail (*http://mail.yahoo.com*)
- Google Gmail (*http://gmail.google.com*)

Some of the leading software applications for *desktop e-mail* include:

- Microsoft Outlook (*www.microsoft.com/outlook/*)
- Qualcomm Eudora (*www.eudora.com*)

Two of the leading *corporate e-mail* applications that offer desktop and Web-based e-mail access, as well as shared contacts, calendars, and other collaboration tools are as follows:

- Microsoft Exchange (*www.microsoft.com/exchange/*)
- IBM Lotus Domino (*www.ibm.com/software/lotus/*)

The obvious advantage of Web-based e-mail is the ability to access your messages anywhere you can access the Internet. The advantage of desktop e-mail is the potential to centralize, integrate and synchronize with the contacts, calendar events, tasks, and other data stored on your PDA. Lastly, if the content of your e-mail is confidential or sensitive in nature, you may consider:

- Mail It Safe (*www.mailitsafe.com*). Provides e-mail encryption for a fee. Mail It Safe is especially useful for entrepreneurs with patents pending or other intellectual property they are seeking to protect.
- PGP (Pretty Good Privacy) Desktop (*www.pgp.com*). Provides encryption of e-mail, selected files, and instant messenger traffic for a fee. PGP Desktop is an effective tool for providing security that is easy to use and integrates well with other applications such as Microsoft Outlook.

E-mail List/Discussion Groups/Discussion Forums

An *e-mail list* or *e-mail listserv* is an e-mail address that distributes to multiple e-mail addresses. A *discussion group* or *discussion forum* is an online forum where members can post, read, and respond to messages. List or group administrators are designated to approve members and/or approve postings. Most e-mail lists, discussion groups, and discussion forums allow you to opt in or opt out, and some also restrict their postings to members only. These tools are useful for maintaining communication among teams or subteams by allowing users to create and join discussion groups, create mailing lists, create shared calendars, poll members, plan group events, and store links. Two tools among the free favorites are:

- Yahoo! Groups (*http://groups.yahoo.com*)
- Google Groups (*http://groups.google.com*)

Also consider blogs (described in a later section) as tools that support group communication.

Voice Communications

Unless you solely rely on a mobile telephone, you will also need to utilize *voice communications* technology. The traditional choice has been a standard, analog, *landline telephone* (or wireline telephone) using POTS (plain old telephone service), with options for voice mail, caller ID, call waiting, and the like. Leading vendors include Verizon, AT&T, and Sprint.

Nowadays, there is a second option known as VoIP (Voice over Internet Protocol), which is more commonly known as a digital *Internet phone* or a *broadband phone*. An Internet phone places telephone calls by transmitting your voice over the Internet. Because VoIP uses the Internet to route calls, as opposed to the physical routing of landline phones, you can send and receive calls to and from the same telephone number anywhere you have Internet access. Internet

---

■ Virtual Phone Systems

Virtual phone systems allow your company's phone number to look and sound like a large established firm at a low cost for a small business. For a monthly fee (as low as $9.95), these services offer a toll-free or local number with the following features: custom main greeting, multiple mailboxes, unlimited voice mail, live call forwarding, music on-hold, message notification, Web and e-mail delivery (voice mail and faxes are e-mailed as attachments), dial-by-name directory, and more. Available choices include GotVMail (*www.gotvmail.com*), Virtual PBX (*www.virtualpbx.com*), Onebox Executive (*www.onebox.com*), and Ring Central (*www.ringcentral.com*).

phones can also take advantage of other services on the Internet such as an address book, audioconferencing, videoconferencing, or information exchange, to name a few. The current shortcomings of Internet phones are the quality and reliability of the calls because of the reliance on the Internet, the inability to send or receive calls if there is a power outage, and the inability to send faxes. Despite these drawbacks, an Internet telephone can be an attractive alternative to a landline telephone. Several cable television and Internet service providers offer VoIP services, such as RCN, Comcast, Cox, Time Warner, and Verizon's VoiceWing. Two additional choices you should be aware of are as follows:

- Vonage (*www.vonage.com*). A leading provider of broadband telephone services.
- Skype (*www.skype.com*). Ebay's popular VoIP option, Skype has come to be known for its free domestic and international PC-to-PC calling. While you must originate a Skype call using your computer, you can use Skype to call a landline or wireless telephone anywhere. Skype also offers desktop videoconferencing and instant messaging services through its user interface.

Fax and E-fax

Facsimile or *fax* technology is well known for its ability to transmit documents over the telephone from one fax machine to another. An alternative to traditional fax is *electronic facsimile* or *e-fax*, which allows you to send and receive a fax from anywhere you can access e-mail. E-fax works great if you're constantly on the move or prefer the immediacy and convenience of using your computer. To fax a document, you send it as an attachment to an e-mail address, which includes the fax number, and it ends up as a piece of paper in the recipient's fax machine. Conversely, faxes sent to you are converted to a digital format (i.e., an image of a PDF document) and sent as an e-mail attachment to your e-mail address. Some of the top choices include the following:

- eFax (*www.efax.com*). Offers the free eFaxFree, as well as eFaxPro and eFaxPlus for a fee.
- MyFax (*www.myfax.com*). A top-rated fee-based e-fax service.
- Send2Fax (*www.send2fax.com*). A top-rated, low-cost, easy-to-use e-fax service.
- CallWave (*www.callwave.com*). Also offers voice mail via e-mail, and an Internet answering machine service.

Conference Calls

Conference calls or *audioconferences* provide a bridge for multiple parties to listen and talk to one another via telephone. Two free conference call services are:

- FreeConference.com (*www.freeconference.com*)
- FreeConferenceCall.com: (*www.freeconferencecall.com*)

These services definitely come in handy when three or more members of your team need to talk remotely.

Text Messaging/Instant Messaging

Text messaging and *instant messaging* (IM) both entail the real-time delivery of a short text message, which may include multimedia elements. This is typically accomplished from a mobile phone or smartphone to another mobile phone or smartphone (text messaging), or from an Internet device (i.e., computer, smartphone) to another Internet device, respectively. Text messaging and instant messaging are useful for quick, real-time communication among your team. The following are free favorites for instant messaging:

- AOL Instant Messenger (*www.aim.com*)
- Yahoo! Messenger (*http://messenger.yahoo.com*)
- eBay's Skype (*www.skype.com*)

Web Sites

Web sites are centralized repositories of pages available on the Internet, which include text, graphics, images, multimedia, and other interactive features—all located at a particular address or domain name such as CampusCEO. com. Hosted by an Internet Service Provider (ISP) or Web-hosting company, a basic Web site is extremely useful from a marketing and advertising standpoint, especially for prospective customers, partners, or even investors seeking more information about your company.

A Web site is a must for any business owner. An online presence isn't an optional, nice-to-have feature, but an absolute necessity. Perhaps the biggest business equalizer to help compete with bigger players, a well-designed Web site conveys professionalism. It can make your company look larger than it is. Just because you're a business of one doesn't mean the world has to know it. For that matter, the Web also gives you anonymity when it comes to age, and even experience. You needn't necessarily broadcast to the world that you're a 20-year-old student, unless, of course, it would be seen as a plus in your business. My point is that a Web site allows you to put your best foot forward, from an image standpoint, and to positively influence potential customers by showing that you have the skills, capacity, and know-how to meet their needs.

Some free resources for Web hosting and Web site publishing are in the following list. All these tools offer some combination of Web hosting, Web site statistics, personalized domain name and e-mail addresses, online photo albums, polling, and an easy-to-use Web site builder (some of which are specifically geared for small businesses). All of these tools are also free, except for Network Solutions, which offers many of these features at a low cost. Be sure to include a "Contact Us" link on your Web site, a feedback form, and, if appropriate, a "Frequently Asked Questions" (FAQ) page.

- Yahoo! Geocities (*http://geocities.yahoo.com*)
- Microsoft Office Live Basics (*http://officelive.microsoft.com*)
- FreeWebs (*http://members.freewebs.com*)
- DotEasy (*www.doteasy.com*), which uses the FreeSiteDesigner.com (*www.freesitedesigner.com*) Web site design tool
- Network Solutions (*www.networksolutions.com*)

For custom-designed Web sites requiring a level of sophistication beyond what's provided by the easy-to-use design tools mentioned previously, take a look at CrystalTech Hosting (*www.crystaltech.com*) for your hosting needs. In addition to offering infrastructure that can support basic and advanced custom-designed Web sites and Web applications, the company also offers CrystalTech Financing, a suite of small-business services, including financing, through Newtek Small Business Finance.

Web Site Statistics and Web Analytics

At a minimum, make sure your Web site utilizes a *Web site statistics* package so you can perform *Web analytics,* or analysis of the data generated by the traffic to your Web site such as the number of visitors, the most frequently visited pages, and the search-engine terms that commonly refer visitors to your Web site. Your Web-hosting company may provide these tools, or you may obtain a third-party service. Google Analytics (*www.google.com/analytics*) and WebStats4U (*www.webstats4u.com*) offer free services, while the following are for a fee:

- WebTrends (*www.webtrends.com*)
- SmarterStats by SmarterTools (*www.smarterstats.com*)
- Microsoft's FastCounter Pro (*www.fastcounterpro.com*)
- ClickTracks (*www.clicktracks.com*)

Each of these tools is well suited to small and medium-size businesses.

Web Site Search Engine Submission and Optimization

These tools submit your Web site to search engines, help optimize your site so it is easier to find via search engines, and provide detailed reports to track your site's visitors, traffic, and rankings at major search engines. A few options for *Web site search engine submission and optimization tools* are as follows:

- Network Solutions Search Engine Submission Program (*www.network solutions.com/web-site-promotion/search-engine-submission.jsp*)
- Microsoft bCentral's Submit It! (*www.submit-it.com*)

If you can't afford these services, don't worry. Without these tools, you can still go to many of the major search engines and submit your Web site directly to them.

Social and Professional Networking Sites

Social and professional networking sites allow you to create a profile or a profile page and invite others to join your network, as well as accept invitations to join others' networks. Profile pages may include journals, blogs, diaries, pictures, videos, music, and links to the profile pages of others in your network. These sites allow you to connect with friends, explore new personal and professional relationships, and expand your network. Many of these sites extend their offering to wireless devices, thus allowing users to post information from their mobile phones. The value of these sites from a business perspective is the opportunity to network and seek out potential employees, customers, and partners, as well as to advertise your products and services. Six of the more popular sites are:

- MySpace (*www.myspace.com*). The most popular social networking site on the Internet. Users can send private messages to one another. Profiles allow the greatest amount of customization when compared to the other sites.

- Facebook (*www.facebook.com*). Social networking Web site geared toward high school students, college students, and alumni (started by a Campus CEO!). Users are confined to their schools' networks; that is, they can access the profile pages of those who attend their schools. Certain companies can also log into Facebook for recruitment purposes and to post jobs.
- Friendster (*www.friendster.com*). A social networking site that includes classified advertisements ranging from résumés to jobs to business services.
- LinkedIn (*www.linkedin.com*). A professional networking site. LinkedIn can be used to find jobs, post employment opportunities, make new connections, establish partnerships, and seek out entrepreneurial opportunities.
- Xanga (*www.xanga.com*). A blog-based networking site comprised of online journals and diaries.
- Doostang (*www.doostang.com*). An invitation-only online community to connect and share career and professional information with others.

■ Safety and Privacy at Networking Sites

As the number of users of networking sites has grown, so have legitimate concerns about safety and privacy. Accordingly, here are a few tips:

- Beware of other users with inappropriate intentions

- Familiarize yourself with the features of each site and utilize the options that protect your safety and security, such as blocking a user, reporting site abuse, or restricting others from accessing certain information in your profile

- Limit the amount of personal information you disclose or other information that reveals your full identify

- Review the policies for each site, particularly as they relate to who can access your profile or post to your profile

- For more information, visit OnGuard Online (*www.onguardonline.gov*), an online resource sponsored by the U.S. government that provides tips for users of social and professional networking Web sites to protect themselves, as well as other technology topics

---

To separate your personal endeavors from your business endeavors, you may consider creating two separate profile pages, one for you and one for the company. As a Campus CEO, however, you should be careful to post only content that reflects a professional image by avoiding inappropriate comments, language, pictures, videos, and the like. You not only represent yourself, but also your company, so you wouldn't want to jeopardize either reputation. It is becoming more and more common for schools to take disciplinary action against students, as well as for companies to look unfavorably upon students based on the content placed on their profile pages.

Online Office

Online office refers to Web-based tools that make business applications available online including document repositories, calendars, databases, contact information, project management tools, and more. Online office tools are useful when you and your team need to collaborate on projects and documents online, or need access to shared information remotely. For example, if you have team members who are not on campus or who tend to be in different places at different times but still need to work together, an online office tool may be something to consider. Using online office tools, you can centralize and share contacts and calendars, work collaboratively on documents, and build customized databases, all of which can be accessed through a Web browser. Two online office tools to consider are:

- WebEx WebOffice (*www.weboffice.com*)
- Microsoft Office Live Collaboration (*http://officelive.microsoft.com*)

Videoconferencing and Web Conferencing

If your company must conduct many meetings, training sessions, sales presentations, or product demonstrations, then *Web-conferencing* tools may be just the thing you need. Web-conferencing tools allow you to host meetings, give presentations, conduct training, or perform demonstrations remotely. Using these tools, one or more meeting participants can see exactly what's on your screen, i.e., Web sites you're visiting, software applications you're demonstrating, presentation slides, etc., or you can control someone's computer from yours. There are also options for audioconferencing, instant messaging, real-time document collaboration, support for drawing or a whiteboard, and the ability to record your meeting to playback for future purposes. If your prospective customers are not within close proximity to campus, Web-conferencing tools can eliminate the need for travel. All they need is a Web browser and an Internet connection to participate. While there are no free options I am aware of, following are five tools you should take a look at. All of the products except GoToMeeting offer *videoconferencing* and integrate with either Microsoft Outlook or the entire Microsoft office suite.

- Citrix GoToMeeting (*www.gotomeeting.com*)
- WebEx Meeting Center (*www.webex.com*)
- Genesys Meeting Center (*www.genesys.com*)
- Raindance Meeting Edition (*www.raindance.com*)
- Microsoft Office LiveMeeting (*www.livemeeting.com*)

GoToMeeting is perhaps the most cost-effective tool and the least expensive of the five products listed. WebEx is the top-rated, market-leading product, but also on the higher end of the pricing scale.

Blogs

In addition to a Web site, you can use a *Weblog* or *blog*—an online journal—to heighten the connection between yourself and your clients. Blogs are increasingly popular ways for companies of all sizes to connect with the marketplace. What's more, they're free or supercheap to set up and run. Blogs include text, photos, RSS (Really Simple Syndication) feeds, and Atom feeds (feeds are syndicated content such as news that can be automatically distributed and updated), and mechanisms for users to post content from their mobile phones, or for visitors to provide comments or feedback. A few prominent tools for blogging are as follows:

> **■ Cool Software and Other Student Freebies**
>
> Be sure to check your college computer store or other campus retailers to learn what special student deals they have going from season to season. You can also explore potential deals on equipment and other technology products at eBay (*www.ebay.com*). Some product vendors sell their overstocked or clearance items there on occasion.

- Blogger.com (*www.blogger.com*). A free site for publishing blogs within an online community of other bloggers; owned by Google.
- Six Apart (*www.sixapart.com*). Offers three blogging tools:
  - TypePad (*www.typepad.com*). A tool for individual, professional bloggers.
  - MovableType (*www.movabletype.com*). A platform for small and medium-size businesses.

- LiveJournal (*www.livejournal.com*). A free online community organized around personal journals.
- Blog.com (*www.blog.com*). Offers a free blog service and premium blog service for a fee, along with group blogging support.

Blogs can allow you to personally communicate and connect with your customers. If you'd like to highlight the latest, exciting developments at your company, describe a new suite of products and services you're preparing to launch, or share your thoughts about trends in your industry, then you can post comments on these and countless other matters in your company's blog. Moreover, you can solicit feedback or engage in a two-way conversation with customers through your blog. In this way, blogs can be useful for marketing, advertising, public relations, customer service, and general information dissemination. A number of companies, including some Fortune 500 firms, are encouraging their executives to blog on a regular basis.

Podcasting

A method for distributing audio, video, and multimedia content that continues to grow in popularity is *podcasting*. Podcasts are increasingly being used by businesses to broadcast relevant, entertaining, and valuable content to their customers. A popular outlet for distributing video podcasts is YouTube (*www.youtube.com*), which is owned by Google. For more information on the what, why, and how to publish a podcast, visit Podcast Secrets Revealed (*www.podcastsecretsrevealed.com*) and sign up for a free minicourse.

E-Newsletter

Just like a printed newsletter, an *electronic newsletter* or *e-newsletter* helps keep your customers abreast of news and information, trends in your industry, and happenings at your company. If that e-newsletter is full of relevant news your customers can use, they'll look forward to receiving it and you'll also build your subscription base when they forward it to their colleagues, family, or friends. The following tools make it simple to design, publish, and distribute e-newsletter content, including easy-to-use templates:

- Constant Contact (*www.constantcontact.com*)
- Topica (*www.topica.com*)

If you would like to publish a newsletter or e-newsletter, but are not in a position to do it now, you can still begin to build your mailing list and electronic mailing list by storing the names and contact information of interested parties in a spreadsheet or database, as well as providing a way for visitors to your Web site to opt in. Then, once you are ready to publish something, you'll already have a list of interested recipients.

> ### ■ The Student Advantage Tech Store
>
> Check out the Student Advantage Tech Store (*www.studentadvantage.com/tech*), which is an authorized academic reseller of hardware and software products. If you're a student, the Tech Store lets you save up to 85 percent off the retail price on top-tier brand consumer electronics, hardware, and software.

Contact Management/ Customer Relationship Management

Have you ever called a customer-service number only to wonder how they had so much information about you, such as the date of your last call? The answer is that they were probably using some kind of *contact management* or *customer relationship management* (CRM) tool. Depending on your business, you may want to look into obtaining one yourself.

CRM software helps you manage customer relationships by offering features such as contact management (i.e., storing contact information, buying history), marketing and sales force automation (i.e., targeted mass mailings), sales tracking (i.e., sales leads and sales transactions), and generation of reports (i.e., largest customers) that can help focus your efforts. Some CRM tools also integrate with your accounting and finance software. Naturally, to make full use of a CRM tool, you need the time and human resources to enter and manage this data, but when this is done well it can be incredibly helpful to your customer service and marketing and sales efforts. Whether you're trying to support your sales and outreach efforts to potential clients or are looking for new and better ways to service existing clients, CRM tools are something to consider. Two tools to take a look at are the following:

- ACT! by Sage (*www.act.com*)
- FrontRange's GoldMine (*www.goldmine.com*)

ACT! offers integration with editions of Microsoft Outlook, Microsoft Office, Lotus Notes, Peachtree, and QuickBooks, while GoldMine integrates with editions of Microsoft Outlook, Microsoft Exchange, and QuickBooks. Both packages offer the ability to synchronize data with handheld and mobile devices.

■ FIVE TIPS FOR GAINING THE TECHNOLOGY EDGE

Here are five final tips for you to gain the technology edge:

1. *Remember the guiding principle of "business-driven, technology-enabled."* There should always be a compelling business case when making the decision to incorporate a new technology into your business. What are your business priorities? What are the greatest challenges facing your business? What are critical areas in need of improvement? Determine the answer to these business questions and the direction you would like for your company, and then use technology as an enabler to help you get there.

2. *Match needs with technology.* Determine your need, then find technologies to help meet that need. If you invest in technology just because it's cool, without a well-identified need, you will be wasting your money and time.

3. *Link organizational processes with technology tools.* Organize or reorganize your business processes, and create standard operating procedures that take full advantage of technology. For example, rather than collecting business cards and placing them in a business card holder, whenever you receive business cards, immediately scan them in and enter them into a spreadsheet or contact database. Whenever someone visits your Web site, give them the option to sign up to receive information and enter it into the same database. You can later use the database to publish an e-newsletter or conduct a targeted marketing effort because you will have a process in place that made it easier.

4. *Evaluate the total cost of technology ownership.* According to our president and CTO at BCT Partners, Lawrence Hibbert, "There are costs associated with technology that lie beyond the initial purchase. Therefore, any technology investment should take into account what it will also cost to maintain and support it after it's been acquired." Lawrence advises our business clients of the "80/20 rule," which says when budgeting for technology you should allocate 20 percent for hardware, software, equipment, and peripherals, and 80 percent for training, maintenance, upgrades, and support. "Some businesses overlook the 80 percent, and that's where you find a significant part of the total cost of technology ownership," Lawrence adds.

5. *Recognize that innovation is in the appropriate use of technology, not in the technology itself.* Technology does not translate into innovation unless

it's used strategically. Some people are easily fooled, but simply having technology for technology's sake does not necessarily make a difference. Lots of technologies gather dust without proper planning, organizational changes, and disciplined oversight that they are being used in the ways intended.

The key for you as a Campus CEO is to explore ways that technology can make your life easier and help you operate more efficiently *and* effectively. And because time is your most precious commodity, any technological advancement (especially free ones!) that helps you automate your business or better service your customers will improve your overall operations. If you master the integration of technology into your entrepreneurial endeavors, you can stay better connected to your business in every facet—from knowing firsthand what your customers think to collaborating with your entire team, even if you happen to be in a remote location. You don't have to be an IT guru to exploit the technology that's available to you right on campus. And don't forget to check Campus-CEO.com (*www.campusceo.com*) for an updated list of tools.

CAMPUS CEO CHECKLIST

After reading Chapter 5, take these steps to assess your business's technology needs:

☐ Consider ways technology can help your company to save time, save money, streamline communications, centralize resources, or remain connected. Identify which technology tools would increase your company's efficiency along these lines.

☐ Consider ways technology can help your company to connect with customers, serve your clients, or build awareness. Identify which technology tools would increase your company's effectiveness along these lines.

☐ Identify which enabling technologies would make the best use of tools designed to increase your company's efficiency and effectiveness.

☐ Investigate what software and technology resources are offered for free on your campus.

PROFILE OF A CAMPUS CEO

■ **Name:** Sergey Brin and Larry Page

■ **Business:** Google

■ **Web site:** *www.google.com*

■ **Founded:** 1998

■ **Their Story:** Sergey Brin and Larry Page first met at Stanford University in the mid-1990s, while they were each pursuing PhDs in computer science. They forged a friendship while developing a new approach to searching the Internet out of their college dormitory. In the late 1990s, the duo pulled together $1 million from family, friends, and investors, and on September 7, 1998, Google officially launched. At first, Google received 10,000 queries per day; now that number tops 200 million daily. Despite a wildly successful initial public offering that made Brin and Page both billionaires, those who know them say they still live relatively modest lives and haven't been caught up by the excesses—like having stables of exotic trophy cars or multiple mansions all over the world—that have been done by some other Silicon Valley entrepreneurs. By the way, *googol* is the mathematical term for a 1 followed by 100 zeros. The term was coined by Milton Sirotta, nephew of American mathematician Edward Kasner. Brin and Page say "Google" is a play on the term and reflects the company's mission to organize the immense amount of information available on the Web.

■ **Advice for Student Entrepreneurs:** "We have a mantra: 'Don't be evil,' which is to do the best things we know how for our users, for our customers, for everyone."

—**Larry Page** to *ABC News* (December 29, 2004)

■ PART 2

Financing Your Business

Show Me the Money—
Raising Capital

6

Cash. It's the lifeblood of any business. For example, according to the U.S. Small Business Administration, 50 percent of small businesses fail within their first year, while 95 percent fail within five years. The most commonly cited reason is insufficient financial capital. This chapter is focused specifically on different approaches to accessing financial capital because it is so critical.

Business owners of all kinds often dream of finding an angel investor or venture capital fund willing to provide the money required to get their venture off the ground. In fact, investors and lenders are out there that earmark millions of dollars to fledgling enterprises, campus start-ups included. But the lament of entrepreneurs everywhere is that access to capital is hard to come by, particularly for start-up operations. In many cases, your enterprise may not yet have grown in size, stature, client status, or revenue to the point that you'd be reasonably able to entice investors. Either way—whether you can get investor funding or not—money obstacles don't have to prevent you from becoming a successful Campus CEO for two reasons.

First, a variety of financing sources are available to anyone starting a college business. In this chapter, I'll tell you how to significantly improve your chances of getting money to fund your start-up, from investors, banks, personal resources, and nontraditional lending sources that can help finance operations. Second, while it's certainly true that financial capital is important, do not overlook the other forms of capital—human, intellectual, social, and cultural—as well as sweat equity, introduced in Chapter 2. These are also valuable assets that can help you get the things you want and need for your business with or without cold hard cash. Be sure to keep this bigger picture in mind as you consider the resources available to launch your company.

■ THREE TYPES OF FINANCING: EQUITY, DEBT, AND BOOTSTRAP

Financing options fall into two primary categories: *equity financing* and *debt financing*. There is also a third option that may or may not combine elements of equity and debt called *bootstrap financing*. All three options are radically different. But before I describe them, take a guess as to which one is most common for entrepreneurs. I'll answer that shortly. But first, let's break down the different types of financing.

Equity Financing

Equity financing represents an investment in the company, which translates into ownership of the company and an expected return on the investment (15 percent to 50 percent). Equity comes in two forms: *public equity* and *private equity*. *Public equity* is acquired by offering stock, or shares of your company, in exchange for money or capital. This is accomplished by way of an initial public offering (IPO) that gives the public the opportunity to purchase shares of your company and gives your company the opportunity to raise money from their

■ CircleLending: Online Loans with Friends and Family

CircleLending (*www.circlelending.com*) is an online resource that helps facilitate interpersonal, informal loans between family, friends, and other associates. For any private loan transaction, CircleLending can structure the loan, help establish a mutually-agreed-upon interest rate, broker payments between the parties, and arrange a payment schedule that meets everyone's needs. Loans can be secured by real estate, and established for personal or business purposes. CircleLending's services include a "Small Business Fundraiser" that can generate request packages for potential lenders and a "Small Business Builder" that can arrange a small business loan between family, friends, and associates.

sale. For example, in March of 1986, Microsoft's IPO sold its shares to the public for $21 per share on the New York Stock Exchange. The initial public offering raised $61 million and, as a result of the company's valuation, Bill Gates was immediately made the world's youngest billionaire! Returns on an equity investment come in the form of dividend payments or the profits made from selling the stock ("capital gains").

Private equity is obtained through *family and friends, angels,* and *venture capital firms. Family and friends* are common investors at the seed stage when you have nothing but an idea. Some family and friends may choose to bypass ownership or expectations of a return on their investment as a consideration to you as an aspiring entrepreneur. An *angel* investor, which can be an individual or a group of individuals who pool their investments, is common for businesses seeking up to $1 million. Angels tend to invest early in the life of a company. In return for their investment, Angels retain ownership of the company. Some angels take a passive, silent role, while others look to be more involved in your company's operations.

> **■ Angel Capital Association**
>
> The Angel Capital Association (ACA) (*www.angelcapitalassociation.org*) is comprised of angel investors throughout North America. They hold annual regional and national conferences that gather angels and angel networks together, disseminate information and resources, and maintain a database of angels that is organized by region.

Venture capital firms or *VC firms* tend to make investments at $1 million and above. They invest in both the early and later stages—or rounds—of financing. In retaining ownership of the company, some VC firms also choose to play a significant role in the operations of the company. This can include everything from serving as formal advisors to sitting on the board of directors to replacing members of the executive management team. The number of angels is significantly larger than the number of VC firms.

Equity investors tend to look at the growth potential of the market, the growth potential of the company, the anticipated return on their investment, and the time horizon over which they will see that return (typically three to five years). Equity investors will want to know their *exit strategy*, that is, how they will eventually reap the full rewards of their investment (i.e., acquisition, IPO, buyback of shares) and then terminate their involvement in the company. Equity investors are not guaranteed to receive any return on their investment. In fact, if the company fails, they could end up losing their entire investment.

Figure 6.1 shows the types of equity investments you should consider at a given stage of your company's growth. At the seed stage, when you have just an

FIGURE 6.1 Equity Investors for Each Investment Stage

Stage	Equity Investor
Seed stage	■ Friends and family ■ Angel
Early stage	■ Angel ■ Venture capital
Later stage	■ Venture capital

idea, you should look primarily to friends and family or angels. While it is certainly an option, venture capital is not likely a source of financing at this stage. During the early stages when your company is actually up and running, you may consider angels and perhaps venture capital. Lastly, during later stages and growth stages, you should explore the possibility of obtaining venture capital if you believe you can generate the kind of returns that would be attractive to a VC firm.

■ Community Development Venture Capital Alliance

Established in 1993, the Community Development Venture Capital Alliance (CDVCA, *www.cdvca.org*) is a network of community development venture capital funds (CDVCs). CDVCA describes its member organizations as providing "equity capital to businesses in underinvested markets, seeking market-rate financial returns, as well as the creation of good jobs, wealth, and entrepreneurial capacity." CDVCs are a growing subset of the larger venture capital community. If you're considering a social enterprise, community development venture, or business opportunity in an underserved market, you should browse the CDVCA Web site to see if one of its member funds is located near you.

A word of caution for those of you planning to solicit equity investors: be sure to familiarize yourself with the rules and regulations governing someone who is and someone who is not an *accredited investor*. An *accredited investor* is an individual (or a legal entity such as a corporation), including an executive, corporate director, or someone with a net worth exceeding $1 million and annual earnings of $200,000 ($300,000 with a spouse). These individuals are considered sufficiently experienced to make investment decisions, which allows for certain exemptions from the Securities and Exchange Commission (SEC) when raising money. You can learn more by visiting the SEC's Web site (*www.sec.gov/answers/accred.htm*). Before soliciting equity investors, consult an attorney who specializes in security law.

Debt Financing

Debt financing entails borrowing money from a lender with the obligation of repaying the funds (with interest) over a specified period of time. Debt is borrowed at either a fixed or a variable interest rate that then determines the amount of each payment. Servicing debt involves making regular payments of the principal amount of the loan, as well as the interest that has accrued. Some loans provide an interest-only option, in which case payments on the principal amount are optional. In most cases, payments are made monthly and commence shortly if not immediately after the loan is signed.

Banks are the most common providers of loans; even most government loans are simply bank-issued, but government-backed or guaranteed. The factors that debt lenders take into consideration include the following: your credit history; your financial history; the company's past financial history; evidence of a strong, if not growing market; evidence of the company's projected profitability (and, therefore, ability to repay the loan); and evidence of personal collateral or business collateral to secure the loan (i.e., savings, real estate, other assets). Debt lenders do not retain any ownership or control of your company.

The best way to think about equity versus debt is to consider your tolerance for *risk* versus your desire to maintain *control* as shown in Figure 6.2. Debt financing increases risk because you are obligated to repay the loan and may be using personal assets to secure the loan, which could be seized. Equity financing reduces control because you are transferring partial ownership of the company to others.

A few final rules of thumb for equity and debt financing are as follows:

- Debt financing is generally easier to acquire than equity financing.
- Never assume more debt than you can confidently service.
- Avoid giving up so much equity that you lose a controlling interest in your company.
- Work hard to precisely determine your cash needs by generating pro forma financial statements (discussed in Chapter 7) that are as accurate as possible; the worst thing you could do is to burn through investment capital quickly, only to have to attempt to raise it again. In fact, the better

FIGURE 6.2 Equity versus Debt = Control versus Risk

you can forecast your financial needs, the better your ability to plan for your company's future.

■ Take care of and manage investment capital (equity and debt) as if it were your own!

There is no silver bullet when it comes to deciding between equity and debt. In fact, many companies are financed through a combination of both. Ultimately, the decision will rest on the needs and circumstances of you and your company, weighed against your short-term and long-term goals.

Bootstrap Financing

Earlier I asked you to guess the most common form of financing for business owners. Without any doubt, the clear-cut answer is *bootstrap financing*. Believe it or not, the majority of companies aren't financed, but rather, are bootstrapped, which is also referred to as "bootstrap equity." *Bootstrap financing* may involve very modest equity investments from friends and family, an option I think many student entrepreneurs would be wise to consider. More often than not, bootstrapping involves more creative forms of investment such as personal savings, credit card debt, loans against real estate, and liquidating a retirement account. Credit cards are not the best route, but they often are a necessary evil for many start-ups. The interest rates on personal credit cards are higher than those on business credit cards—typically averaging 15 percent and above. So be

FIGURE 6.3 Amount of Start-up Capital Raised by the Inc. 500 Fastest-Growing Companies. Source: *Inc.* magazine

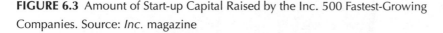

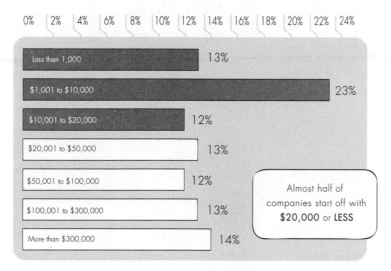

Less than 1,000	13%
$1,001 to $10,000	23%
$10,001 to $20,000	12%
$20,001 to $50,000	13%
$50,001 to $100,000	12%
$100,001 to $300,000	13%
More than $300,000	14%

Almost half of companies start off with **$20,000** or **LESS**

careful about using credit here and don't overextend yourself and wind up with a pile of business debt. Regardless of how you cut it, bootstrapping a company means doing everything you can to pull together whatever financial resources are available to launch your venture, and then reinvesting the profits to continue to fuel its growth. Its name derives from the fact that you are, literally, pulling yourself up by your bootstraps.

Bootstrapping is the most common way to finance a business. This often comes as a surprise to entrepreneurial newcomers. A look at the Inc. 500 list of the fastest-growing companies in America makes this point crystal clear. Figure 6.3 charts the amount of start-up capital raised by the Inc. 500 companies. Start-up capital refers to the funds raised before any product or service was delivered. The chart clearly shows that almost half (48 percent) of the companies started with $20,000 or less and just over one in every ten (13 percent) started with $1,000 or less.

Figure 6.4 shows the source of start-up capital raised by the Inc. 500. "Personal assets" includes personal savings, a mortgage or other personal loan, credit card debt, liquidation of a retirement account, etc. Here it's clear that the personal assets of the founders alone represent the overwhelming majority (70 percent) of the sources, while other sources such as venture capital and private equity are minor (4 percent or less) by comparison.

Clearly, the ability to successfully bootstrap a company often separates the winners from the losers in entrepreneurship. But as a Campus CEO you have

FIGURE 6.4 Sources of Start-up Capital Raised by the Inc. 500 Fastest-Growing Companies. Source: *Inc.* magazine

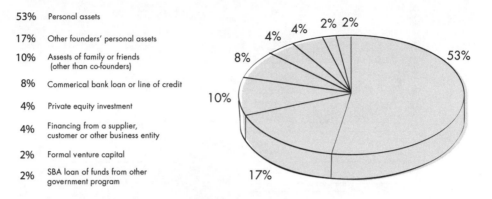

53%	Personal assets
17%	Other founders' personal assets
10%	Assests of family or friends (other than co-founders)
8%	Commerical bank loan or line of credit
4%	Private equity investment
4%	Financing from a supplier, customer or other business entity
2%	Formal venture capital
2%	SBA loan of funds from other government program

access to unparalleled resources that can only increase your chances of success. It's not easy, but first-time entrepreneurs are making it happen every day and so can you. Here, again, the importance of taking the time to forecast your needs via pro forma financial statements is important. When you're first getting started this means finding someone familiar with your industry, or an example of a business plan for a company similar in nature to yours, to minimize your guesswork (refer to Chapter 3 for tips on finding sample business plans). The longer you're in business, the easier it will become because you will have historical data to rely on. Good forecasting enables you to make better decisions with what may be limited financial resources.

Like many entrepreneurs, including us, you are often called on to bootstrap your company because no other viable options exist. This doesn't suggest that you should overlook alternative sources of capital. However, it does suggest that you should be prepared to do whatever you can, within reason, to get your venture off the ground if those sources don't pan out. Again, the goal is to obtain the necessary financing (or sufficient financing) without incurring too much risk and without giving up too much control. Accomplishing this feat is truly the art, not the science, of entrepreneurship. The summary lesson is simple: consider all your options—equity, debt, and bootstrap financing—but don't let the absence of equity and debt financing stop you from pursuing your dreams.

■ OTHER TYPES OF FINANCING

Looking beyond traditional forms of equity, debt, and bootstrap financing, there are a number of other types of financing to consider. Business plan competitions, as previously suggested in this book, are a great way to get money to launch your business. For more information on business plan competitions, please refer to Chapter 1 where we talked about them extensively, and how they can be helpful to any campus business. The remaining alternatives include the following:

- People-to-people lending
- Term loan
- Line of credit
- Government loan
- Asset-based financing
- Factoring
- Insurance-backed financing
- Trade credit
- Microloan

Some of these options are better suited to mature companies. Others can be explored right away by a start-up or small business. I present all of them in the following sections so at least they are on your radar, and at most you can one day take advantage of them.

People-to-People Lending

People-to-people lending is a market-based approach to lending being popularized by Prosper.com (*www.prosper.com*). At Prosper.com, in a manner similar to an auction, you can post a loan offer for the dollar amount you're looking for—up to $25,000—and the interest rate you are willing to pay on that amount. Based on certain criteria (i.e., credit score, debt-to-income ratio, etc.), people then bid the amount and interest rate they are willing to pay. After a maximum of two weeks—as long as there are enough bids to fulfill your request—your final loan amount and interest rate are determined by the bids with the lowest interest rate. The loan is unsecured with a fixed rate with a term of three years (no penalty for prepayment). Lending at Prosper.com can also be organized in groups. As a member of a group, if you repay your obligations, then members of your group earn money from the transaction. If you miss payments or default on payments, then the group's reputation is damaged. Groups help exert a social pressure for borrowers to honor their commitments. People-to-people lending is a new and emerging area of financing in the United States, having already gained considerably more traction in overseas markets such as Zopa.com in Great Britain (*www.zopa.com*).

Term Loan

A *term loan* gives your company a lump sum amount of money up front. You then repay the money in predetermined monthly installments for the duration of the loan. So if it were a five-year loan, you would make 60 monthly payments to repay the principal and interest connected with that loan. Term loans are typically obtained via banks; however, most banks will require one to three years of operating history before they'll front you money. Financial institutions also want to see that you have cash flow to support the repayment of a term loan. Additionally, term loans often are used if you're financing big-ticket items, such as equipment, vehicles, or property, or if you simply need money for expanding your business.

Line of Credit

A *line of credit* gives you access to funds up to a certain limit, for example, $10,000. You tap the credit line on an as-needed basis, and then you pay back the loan (plus interest) based on the amount of your outstanding loan balance. Again, you can obtain a line of credit through a bank, credit union, or traditional lenders, and they will likely require one to three years of operating history. Even though these sources may lend the money to your business, they may require you as an individual to sign a pledge guaranteeing repayment of the loan. This means that if something goes wrong with your company—for instance, it goes out of business—you still are personally on the hook to make good on the loan. Certain lenders will also ask you to put up collateral, such as business assets or a home if you own one, to back your line of credit. Ideally, lines of credit are treated as revolving accounts as opposed to outright loans. In this manner, money is borrowed against the line to cover short-term expenses for which cash is not immediately available, but, rather, is expected in the foreseeable future. Once the cash is received, it is used to pay the line of credit back down.

■ Corporate-Supported Entrepreneurship Programs

Two excellent examples of corporate-supported entrepreneurship programs are the Prudential Young Entrepreneur Program (*www.microenterpriseworks.org/index.asp?bid=137*) and the Miller Urban Entrepreneurs Series (*www.millerurbanentrepreneurs.com*). PYEP, established in 1999 by The Prudential Foundation and Prudential Financial, offers a range of assistance for young urban residents in Newark and Philadelphia between the ages of 18 and 30 to help them start and grow their own businesses, including loans up to $15,000. MUES, also launched in 1999 by the Miller Brewing Company, responds to the needs of adults ages 21 and older seeking to achieve economic empowerment through entrepreneurship by awarding up to $50,000.

Government Loan

The most popular *government loan* for small business owners comes from the Small Business Administration (SBA), which either guarantees loans made by other institutions or supplies loans directly to entrepreneurs. While the SBA qualifying standards are more flexible than other types of loans, you will nonetheless still be required to supply the SBA with comprehensive information about your company, yourself, and a detailed description about why you need funding. According to the SBA's Web site (*www.sba.gov*), you should expect to turn over the following documentation to get an SBA loan:

1. *Business profile.* A document describing the type of business, annual sales, number of employees, length of time in business, and ownership.
2. *Loan request.* A description of how loan funds will be used. Should include purpose, amount, and type of loan.
3. *Collateral.* Description of collateral offered to secure the loan, including equity in the business, borrowed funds, and available cash.
4. *Business financial statements.* Complete financial statements for the past three years and current interim financial statements. Your business financial statements should include balance sheets, income statements, and cash flow projections.
5. *Personal financial statements.* Statements of owners, partners, officers, and stockholders owning 20 percent or more of the business. These statements involve detailed lists of your personal assets and liabilities, along with your personal income tax records (typically for the past three years, if available).

As you can see, the process of obtaining loans through traditional lending sources can be somewhat rigorous.

Asset-based Financing

Let's say you need to buy computers, tools, or machinery of some type. Equipment financing and leasing allows you to secure these items. You could also put up some assets you own as collateral in exchange for financing. This is known as *asset-based financing*, and it may tip the scales in your favor with a potential lender who has the comfort of knowing that if you don't repay the loan, it has the right to seize or sell whatever assets you've put up as collateral.

Typical collateral sources include inventory or certain business assets you may own, but in most cases it is your accounts receivable that collateralize an asset-based loan. So if you have money coming in from a corporate client, but perhaps it is just slow to pay, or the norm within your industry is to get paid within, for example, 60 to 90 days, you may be able to put up your accounts receivable as collateral and receive up-front money or a line of credit in exchange for those receivables. The terms vary among lenders, but most will not loan more than 80 percent or so of the value of your receivables.

Commercial finance companies, major banks, and other financial institutions offer asset-based lending to businesses that are highly leveraged but have tight cash flow. With asset-based financing, the lender is primarily concerned with the quality of the collateral you put up, along with how liquid that collateral is (i.e., how readily it can be sold, if necessary, to repay your loan). This is why only commercial accounts receivable are eligible for loan consideration. (Sorry, that IOU from your uncle or your frat brother doesn't qualify!) Lastly, asset-based financing is designed for businesses seeking acquisitions, expansion into new markets or products, funding for capital-intensive industries, and rapid growth. For this reason, many asset-based lenders have loan minimums, such as $100,000, $250,000, or even $1 million. You can find lenders that specialize in asset-based financing on the Internet, in your local phone book, or by asking your professors, business mentors, and others for referrals.

Factoring

A somewhat similar strategy to asset-based lending, in terms of financing, is called *factoring*. Factoring is when you convert your accounts receivable into cash by selling those outstanding invoices to a so-called factor, the lender, at a discount. The lender typically supplies you with 80 percent or so of your accounts receivable (again, this is based on the credit quality of those invoices), giving you the immediate cash you need to manage your operations. Factoring works extremely well when you have a reputable client, such as a large corporation or a government agency, that typically takes a long time to pay you. By factoring the receivables for that client, you can get access to that money sooner, rather than later.

I remember a point in time where MBS trained more than 2,000 interns over the course of a summer for a big client, General Motors. We had to bring our largest workforce to date—at that time, about eight trainers—out to GM's facilities in Detroit and we worked there four consecutive days facilitating four concurrent sessions all day, each day. Some of our staff were students; others worked full-time jobs elsewhere, yet they flew out to Detroit and did the work for us. Not surprisingly, they wanted to be paid for their efforts, but we couldn't afford to pay them until GM paid us. We had a $120,000 receivable, but no sizable amount of cash on hand. If we had known about factoring, we would have likely obtained a percentage of the money GM owed us, and then used that money to pay the people we owed in a more timely fashion.

■ Social Venture Funds

Here is a sampling of some well-known venture funds that promote social responsibility and social entrepreneurship. Contact these groups if you need seed funding and other assistance to support your socially conscious business pursuits:

- Youth Venture
  (*www.youthventure.org*)
- DoSomething BRICK Awards
  (*www.dosomething.org/awards/brick/*)
- Echoing Green Fellows Program
  (*www.echoinggreen.org*)
- Ashoka Fellows Program
  (*www.ashoka.org*)

- Investors' Circle
  (*www.investorscircle.net*)
- Open Society Community Fellows Program (New York and Baltimore Only)
  (*www.soros.org/initiatives/cf/*)
- Blue Moon Fund Urban Fellows Program
  (*www.bluemoonfund.org*)
- Draper Richards Foundation Fellowship
  (*www.draperrichards.org*)
- Community Development Venture Capital Alliance (*www.cdvca.org*)

For an up-to-date list visit the Campus CEO Web site (*www.campusceo.com*).

Insurance-backed Financing

Here's a source of financing you probably haven't considered yet: If you (or your parents or someone else) has a sizable cash surrender value in a life insurance policy, you can typically borrow money against that policy. The customary way business owners accomplish this *insurance-backed financing* is to borrow against the policy and then relend the money to their own business at the same interest rate. Under the tax law, the IRS permits the business to then take an interest deduction on the loan, because you don't earn taxable interest income on the transaction.

Trade Credit

Using *trade credit* is another smart way to finance your company's operations. Trade credit is when a supplier in your industry allows you to purchase goods and pay for them over time. For example, you start a food-service business and you buy frozen pizza in bulk. If your supplier gave you 30 days to delay paying for that pizza, then you've just received trade credit. You didn't incur any immediate out-of-pocket costs, yet you were still able to get the product you needed. What's more, if you are managing your business right, you should be able to sell those pizzas within 30 days, get the money from your customers, and then use the funds to repay your supplier on time.

This type of vendor or supplier financing is commonly done for small and expanding businesses. So ask about getting trade credit— for 30, 60, or 90 days as needed—from potential suppliers with whom you plan to do business. This may include computer manufacturers and office supply stores in addition to equipment vendors. By using trade credit, you can also spread your repayments over time. You don't always have to pay for inventory or supplies all at once. And in most cases, if you pay what you owe in the agreed-on time, your suppliers won't charge you any interest; or if interest is charged, it will be very nominal.

Microloan

A *microloan* or *microfinancing* is a small loan (i.e., $35,000 maximum) that is awarded to a *microenterprise,* or a very small business that meets certain criteria. Microloans are typically awarded by nonprofit intermediary organizations that work directly with business owners. This includes small business assistance centers, community organizations, and community investment and economic development funds. The criteria and focus for microloans vary from lender to lender based on their credit requirements, which can include the need for collateral or some other type of guarantee. Some microlenders focus on small businesses of a certain size (i.e., five employees or less), while others focus on small businesses that are owned and operated by certain individuals (i.e., local residents, low-income residents, or residents of underserved communities—as a tool for economic empowerment). To receive a microloan from certain lenders, the business owner is sometimes required to participate in and complete certain training. Here are some useful links to microloan lenders and intermediaries:

- The U.S. Small Business Administration's microloan program (*www.sba.gov/financing/sbaloan/microloans.html*) is geared toward start-up and emerging small businesses. The average SBA microloan is $13,000 and the maximum term is six years. Visit SBA's Web site for a complete list of microlenders.

- The Association for Enterprise Opportunity (AEO) (*www.microenterpriseworks.org*) organizes conferences, training, and technical assistance for its member microenterprise development organizations (MDOs). These MDOs, in turn, work with local microenterprise entrepreneurs.

- ACCIÓN International (*www.accion.org*) is a leading international microenterprise organization offering loans as low as $500.

- Trickle Up (*www.trickleup.org*) provides seed capital to low-income people across the globe to launch microenterprises.

- Count Me In (*www.countmein.org*) is an Internet-based model for credit scoring and lending to women. With first loans up to $5,000, and second loans up to $10,000, Count Me In takes a variety of factors into account, such as prior experience, the type of business, and the intended use for the funds, that are often overlooked by traditional lenders.

The idea underlying this approach is that even a small amount of financing can make a big difference, especially for a start-up company that is severely capital-constrained.

■ Ownership Matters

A word of caution about accepting financial investments in your business: don't be so quick to take money—or to give up the reins to your business unnecessarily. If you've invested considerable time, energy, and financial resources to launching a company, it would be foolish to sell a majority stake in your venture prematurely. Take a lesson from Mark Zuckerberg, who started Facebook.com, the online social directory, from his dorm room at Harvard. Zuckerberg supposedly met with a couple of VCs in Silicon Valley during his junior year. At the time, the then 20-year-old Zuckerberg was intent on retaining control of his company. Good thing he did: Facebook.com is now the seventh most trafficked Web site in the United States and the number one photo site on the Web, with more than 1.5 million photos updated daily. Unlike with many start-ups, Zuckerberg didn't want to take the money in exchange for a loss of control, so he negotiated that in the terms of his deal. Some students will practically give their right arm for funding. But Zuckerberg had precisely the opposite attitude, which apparently gave him leverage when it got down to finalizing terms with those Silicon Valley VCs. "I didn't really want or need venture money, and they wanted to invest," Zuckerberg was quoted as saying in an October 2005 article in *BusinessWeek*.

■ FINAL WORDS ON FINANCING

When it comes to borrowing money, be sure to distinguish between a revenue gap and a cash flow gap. A cash flow gap is merely when you don't have the money on hand today to cover your existing debts, but soon you will have the funds coming in the door to pay those obligations. Perhaps you have a seasonal business or vendors that are slow to pay. In these instances, you may experience a cash crunch. A revenue gap, however, is a far more serious issue. This describes a situation where you don't have the money to meet your obligations, and you don't have any accounts receivable coming in, or you don't see where the money will come in the door to fund ongoing operations as necessary. If this describes your situation, and month after month you seem to be in the hole without the proper revenues to support your venture, you need to reassess your business strategy and take a fundamental and realistic examination of how much money your company is truly generating. If you are not careful, you could get seduced into thinking that you're financing a cash flow gap, when in reality you're financing a revenue gap. Don't turn a blind eye, consciously or unconsciously, to the health of your business. To ignore a revenue gap is to risk going into debt—at best—or going out of business—at worst. Toward this end, the next chapter provides you with advice on how to understand financial statements, including income statements, cash flow statements, and balance sheets.

CAMPUS CEO CHECKLIST

After reading Chapter 6, take these steps toward financing your business:

- ☐ Write down the three most realistic potential sources of funding for your business.

- ☐ Visit the Angel Capital Association Web site (*www.angelcapitalassociation.org*) to find an angel investor near you.

- ☐ Visit a local bank to learn about their lending options for businesses such as a line of credit, term loan, asset-based financing, and insurance-backed financing.

- ☐ Visit the SBA's Web site (*www.sba.gov*) to learn about government resources for start-ups.

- ☐ Explore funding options with the Community Development Venture Capital Alliance (*www.cdvca.org*) and various other social venture funds if you're a social entrepreneur.

- ☐ Investigate what trade credit is available from your suppliers and vendors.

- ☐ Write down five ways you can "bootstrap" your business or minimize your startup capital needs by acquiring goods, services, or expertise you need free of charge.

PROFILE OF A CAMPUS CEO

■ **Name:** Courtney Klein

■ **Business:** Youth Re:Action Corps

■ **Web site:** *www.yrcorps.org*

■ **Founded:** 2005

■ **Her Story:** Courtney Klein started her work as a social entrepreneur at a young age and had a vision for Youth Re:Action Corps at the age of 18 while volunteering in a small rural village in the Yucatán peninsula of Mexico. The people she met, the ways in which she lived, and the work that she did in her short time there have profoundly impacted her life forever. Later, as a student at Arizona State University (ASU), Klein started her company with the help of several fellow students and ASU's Edson Student Entrepreneur Initiative, which provides funding, training, office space, and networking opportunities for aspiring entrepreneurs. Klein graduated from ASU in 2005, receiving a degree in nonprofit leadership and management. She is now earning a graduate degree in nonprofit leadership and management. Youth Re:Action Corps's mission is to educate, empower, and invest in young people to change the world. The organization offers a high school program that engages students in the community, developing initiatives that they feel will solve the problems in their community. To get the nonprofit off the ground, Klein used about $1,000, and sold a BMW that her mother had bought her for her college graduation. Since then, Klein's nonprofit has received several funding awards, including multiyear financial and human capital investments from Social Venture Partners Arizona.

■ **Advice for Student Entrepreneurs:** "You don't hit roadblocks. They're just things you know you have to get through—and you get through them because you're passionate about what you're doing."

—**Courtney Klein** to *ASU in the Community* (March 15, 2006)

Financial Statements 101—
Understanding the Basics
of Business Finance

Creating financial statements is an integral part of learning how to manage your business, and these documents will also be among the most pertinent information that you show potential investors or lenders. In Chapter 3, I told you the primary financial statements you need to include in your business plan are as follows:

- *Income statement*
- *Cash flow statement*
- *Balance sheet*

Now I will explain each of these documents in more detail, tell you what information must be included in each, and define some basic financial accounting terminology you need to know. Figure 7.1 provides a brief overview of the three all-important financial statements. Taken together they can quickly show you the financial health and strength of any business.

■ FINANCIAL STATEMENTS AND ANALYSIS

Each financial statement can be generated as an *actual* statement or a *pro forma* statement on a monthly, quarterly, or annual basis. An *actual* statement looks backward in history and reports the real performance of your company.

FIGURE 7.1 The Three Financial Statements

Financial Statement	Description	Purpose
Income statement	Captures the total income, total expenses, and net profit generated by the company over a period of time	To determine whether the company is (or is not) profitable
Cash flow statement	Captures incoming and outgoing money (or cash) to the company over a period of time	To determine whether the company can (or cannot) meet its obligations (i.e., pay its bills)
Balance sheet	Captures the value of the company at a specific period in time (a financial "snapshot")	To determine the financial condition of the company

A *pro forma* statement or *forecast* looks forward into the future and projects the anticipated performance of your company. The former is useful in understanding your company's progress over time, and is of particular interest to lenders to better understand your track record to date. The latter is useful for anticipating your company's development moving ahead, and is of particular interest to investors to better understand your trajectory and growth.

Preparing an Income Statement

The *income statement* for your business is sometimes referred to as the "profit and loss" or "P&L" statement. This financial statement demonstrates whether your company is "in the black," or earning more money than it is spending. If not, your company is said to be "in the red," or operating at a loss. Income statements show the profits earned (or losses posted) by your business for a given month, quarter, or year.

Sales. The first entry on your income statement will always be "Sales" or "Revenues." They mean the same thing and are often used interchangeably. Sales or revenues refer to the money your company generated directly from selling its products or services. Some people also call your revenue figures your "top-line" numbers, because they are found at the top of the income statement. Also, some top-line figures on certain income statements are labeled

"Income." This, too, is synonymous with the overall sales or revenues your business generated during the reporting period. In this case, "Income" refers to the gross income or total amount of sales your company reaped from selling your product or service.

■ Tools to Assist with Your Financial Statements

Once you are ready to pull together all your financial statements, several software programs can aid you in this endeavor and your accounting, including:

■ *Microsoft Excel.* Part of the Microsoft Office suite, Excel is good for generating actual and pro forma financial statements.

■ *Lotus 1-2-3.* Part of the Lotus SmartSuite, Lotus 1-2-3 is also useful for generating actual and pro forma financial statements.

■ *Intuit Quicken Personal and Business.* Personal and business accounting software (excluding inventory and payroll) that is particularly useful for sole proprietors and other self-employed individuals.

■ *Intuit QuickBooks.* Business accounting software that contains additional modules to manage payroll, cut checks, accept credit cards, and facilitate retail point-of-sale transactions. It's available for PC and Mac users for a one-time fee or online via subscription.

■ *Sage Peachtree.* Business accounting software that offers certain modules with the ability to integrate with Microsoft Excel, Outlook, and Word. Additional modules are available for payroll, check payments, accepting credit cards, time and billing, Web site tools, and integration with ACT! (a customer-relationship management tool). Sage Peachtree is available for PC users for a one-time fee or online via subscription.

Other Income. Depending on the type of business you have, or the income that your firm produced, you might also have a second line on your income statement called "Other Income." For example, if you sold a division of your company, or reaped business income from something other than selling your product or service, this would be included on the "Other Income" line of your income statement.

Total Income = Sales + Other Income. By adding your top-line figure (i.e., your sales, revenue, or gross income) to any "Other Income" you may have derived, you now have your "Total Income."

Cost of Goods Sold. Next you must calculate what's known as your "Cost of Goods Sold." This is the cost that a business incurs to produce a product for sale to its customers. For example, you're selling custom T-shirts. Part of your cost of goods sold would be the expenses you rack up to buy the T-shirts in bulk, purchase the ink or paint you use to create the artwork on the shirts, and so forth. If you have a service company, or operate a consultancy, there is no cost of goods because there are no raw materials costs. In short, if you make a product or assemble it, you should know how much it costs to manufacture that item.

Gross Profit = Total Income – Cost of Goods Sold. You calculate your "Gross Profit" by subtracting your cost of goods sold from your total income. For a service company, which has no cost of goods sold, gross profit isn't relevant. Gross profit (and gross profit margin as explained in the following section) are relevant for other companies such as manufacturers.

Gross Profit Margin = Gross Profit/Total Income. "Gross Profit Margin" is a ratio or percentage. It is calculated by dividing gross profit by total income. It represents the percentage of gross profit realized on your sales after subtracting the cost of goods sold from the total income. Gross profit margin is a measure of your company's efficiency.

Expenses. Your "Expenses" or "Costs" represent the other costs and indirect costs of running your business, including marketing, advertising, and selling, general administrative (SG&A) expenses. These expenses are generally grouped into two categories: *fixed costs* and *variable costs. Fixed costs* are expenses that generally remain the same regardless of your company's level of activity. *Variable costs* are expenses that generally increase as your company's level of activity increases and decrease as your company's level of activity decreases. As your business grows, however, certain fixed costs can become variable. Examples of fixed costs are rent, equipment, full-time salaries that you pay employees, and insurance payments. Variable costs include such things as utility payments, bonuses, commissions, or part-time salaries. As you might expect, the latter expenses can fluctuate greatly based on either an employee's performance, how many hours he or she works in a given time period, or the amount of revenue generated by your company. Examples of costs that business owners are likely to incur are as follows:

1. Advertising
2. Bank charges
3. Charitable contributions
4. Commissions and bonuses
5. Credit card fees
6. Dues and subscriptions
7. Insurance
8. Interest
9. Internet service
10. Labor (part-time, contract)
11. Maintenance
12. Marketing and publicity
13. Miscellaneous
14. Office expenses
15. Permits and licenses
16. Postage and delivery
17. Professional fees
18. Rent
19. Reproduction
20. Repairs
21. Supplies
22. Telephone
23. Travel
24. Utilities
25. Wages
26. Web design/hosting

Total Expenses = Fixed Costs + Variable Costs. When you add up all your fixed costs, along with your variable costs, this gives you your "Total Expenses."

Earnings before Interest and Taxes = Gross Profit – Total Expenses. Subtract your total expenses from your gross profit to determine your "Earnings before Interest and Taxes" (EBIT) or "Operating Income" or "Operating Profit."

Operating Margin = Earnings before Interest and Taxes/Total Income. "Operating Margin" is a ratio or percentage. It is calculated by dividing your earnings before interest and taxes by your total income. It represents the percentage of total income that translated into profit before interests and taxes. It is a measure of your company's profitability before interest and taxes.

Interest. "Interest" is the cost you incur to service your outstanding debts such as loans or lines of credit.

Net Profit before Taxes = Earnings before Interest and Taxes – Interest. By subtracting interest costs from your operating income, you get your "Net Profit before Taxes."

Taxes. The combination of state and federal "Taxes" imposed on a business can vary greatly based on a company's profits—anywhere from roughly 15 percent to 40 percent. Companies are required to pay sales, income, and other business taxes.

Net Profit (Loss) = Net Profit before Taxes – Taxes. After subtracting these taxes from your net profit before taxes, you finally arrive at what's called "Net Profit (or Loss)" or the "bottom line" because it is the figure found at the bottom of the income statement. This is the last entry in a full-fledged income statement and it can be either a positive or negative number.

Profit Margin = Total Income/Net Profit. "Profit Margin" or "Net Margin" or "Net Profit Margin" is a ratio or percentage. It is calculated by dividing the total income by the net profit. It represents the percentage of total income that translated into net profit. It is a measure of your company's overall profitability.

Obviously, in the best of all worlds you want to see a positive number as your bottom-line figure, which indicates your business has turned a profit. But that's not the only indication of your company's financial well-being. Bankers and investors will also look closely at the gross, operating, and profit margins on your income statement. It's generally a big red flag if your margins are way out of line with industry averages—either much higher than or much lower than the rest of the marketplace. Be sure to check your school's library for *Standard & Poor's Analysts' Handbook, Standard & Poor's Industry Surveys, Dun & Bradstreet Industry Norms and Key Business Ratios,* or other reports, which provide financial figures, margins, and ratios for various business industries.

A sample income statement is shown in Figure 7.2.

Understanding a Balance Sheet

The *balance sheet* provides a financial snapshot of your business at a single point in time. It shows a listing of all your company's *assets*, a listing of your company's *liabilities*, and a summary of the owner's *equity*. The three items are governed by the following equation: *Assets – Liabilities = Equity.*

FIGURE 7.2 Sample Income Statement

Income		
Sales	10,000	
Other Income	0	
Total Income	**$10,000**	
Cost of Goods Sold		
Cost of Goods Sold (COGS)	2,500	
		Gross Margin
Gross Profit	**$7,500**	*75%*
Expenses		
Fixed Costs:		
Advertising	100	
Internet service	50	
Miscellaneous	125	
Supplies	150	
Telephone	100	
Wages	500	
Web design/hosting	250	
Variable Costs:		
Commissions	100	
Labor (part-time)	100	
Total Expenses	**$1,475**	
		Operating Margin
Earnings Before Interest and Taxes	**$6,025**	*60%*
Interest	25	
Net Profit Before Taxes	**$6,000**	
Taxes (25%)	1,500	
		Profit Margin
Net Profit (Loss)	**$4,500**	*45%*

■ *Assets.* Assets can be *current assets* or *long-term assets. Current assets* include cash and marketable securities such as stocks and bonds, as well as *accounts receivable,* or the amount that customers owe the company. Deferred income taxes, investments, and inventory—whether finished goods, work in progress, or raw materials—also qualify as current assets as long as they can be liquidated (i.e., sold) within one year. Under the category of *long-term assets* are plant, property, and equipment (PP&E), as well as other assets that can only be liquidated after one year. By adding your short-term and long-term assets, you have your *total assets.*

- *Liabilities.* Liabilities can also be grouped into *current liabilities* and *long-term liabilities.* Among *current liabilities* are accrued wages, bank notes, accrued interest payable, accrued taxes due, and *accounts payable,* or the amount the company owes to suppliers. *Long-term liabilities* are those obligations that must be paid out over more than one year. By adding short-term liabilities to long-term liabilities, you have a complete picture of your firm's total liabilities.
- *Equity.* Owner's equity, also known as *shareholder's equity, stockholder's equity,* or *net worth,* is the amount remaining after liabilities are subtracted from assets. In other words, assets minus liabilities equal shareholder's equity. Owner's equity can be interpreted as the actual value of the business to the owner(s).

Part of the reason the balance sheet is so-named is because it is divided into two parts, and both parts must show the same total or balance out. The first part is where you list assets. The second part is where you place liabilities and equity. Using the *Assets – Liabilities = Equity* formula, you can see that if your assets are greater than your liabilities, your business has a positive equity or net worth. If assets are less than liabilities, your company's equity or net worth is negative.

When you (or other professionals) analyze your balance sheet, something you will also want to understand is the *working capital* or *operating capital* needs of your business, which represents your company's liquid assets, or assets the company can readily convert into cash if needed. Working capital is calculated as the difference between current assets and current liabilities. It is another indicator of your company's ability to cover its day-to-day obligations. Lenders also want to determine if you have adequate assets to sell in the event you can't repay a loan. If your company's financial health deteriorates, a lender will typically look at three areas as a secondary source of repayments:

- *Accounts receivable.* Lenders generally assign a value to accounts receivables of roughly 60 percent of what a business shows on its books.
- *Inventory.* Lenders are all over the place on this one, assigning a monetary value of anywhere from 0 percent to 50 percent of the inventory you have on hand. The greater a commodity the inventory is, the higher the value assigned to it.
- *Equipment.* Lenders usually ascribe a value to your equipment of about 60 percent of its net book value.

You should be aware that even equity investors scrutinize balance sheets, mainly because they are more inclined to put money into activities that will generate a return on their investment, such as critical purchases of equipment, acquisition of software, or product development activities. They are less inclined to put money at risk to finance working capital needs. Investors are often also reluctant to put up money if their equity investment will be spent repaying creditors. That's why investors look closely at your accounts payable section of the balance sheet. They don't want it to be too high. If you do need money to pay off old debts, however, you can certainly make a case to an investor that for your company to grow, you have to get in good standing with suppliers. Explain that their investment dollars will help position your company for faster growth if you can get past-due debts behind you.

■ Resources for Creating Financial Statements

Here are some other resources that can help you to create financial statements:

■ *Financial Statements: A Step-by-Step Guide to Understanding and Creating Financial Reports* by Thomas R. Ittelson.

■ *Financial Statements.xls: A Step-by-Step Guide to Creating Financial Statements Using Microsoft Excel,* Second Edition, by Joseph Rubin (includes CD-ROM with sample financial statements). More information at *www.exceltip.com.*

■ *SBA Online Library of Forms,* which includes templates for income statements, cash flow statements, and balance sheets. More information at *www.sba.gov/library/forms.html.*

■ *SCORE Business Templates,* which includes templates for income statements, cash flow statements, and balance sheets. More information at *www.score.org/template_gallery.html.*

Understanding a Cash Flow Statement

While the income statement shows your firm's financial performance over time, and the balance sheet captures your firm's financial status at a particular point in time, the *cash flow statement* shows changes in your company's financial position over time. Your firm's cash flow statement focuses on the inflows and outflows of cash to your business resulting from various *operating, investing,* and *financing* activities, which collectively determine the strength (or weakness) of your company's cash position. These include:

- *Operating cash flows. Operating cash flows* are determined by changes to a company's current assets and liabilities resulting from operations. For example, changes in inventory, accounts receivables or accounts payable, and accrued wages are all part of a firm's normal day-to-day operations, and therefore affect cash flow from an operating standpoint.

- *Investment cash flows.* If your business acquires property, plant, or equipment or generates proceeds from the sale of a business unit, that too affects cash flow—only this time it's *investment cash flow.* You might also decide to make a long-term commitment to purchase expensive software that will help you better manage or grow your business. If so, that purchase would be reflected in the investing activities section of your cash flow statement.

- *Financing cash flows.* Lastly, the third part of your cash flow statement relates to your financing decisions. *Financing cash flows* can be either short term or long term. If you issue stock or debt, make payments on loans or lines of credit, or have an increase or decrease in cash or cash equivalents, all these financing activities produce a cash inflow or an outflow.

The last line in a cash flow statement reveals your firm's cash position at the end of the accounting period in question. If the sum of cash inflows from operations, investments, and financing is positive, then your business experienced a cash inflow. If the sum is negative, the result is a cash outflow. Ultimately, by looking at your statement of cash flow, you (or an investor or lender) can see where your firm generated cash—and how that money was used.

Lenders and investors use your cash flow statement to ascertain whether you can do everything from make payroll to repay existing debt or lines of credit. What's more, many investors believe that while income statements can be "managed," your cash flow statement is far more transparent and tells it like it really is. A person skilled in cash flow analysis will be able to readily determine from your cash flow statement how capital-intensive your business is, the extent to which your operations are impacted by seasonal factors, and the rate at which accounts receivables turn over. The latter point is especially important because high accounts receivable can severely compromise your cash position. The longer someone owes your business money, the more you must rely on existing cash to cover your short-term expenses and other obligations. If your company is growing, having very lengthy collection periods means a higher likelihood of facing a cash flow crunch, unless you have access to money that can "float" you, or cover you, during the interim. You can help ward off this potential problem by paying close attention to your cash flows and by preparing monthly cash flow statements.

■ HOW EQUITY INVESTORS AND DEBT LENDERS USE FINANCIAL STATEMENTS

Interestingly, equity investors and debt lenders will likely view your financial statements in very different ways. Because lenders are loaning you money, they really aren't taking the same level of risk that an investor is who fronts you money to launch or expand your business. At the bank, for example, chances are your loan will be fully collateralized, personally guaranteed, or both. So if you don't have large fixed assets, but are awaiting several payments from customers, banks are more likely to offer you accounts receivable financing instead of a traditional term loan. The bank's primary concern is to understand your actual financial statements and to make sure you have the financial wherewithal to repay any loan or financing offered. This is not the case with investors. In most instances, investors aren't looking at your ability to repay debt, but at your company's ability to grow. That's why investors scrutinize not just your company's historical financial data, but also your forecasts concerning future financial performance. For the investor, the goal is to try to see how much capital will be required to help your company grow substantially. The thinking is: the more your business grows and the faster it does so, the bigger the upside payoff is for the investor. But in terms of repayment terms with a bank, regardless of whether your revenues or profits double or triple, the bank is still going to receive the exact same return from you. Here are some final tips to help in preparing financial statements for investors or lenders:

- Make sure you *completely* understand how your figures were generated and the key assumptions underlying them, regardless of whether you created the statements yourself.
- Make all assumptions as explicit as possible, so it is easy to follow the logic behind your statements.
- Explore a few "what-if?" scenarios in your spreadsheet to test the durability of your assumptions. In particular, explore scenarios where your performance falls short of what you've projected. For example, what if your revenue is 10 percent below what you've projected? How does that affect your bottom line? Be prepared to explain how your company will deal with these situations.

- Write a summary of your financial statements, highlighting important points you would like to draw to their attention.

Depending on whether you are presenting your financial statements to equity investors or debt lenders, the same guiding principle that applies to the business plan overall also applies to your financial statement: know your audience.

CAMPUS CEO CHECKLIST

After reading Chapter 7, take these steps to prepare your company's financial statements:

☐ Research and select the appropriate financial and accounting tool for your business.

☐ Obtain templates to assist in creating an income statement, cash flow statement, and balance sheet.

☐ Visit your school's library to research typical financial figures, margins, and ratios for companies in your industry.

☐ Create actual financial statements for your company every month or every quarter.

☐ Create quarterly detailed versions of pro forma financial statements for up to three years.

☐ Create annual summary versions of pro forma financial statements for up to five years.

PROFILE OF A CAMPUS CEO

■ **Name:** Charles D'Angelo

■ **Business:** Start To Lose

■ **Web site:** *www.starttolose.com* and *www.charlesdangelo.com*

■ **Founded:** 2004

■ **His Story:** At age 17, Charles D'Angelo weighed a whopping 334 pounds. He'd struggled with weight for most of his adolescent life. But then he began a strict program of healthy nutrition and exercise, and within 15 months lost 120 pounds. When he realized the difference his weight loss made in his life, D'Angelo decided to mentor and coach others who were battling their own weight-loss issues. He launched Start To Lose, a nutrition counseling business, while a student at Saint Louis University. Currently, D'Angelo meets clients biweekly, offering telephone or in-person consultations to help children, adolescents, and adults who are trying to shed pounds. He is also pursuing a degree in premedicine and psychology at Saint Louis University and plans to graduate in 2008.

> ■ **Advice for Student Entrepreneurs:** "Anything you want to do is possible if you put your mind to it. Don't ever limit yourself. Don't let anyone stop you."
>
> —**Charles D'Angelo** to *Young Money* (June 12, 2006)

Follow the Rules—
Managing Risk and Playing It Safe

66 *Successful entrepreneurs take calculated risks.* **99**

—Gerald Hills, Founder of The Collegiate Entrepreneurs' Organization (CEO)
in interview with Bankrate.com (August 11, 2006)

8

In business, so many people envision entrepreneurs as the ultimate risk takers. They picture business owners throwing caution to the wind, mortgaging their homes, and spending every dollar they have on making a business work. Well, smart entrepreneurs rarely take risks that aren't fully calculated and considered. There's a great book I recommend on this subject that you should pick up if you haven't already. It's called *Never Bet The Farm: How Entrepreneurs Take Risks, Make Decisions, and How You Can, Too.* The authors of the book are none other than Anthony Iaquinto, a leading entrepreneur, and Stephen Spinelli, the founder of Jiffy Lube and head of the Blank Center for Entrepreneurship at top-rated Babson College.

I know that for myself, I am a bit of a thrill seeker. I truly believe where there is no risk, there is no reward. As a business owner, I sometimes have to move outside of my comfort zone—and so will you. Not only that, but you'll have to take calculated risks, deal with unexpected events or problems, and manage a host of unforeseen business challenges as well.

Because business risks and rewards almost go hand in hand, no book about launching and growing a business would be complete without some advice about how to confront the inevitable pitfalls you'll encounter. So in this chapter, I'll share with you a few ideas about how to manage risk, and how to protect your campus business from certain financial dilemmas, such as cash flow crunches, when you should or should not borrow money, and how to minimize the sales cycle in landing new business.

■ CASH FLOW IS MORE IMPORTANT THAN . . .

As an entrepreneur, you'll find that cash flow is a perpetual problem for virtually every small or growing business. In fact, my experience is that *cash flow challenges represent the number one headache for entrepreneurs.* Most people think it's happening only to them. It's like the dirty little secret of entrepreneurship. But if you do find yourself in a cash crunch, don't despair. You're definitely not alone. In one of my entrepreneurship classes at MIT, a professor once wrote this acronym on the board: CFIMITYM. He said it stood for "Cash Flow Is More Important Than Your Mother." Now I know that cash flow is not more important than my mother, but as a business owner, it's been such a headache that it sometimes makes me run home to my mother! Besides obtaining a loan, there are five primary ways to manage cash flow:

> ### ■ Young Entrepreneur
>
> Based in Blaine, Washington, Young Entrepreneur (*www.youngentrepreneur. com*) is a member-based Web site that offers advice and information for up-and-coming businesspeople, along with help in tracking down funding.

- Collect money up front
- Collect accounts receivable
- Stretch out accounts payable
- Liquidate inventory
- Retain cash

Collect Money Up Front

In many industries, people and companies pay for goods and services as they receive them. But that's not always the case. Depending on your industry, it may be customary for you to commence work or to ship goods without being paid up front. When you take on new assignments or deliver products to customers, at the very least you should secure some money from those clients. Ask for a third—or better yet, half—of the total invoice due, with the balance due at a fixed time or on completion of the work or final delivery of whatever goods you may be selling. In other words, try to get as much money up front as possible from your clients.

Collect Accounts Receivable

You can collect more quickly on the invoices owed you by other individuals and companies. You do this by first monitoring and tracking who owes you and not allowing invoices to get stale. Second, you ensure collection of these monies by devoting time and resources to the collections process. Consider investing in a good bookkeeper and assigning responsibility to someone specifically for collections. Often the time or money earmarked for that person is more than justified by the work he or she puts into keeping those receivable accounts coming in the door in a timely fashion. Politely remind clients about past-due bills. It's especially important to make sure you get paid as soon as possible in case one of your customers experiences its own financial problems down the road, so try to establish favorable terms in your contracts on which payment should be received, such as "Invoice payable in 30 days" (or lower). Finally, companies can avoid many cash flow problems simply by having the proper accounting controls in place to ensure prompt payment of invoices.

Stretch Out Accounts Payable

You can stretch out the time you are required to pay other people and businesses. You accomplish this chiefly by arranging payment terms in your contracts, such as "Invoice payable in 90 days" (or higher), with suppliers, vendors, and others. As mentioned earlier, this is also achieved by obtaining trade credit. If you have contractors working for you, you can write into your contracts with people that you're only going to pay them when you get paid. That's what we should have done with our contractors when we had the GM training assignment. It sure would have saved us from having to answer a lot of phone calls! Learn

■ Junior Achievement

Junior Achievement (JA) uses hands-on experiences to help young people in grades K–12 throughout the world to understand the economics of life, including the basics of business, finance, and entrepreneurship. Visit *www.ja.org* to find a JA program near you.

from my mistake, and cover yourself as necessary when it comes to handling your financial obligations—especially payroll.

Liquidate Inventory

In cases when cash flow is hurting, but your company is carrying inventory that can be liquidated or converted to cash quickly and easily, it may be in your best interests to do so. For example, certain inventory can be returned for a full refund, possibly with a restocking fee, while other items can be liquidated through sales, discounts, or even sold on eBay.com.

Retain Cash

At the end of the day, when it comes to managing cash flow, one principle will always remain: *cash is king*. Retaining cash is perhaps the only surefire method to avoid cash flow headaches. There will always be instances where it makes sense to borrow money—for example, you need growth capital or your clients are stretching out their payments to you—but cash gives you the greatest flexibility.

Know Your Worth

One way to avoid a cash crisis altogether is to know the value of your product or service in the marketplace, and don't be afraid to ask for it. If you're proposing a price for customized or project work, it's far better to come in high, and be negotiated down, rather than throw out a very low number and watch your client (or potential client) just look at you silently, or accept in a hurry, because they're thrilled about your lowball offer and they know you've underpriced yourself. We made this mistake often with MBS when we offered educational seminars. We developed a full-blown business plan for the company. We benchmarked ourselves against competition. We looked at pricing arrangements from leaders in our arena such as Franklin Covey. Yet we were always reluctant to price ourselves in line with the competition. I know now that was a mistake. At any given presentation, our audience size could range from 20 interns at AT&T to 2,000 employees at General Motors. We organized entire conferences for under $5,000, while competitors would charge $20,000 or more for the same event. Clearly, we missed the boat on pricing in those earlier days, largely because we foolishly discounted ourselves based on the fact that we were students.

Learn to Say "No"

For many start-ups it can be incredibly difficult to turn down work. But believe it or not, in some cases, it's probably in your best interest to say "No" to a project that is clearly going to be unprofitable unless there are mitigating considerations. For example, the project may serve as a useful reference for future projects, it may provide a valuable entry point to a new line of business, or it may provide much-needed exposure leading to other, related opportunities.

One way to tell whether a project will be profitable is to estimate the number of hours it will take you to complete the job. Let's say you believe you can accomplish a given project in 20 hours. Now go ahead and add 50 percent to that figure because it's been my experience that most assignments take far more time than you anticipate. If you anticipate 30 work hours and you are being paid $1,200 for an assignment, then that means your hourly rate is $40. As long as that $40 an hour is enough to pay your workers, cover all your costs, and still leave you with cash left over, then the job will be profitable. Establish a target for profitability on every project, and then have the discipline to adhere to those targets when it comes to accepting project work.

Always keep in mind that taking on money-losing projects can sometimes do more harm than good because you sell yourself short in the marketplace, and because there's an opportunity cost tied to the fact that your time and energies are now devoted to subpar business (from a financial standpoint), so you're not freed up to seek more lucrative business.

For student entrepreneurs, there's no question that at times you might offer your labor, products, or services free of charge. In these cases, your goal is to gain work experience, make connections, learn about an industry, or reap some other reward besides an immediate and tangible financial benefit. Just don't make a practice of giving away your work, however. Remember that what you're offering is of value to the marketplace—and the right clients who need your product or service will be willing to pay you for it.

■ WHEN SHOULD I BORROW THE MONEY?

It is not a trivial decision to borrow money to finance your business. As I mentioned in Chapter 6, the more debt you incur, the more risk you assume, because you are ultimately responsible for repaying the obligations. Here are some guidelines about when you should borrow money—and when you should not.

It's OK to Borrow Money When . . .

Several reasons for borrowing money include:

- *You're financing capital expenses.* Getting a new phone system, office equipment, or computers to help you manage your business is smart decision making because it's an investment in the growth of your enterprise. Plus, these are big-ticket items that you may not have enough cash on hand to pay for outright.
- *You're managing cash flow.* For example, you are certain to receive payment from a client in the near future, but charge operating expenses such as your telephone bill or business card printing on your credit card. As long as you pay the charges off by the time the bill rolls around, borrowing money on your credit cards in this way is fine.
- *You're taking advantage of a viable opportunity.* When you've conducted your due diligence on a potential opportunity for your company (i.e., legal assistance for a promising partnership agreement, brochures for an ideal marketing event, etc.), it can be a smart thing to use borrowed funds to finance that investment. These opportunities will likely be few and far between, so don't make a habit of borrowing money to finance every whimsical "opportunity" that comes your way.

You Should Avoid Borrowing Money When . . .

Some reasons for not borrowing money are:

- *You have no clue how you'll repay it.* Any time you accept credit or a loan, you should know exactly the source of funds (either existing or future money) that you'll use to repay what you owe. To do otherwise is to play the equivalent of financial Russian roulette.
- *You can't afford the loan.* No matter how dire your situation, it's probably best to decline a loan if you can't truly afford the debt. Let's say a hard-cash lender offers you money, but it's at 25 percent interest and would require sizable monthly payments that would seriously hamper your budget. Your best bet is to keep looking for better terms and rates. Any loan you accept shouldn't put such a dent in your cash flow that you have to be worried about repaying that loan.
- *You're trying to pay for fixed expenses.* Fixed expenses are set costs for things such as your monthly Internet service or any payroll obligations

you have to meet. These expenditures are best paid for from the normal cash flow your business generates. If not, there's a problem. And your business is deficit-spending in a way that is bound to cause financial problems down the road.

■ *You have smarter or better alternatives.* As mentioned earlier, it may be smart to borrow for certain capital expenses, but in some instances, you may have an alternative to borrowing, such as leasing equipment or using trade credit with vendors and suppliers.

■ Luring Potential Lenders

You can make yourself more marketable and attractive to potential lenders by following a few key bits of advice.

■ *Maintain good credit.* Most banks will run your credit report and check your FICO score, a credit rating developed by Fair Isaac & Co., as a prerequisite to giving you a loan. You can get your credit history and FICO score at *www.myfico.com.*

■ *Seek out lenders who specialize in your industry.* It'll be far easier to obtain financing if you don't have to walk a bank officer through every single detail about how companies in your industry make money. If you're in a health care consulting business and that bank has loaned money to tons of other health care consultants, chances are it will be able to more clearly see you as a viable business. To find lenders with knowledge of your industry, join professional and trade groups, and obtain referrals from those people in organizations you network with at industry meetings.

■ *Apply for money before you need it.* Don't rush through a lender's doors at the 11th

hour and expect it to turn around a loan within 48 hours so you can meet payroll, buy some equipment you needed yesterday, or pay suppliers what's already due to them. To a loan officer, there's probably nothing worse than a look of desperation on a bank loan applicant's face when that individual hasn't planned ahead and is now facing a serious cash crisis. Along these lines, even if you don't need access to capital right now, you should consider obtaining it in case of an emergency or unforeseen circumstance so it is then readily available.

■ *Explore multiple sources of funding.* This is no time to put all your eggs in one basket. Instead of going to just one bank, or pinning all your hopes on one lender, seek funding from a variety of financing sources: friends and family, private investors, government entities, and so on. Having a broad mix of relationships with potential investors will put you in good stead when the time comes for you to call on those contacts for a loan.

■ MINIMIZING THE SALES CYCLE: THE PATH OF LEAST RESISTANCE

One of the early lessons I learned about securing new clients in the shortest possible time is to pursue the path of least resistance. This means you don't always need to go after the biggest fish in town or chase after a large number of people to try to sell them on your product or service.

Our first contract at BCT was with our church, First Baptist Church of Lincoln Gardens in Somerset, New Jersey. At the time, three of the inaugural five partners worshipped there, so the senior pastor already knew us. That eliminated one big hurdle: no introduction was needed. The church needed a data network installed so the staff members could all get on the Internet. We convinced them to give us that contract. There was no need for bids, no competitors to rival our efforts, and we benefited from a very tight sales cycle, where the time required to close the deal was minimal. For student entrepreneurs—where time and money are likely scarce—all these things can help you grow your business quickly and efficiently. Landing that first contract for BCT also was a big win in other ways. It gave us a reference and an actual project we could point to that we'd handled. As a student, you may not have much formal work experience, but you can often land clients based on project work you've performed.

That church contract was for $45,000. We got a third of the money up front and were tasked with completing a four-month project. That was December of 2000. At the time, the prospect of anyone paying us $45,000 seemed lucrative. We would've done just about any work for that kind of money. As it turns out, the work ultimately took significantly longer than expected and consequently we barely broke even. Still, the experience was a positive one and taught us lots of lessons. So if we had to do it over again, we would have still taken the project because it gave us credibility and positioned us for other opportunities. But we should have at least gone into the work knowing exactly what we were signing up for, which is a common mistake that we made that I will discuss in greater detail in Chapter 15. Following the path of least resistance—going after "low-hanging fruit" or getting business from people who already know you—is a surefire way to reduce the sales cycle and alleviate cash flow problems. In the next chapter, I'll talk more about networking with other students and professors, and mentoring, as ways to establish new relationships that can help you in this regard.

CAMPUS CEO CHECKLIST

After reading Chapter 8, take these steps to minimize risk, manage cash flow, and reduce the sales cycle:

☐ Make it standard practice to ask for as much money up front as possible from customers (i.e., 50 percent).

☐ Establish favorable payment terms with customers that owe money to you (i.e., 30 days net or lower) to minimize accounts receivable.

☐ Assign someone to be responsible for collecting from past-due clients.

☐ Establish favorable payment terms with suppliers or vendors you owe money to (i.e., 90 days net or higher), or a trade credit account, to stretch out accounts payable.

☐ Benchmark your company's prices against those of the competition.

☐ Check your credit history and FICO credit score at *www.myfico.com*.

☐ Research which banks and other lending institutions have experience in your industry.

☐ Identify someone you know personally or have worked with in the past who could serve as an initial reference customer.

PROFILE OF A CAMPUS CEO

■ **Name:** Luke Skurman

■ **Business:** College Prowler

■ **Web site:** *www.collegeprowler.com*

■ **Founded:** 2002

■ **His Story:** When Luke Skurman was a high school student in Marin County, California, he had his sights set on going to college on the East Coast, but he didn't feel he was getting the real scoop on many colleges based on the largely glowing information available to him in magazines, university brochures, and college guide-books. Sure these publications gave out tons of data about average SAT scores, the range of majors available to students, and the credentials of the faculty. But none of these sources, in Skurman's mind, dealt with other issues that students really want to know, such as "What's the dating scene like? Is there a lot of peer pressure to do drugs? And what about crime on campus?" To answer these questions and more, Skurman launched College Prowler while he was a sophomore at Carnegie Mellon University. This book-publishing business tells students everything from how much partying goes on at a particular campus to how good the cafeteria food is. So far, College Prowler has published reviews of 200 campuses throughout the United States. Unlike lists compiled by magazines such as *U.S. News & World Report,* with College Prowler students vote and rank schools. In fact, the College Prowler guidebooks have become enormously popular precisely because they're written by current students for prospective students—giving fresh insights into campus life that students probably wouldn't get unless they visited the campus, which can be time-consuming and expensive. College Prowler employs 8 full-time employees and 214 part-time student-authors nationwide. And Skurman says 2006 marked a record year for his business; already his 2005 revenues from book sales grew eightfold since 2004.

■ **Advice for Student Entrepreneurs:** "To be a strong leader, you have to be honest and credible. If you don't have those two qualities, you don't have anything. People need to hear the truth and to know what's going on—whether it's good news or bad news."

—Luke Skurman

PART 3

Balancing Business and Education

Build a Winning Team—
Tapping a Brilliant Workforce

❝ *Our first 20 employees were Cornell graduates.* ❞

—Todd Krizelman, Cofounder of TheGlobe.com (with Stephan Paternot) in the *Cornell Chronicle* (March 9, 2000)

9

No matter what your business is, you'll need help getting it off the ground and keeping it running smoothly on an ongoing basis. Where should you turn for this assistance? In many cases, you need only look right outside your dorm, or at least right there on campus, because your school environment likely has dozens, if not hundreds or maybe even thousands, of potential individuals who could aid you in your entrepreneurial efforts. Your peers and cohorts obviously don't have their degrees yet, but they often know a great deal more about their subjects—whether it's Web design, marketing, or sales—than a number of high-priced working professionals in the marketplace who never bother to update their skills or take continuing-education classes. In fact, some of these same students may have already interned with major companies in their fields. These are the individuals you want to recruit as student employees and interns—in many cases at no immediate financial cost to you. This readily available, eager talent pool of workers can be motivated by a number of things beyond money, such as college credit or the chance to work in a start-up that may later go public.

■ BUILDING A WINNING TEAM

In *Good to Great,* management expert Jim Collins writes that part of having a great business is recognizing that "people are not your most important asset.

The *right* people are." Building a winning team means not just finding any people; it means finding the right people. For you to build a winning team, it will take a discerning eye, and time to perform the necessary due diligence. It's not painstaking. But it is about being thoughtful. And it is one of the most important roles you can play because *the right people are your most valuable asset*. In this chapter, I'll share some of the ups and downs we experienced at MBS and BCT in building our team, and then I'll offer some tips to help you on working with friends, recruiting volunteers, choosing partners, and building your team.

Building Our Team at BCT Partners

In 2001, the market for MBS's services began to dry up. Fortunately, the seeds were already being planted to establish my next and current venture, BCT Partners. Initially led by the dedicated efforts of a new business partner, Munro Richardson, an Oxford classmate and fellow Rhodes scholar, BCT was able to continue the momentum established by MBS and, in fact, for reasons I'll discuss later, MBS eventually folded just as BCT was on the rise. To build our team at BCT we aligned ourselves with people who believed in the mission, vision, and values of the company. In fact, to ensure consistency between the direction of the company's and our team, we established a completely new mission, vision, and values for BCT Partners. We believed that our mission, vision, and values should not only reflect what we believed in as we sought to launch another venture, but it should also speak to the kinds of people who would want to work for the company. BCT's mission, vision, and values today are as follows;

BCT Mission:
BCT Partners is a socially responsible consulting firm that develops solutions to complex problems with a spirit of excellence, commitment, and integrity. We leverage management, technology, research, and policy expertise to help our clients achieve desired results.

BCT Vision:
As an entrepreneurial institution, BCT Partners' vision is to be a catalyst in developing and sustaining the growth of healthy communities, strong institutions, and constructive public policies. To achieve this vision, BCT Partners will foster an environment that upholds our corporate values, builds upon the expertise, dedication, and commitment of our talented staff, and promotes their development and growth.

BCT Values:

- *Balance.* Balancing work and family, balancing a healthy lifestyle and work environment, and balancing each other's strengths and weaknesses, as well as other areas of individual and collective development.
- *Integrity.* Fostering an environment of truthfulness, honesty, openness, and honoring commitments.
- *Innovation.* Inspiring and encouraging creativity, ingenuity, imagination, and inventiveness.
- *Growth.* Promoting resilience, tenacity, development, advancement, and lifelong learning—personally, professionally, and organizationally.
- *Faith.* Believing and trusting in ourselves and one another; the substance of things hoped for, the evidence of things unseen.
- *Excellence.* Demonstrating quality in the work we do, setting the standard, and striving to be the best.
- *Entrepreneurship.* Supporting risk taking, courage, resourcefulness, initiative, and leadership.
- *Teamwork.* Maintaining respect for the individual and camaraderie in our working relationships through synergy, sacrifice, collective work and responsibility, collaboration and interdependence.

These "governing ideas," as discussed in Chapter 3, were reminiscent of Mind, Body & Soul Enterprises' history as well as certain ideas underlying the entrepreneur's mindset. But they also more accurately reflected BCT's products and services, BCT's market segments, and BCT's direction moving forward. Each element helps guide our business considerations and, perhaps of greatest relevance here, our hiring decisions and interactions between staff and partners. In my opinion, mission, vision, and values represent your company's foundation as it relates to finding the right partners and people.

Working with Friends—Mixing Business with Pleasure?

As a result of the time and effort invested by the initial five partners and me, MBS approximately doubled or tripled its revenues every year during the first seven years of my graduate studies. It was an incredible group of committed and talented people with whom I've been blessed to have the opportunity to work with. My core business partners were friends. However, many entrepreneurs strongly recommend against going into business with family or friends for legitimate reasons. My experience has been a positive one overall, but some would suggest that it is the exception, not the norm. For me, the advantage of going into business with friends was that they were true friends. We believed in one another, supported one another, and wanted to see us all do well. The disadvantage is when someone isn't carrying his or her weight or he or she cannot separate personal matters from business matters and, as a result, issues in one area can lead to issues in the other area.

When I think about my past business partners beginning with MBS and evolving into BCT, five of them have come and gone, but three partners have remained consistent throughout each venture. They are Lawrence, Dallas, and JR—each was able to carry his or her own weight, each could separate personal matters from business matters, and each has remained committed to the company in some manner (Lawrence and I remain full-time with BCT to this day). In my mind, these are the single most important traits you need from a friend with whom you also plan to do business. Our business relationship has been bound by our equity ownership arrangement, as well as our mission, vision, values, faith, and belief in one another. If your friends can't operate with honesty and with integrity, they're not the right people to enter into business agreements with, especially in cases where you have money today and you're broke tomorrow—or vice versa. If you can't ride those inevitable highs and lows that any entrepreneur faces, and separate the friendship from the partnership, then the lines may get blurred and ultimately the friendships may get blurred as well. I'm pleased to say that even among partners who left my past businesses, for the most part, the friendships remained intact. However, there's no question that tensions sometimes arose if it seemed that those friendships were in jeopardy because of the business.

Having a friendship alone doesn't necessarily translate into a great business partnership, especially if your friends know nothing about entrepreneurship or your industry. Align yourself with someone committed to the venture and whose skill set complements yours, rather than partnering with a friend just because he or she is a friend. I've been fortunate in this regard. For example, Lawrence has developed considerable expertise in information technology, gaining corporate experience at General Electric and Merrill Lynch, and now serves as our president and chief technology officer at BCT Partners. Jeffrey is a professor of entrepreneurship who advises the student business plan competition at New York University. Dallas is the dean of finance and administration at our alma mater, Rutgers University, and Munro is now the director of special projects at the Kaufmann Foundation, one of the leading foundations in the areas of entrepreneurship and education.

Working with Volunteers—The Student Volunteer Conundrum

When it comes to volunteers, you have to accept the fact that not all labor—free, paid, or otherwise—is created equal. People often say that "You get what you pay for." And in many cases, that's true. Sometimes when you have volunteers or interns working for your business, you'll be disappointed to find that they don't take the business as seriously as you'd like, they don't finish tasks on time, show up for meetings, or do what they promised to do. In truth, though, that can happen to any business owner—even one who's paying his or her employees! If you recruit people to work in your enterprise, I want you to think beyond the old "You get what you pay for" mentality. Remember the entrepreneur's mindset that it's critical for you to maintain to make your business a success. With an entrepreneur's mindset, you'll recognize that there are several possibilities (beyond money) that could motivate your team members. Generally speaking, people will work if they:

- Get paid for their efforts
- Believe in the mission, vision, and values of your company
- Support you personally
- Gain professional experience
- Want to learn more about an industry
- Obtain exposure in a field of interest

Most student entrepreneurs are in a position to provide at least one of these benefits. Some people will come on board because they really believe in what you're doing, or believe in you. Others can be promised something today that they'll get tomorrow—or at some point in the future. An employee may expect, or a partner may be given, equity with the hope of an economic payoff down the road. Different things motivate people. The challenge is in discerning what it will take to get someone committed to the business. You certainly don't want to exploit or take advantage of anyone. But you definitely need to be realistic and honest about what you can offer. Some people will tell you straight out that they need to get paid up front, while others don't need money at all.

Someone once said, "Volunteers are not paid—not because they are worthless, but because they are priceless." When you're dealing with people you aren't paying, you'd be wise to keep this philosophy in mind.

Choosing Partners—A Decision of Paramount Importance

In a business relationship, I can't stress enough the importance of choosing partners wisely. I've had eight business partners over the course of my various professional ventures, some of whom I brought to the table and some of whom others brought to the table. Every partner was a friend of an existing partner. Everyone was a known quantity. Nevertheless, not everyone worked out. Sometimes people didn't pull their weight; in a few instances, partners didn't bring in contract opportunities when they had an equity stake in the company that required them to land new business, while at other times, individuals had other priorities and were unable to sustain their commitment to the venture. The result is that some partners left of their own accord. Some were escorted out, and others were kicked out. Bringing someone into your company as a partner is a decision of paramount importance and should not be taken lightly. Many say, and I agree, that from a legal and fiscal standpoint, the relationship of "being in business with someone is second only to being married."

Bringing on a business partner means cutting him or her in as an equity owner of the company. You should weigh very carefully the value of what he or she brings to the table to determine whether giving up some ownership of the company is warranted. As shown in Figure 9.1, you can determine a person's value along the same lines of what we discussed in Chapter 2 and your capacity to pursue a new venture. This means evaluating their current or anticipated contributions to the company by asking him or her the following questions:

- What specialty knowledge and expertise do you possess? (*Human capital*)
- What synergy can you bring to the team? (*Intellectual capital*)
- What relationships and contacts can you bring into the fold? (*Social capital*)
- What experience and intuition with our customers or industry do you hold? (*Cultural capital*)
- What monetary contributions or credit are you willing to invest? (*Financial capital*)
- What amount of time and effort are you willing to contribute? What sacrifices are you willing to make? Is this a priority? (*Sweat equity*)

Naturally, financial capital will almost always lead to an equity stake in the company (or a debt obligation). In the remaining categories, there are alternative ways to keep someone valuable engaged with your company without

FIGURE 9.1 Evaluating Others' Contributions—The Five Forms of Capital and Sweat Equity

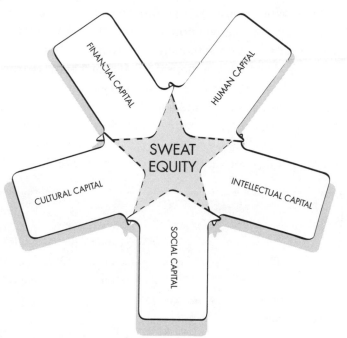

making him or her an owner. He or she could join the team as an employee, contractor, consultant, or advisor. But it may also be the case that your company is lacking in the financial means to pay someone and equity is all that remains to offer. This was true at MBS when we recruited Lawrence, Dallas, and Raqiba as partners, and they all brought incredible value to the company. Furthermore, it is not uncommon for members of the board of directors for a corporation, senior management, and possibly some key advisors to receive equity ownership in a company. Ownership can go a long way in building commitment and buy-in among those who receive it.

Don't make the mistake that many cofounders do when people come together in business and arbitrarily say, "Let's split the business 50-50." That's not always the best strategy. Equity stakes should be divided based on the contributions various partners bring to the table. Again, in this area, it's vital to have partners who can separate the business from the personal.

If you have to discuss an equity stake, it shouldn't get personal. Many times, partners will have strong personalities and each one will have something of value to offer. Take this exercise very seriously, but also don't get too bogged down so that getting the exact equity percentages prevents you from working together. I am sad to say that I've seen potentially great partnerships derail over percentage points. When you're just getting started, 51 percent of nothing is nothing. Obviously, quibbling over nothing is pointless. An equity conversation among would-be partners is an extremely important one, but it should not be a showstopper. If it is, then that is perhaps the first sign that the partnership is not a good fit. Nonetheless, to protect the company against a partner's exit, make sure your partnership agreement includes both a "nondisclosure agreement" (or NDA, discussed in Chapter 3) to prevent disclosure of proprietary information, and a "noncompete" clause, which stipulates that a partner cannot create or work for a competing company for a specified period of time.

■ Looking for Talent?

In addition to finding fellow students at your school's career placement center, the following Web sites can also assist if you are in search of consultants, experts, contractors, part-time assistance, or freelance talent:

- Craigslist (*www.craiglist.com*). Craigslist is one of the largest online destinations for classified advertisements and forums tailored to local communities. Your company can post jobs, products, services, and more for interested parties in your area at no cost.

- Elance (*www.elance.com*). Elance is used by small businesses to obtain free and affordable quotes from a global network of graphic designers, programmers, Web site designers, and writers for hire.

There you can find professionals in areas such as accounting, data entry, market research, public relations, telemarketing, and more.

- Guru (*www.guru.com*). Marketed as the largest online marketplace for freelance talent, Guru is a free service to connect with top professionals in everything from business consulting, law, and advertising, to illustration, photography, and translation.

- Idealist (*www.idealist.org*). While it is geared for the nonprofit community, Idealist is also a good resource for socially responsible organizations seeking consultants. Social entrepreneurs should certainly consider posting opportunities at Idealist.

■ TAPPING A BRILLIANT WORKFORCE

So how do you know if someone would make a great addition to your team? Just because he's your roommate and you hang out together constantly is not good enough. And just because your girlfriend gives you great relationship advice or shares notes with you from Psych 101, that doesn't qualify her to go into business with you.

On one hand, never be afraid to trust your gut instincts. On the other hand, the five forms of capital and sweat equity are also useful when evaluating the possible contribution of any member of your team. In fact, in the absence of financial capital—i.e., someone putting up cash or credit—all you may have left to strengthen your team is the human capital, intellectual capital, social capital, cultural capital, and sweat equity of the people you attract. Along these lines, here are some additional tips when evaluating working with potential volunteers, employees, and partners:

- *Seek out like-minded individuals.* Look for people who share a passion similar to yours and have demonstrated a commitment to that passion. One of the things that made Jeffrey and Aldwyn such excellent business partners for MBS was that they were both already immersed in the areas they would be leading for the company. JR had previously started his own educational services and training company, while Aldwyn was known throughout campus as a music aficionado.
- *Evaluate their track record.* Are they active in student organizations? Are they respected leaders on campus? Have they proven their ability to get things done? Actions speak louder than words, and to the extent they are already making things happen, they may be able to make things happen for your company.
- *Test the waters.* To get a feel for good potential business partners, test the waters slowly, a little bit at a time. Set some initial goals or objectives, or assign some initial tasks to accomplish, and see how they do. If things go well, that's fantastic. But if they can't carry out simple chores, that should raise a red flag that you probably should heed.
- *Clarify roles, responsibilities, and expectations.* I'll be the first to admit that there was a lot of room for improvement in this area when I ran my student businesses. As with any relationship, for each member of the team it pays to clearly define his or her role and responsibilities (i.e., written job description) and performance expectations (i.e., defined goals and objectives over a period of time). Just as important, be sure to communi-

cate this information to everyone on your team so they're all on the same page. This will ward off issues down the road.

- *Maintain ongoing, regular communication.* Maintaining ongoing and regular communication is a must. In Chapter 3, I presented a number of ways to keep your team in the loop by utilizing technology-based and non-technology-based approaches to communication. Leverage tools such as e-mail, conference calls, text messaging, and Web conferencing to keep everyone abreast of what's happening. But despite the wonders of technology, also make sure to schedule good old-fashioned, in-person meetings.

- *Never burn bridges.* If you believe you've given someone every opportunity to prove himself or herself and you have to let them go, be as clear and specific as possible about why you must part ways. Give (and receive) constructive feedback, but also seek to maintain a good relationship thereafter. Former employees or partners can continue to be helpful if the bridge isn't burned.

Placing the Right People in the Right Job at the Right Time

One of the benefits of starting an educational services and training company was that it forced us to apply many of the organizational development principles we were teaching to our customers to our own business. We had to practice what we preached! Through our work, we were fortunate to be exposed to several approaches related to organizational mission, vision, values, leadership, management, team building, and team dynamics, as these are all areas that some entrepreneurs completely overlook. In retrospect, we found this information not only invaluable to our customers, but also foundational to our own ability to identify good people. Perhaps most important, these concepts continue to help us at BCT Partners in building a winning team that reinforces the culture and values we seek to uphold.

One of the more popular seminars we offered was called "Leadership and Management in the Workplace." During this session, attendees learned about their *personality type,* which seeks to describe certain patterns of behavior, traits, and motivations. The purpose was not to pigeonhole, stereotype, or typecast people. Instead, using personality type, we would help people gain greater insight to themselves as well as other members of their team. To determine each participant's personality type, we would administer a precursor to the Keirsey Temperament Sorter II®. Now offered by AdvisorTeam, the Keirsey Sorter is a leading personality assessment tool that is available online at *www.advisorteam.com* (including a version for students). The Sorter is closely related to the work of Katharine Cook Briggs and her daughter, Isabel Briggs Myers (the pair is popularly known as Myers-Briggs). According to their work, personalities can be sorted along four preference scales:

- *How are you energized?* Extroversion (E) and Introversion (I)
- *How do you process information?* Sensing (S) and Intuiting (N)
- *How do you make decisions?* Thinking (T) and Feeling (F)
- *How do you live your life?* Judging (J) and Perceiving (P)

The scales denote certain *preferences* along a given spectrum. It is unlikely that you are completely on one side of a scale or completely on the other side. Your behavior may change based on the circumstances. Usually, however, you have a preference on each of the four scales (E or I, S or N, T or F, and J or P).

Extroverts are energized by people and the outer world of people and things, while *introverts* are energized from within and the inner world of thoughts and reflections. Do you think best when talking with people or do you think best when you're alone? If it is the former, then you may be an extrovert. If it is the latter, then you may be an introvert. *Sensing* people process information using the five senses (see, hear, touch, taste, and smell), while *intuiting* people process information using their intuition or what some call a "sixth sense." Would your friends best describe you as someone who is very realistic and tends to focus on known facts? If so, then you might be more of a sensing person. Or would they best describe you as someone who is very imaginative and tends to look at possibilities? In that case, you might be more of an intuiting person. If you are a *thinking* individual, you make decisions based on logic and objective considerations, while if you are a *feeling* individual, you make decisions based on personal tastes and subjective considerations. Did you decide to purchase your last cell phone only after a careful and analytical review of its features and functions weighed against its cost? Or did you decide it was the right phone for you based on how you "felt" the moment you saw it and held it in your hand? Clearly, the first example suggests you may be more of a thinking individual, while the second example suggests you may be a feeling individual. Lastly, *judging* people live their lives in a scheduled, decisive, and orderly manner, while *perceiving* people live their lives in a flexible, adaptable, and spontaneous manner. As a judging person, when I was in school I would plan and schedule my entire week almost down to the minute. By contrast, as perceiving people, some of my roommates would wait and discover what the week had in store for them.

■ Want to Learn More about Your Personality Type?

There is considerable information available via books and online describing each of the 16 personality types as well as how they can effectively interact with other types. Three books I recommend are:

■ *Please Understand Me II: Temperament, Character, Intelligence* by David Keirsey. This is a best-selling follow-up to Keirsey's initial book on temperament. It includes full descriptions of the temperaments and their relationship to leadership.

■ *Joining the Entrepreneurial Elite: Four Styles to Business Success* by Olaf Isachsen. Isachsen identifies four distinct entrepreneurial styles—the Administrator, the Tactician, the Strategist, and the Idealist—that are related to the temperaments, and describes their relationships to entrepreneurial success.

■ *Do What You Are: Discover the Perfect Career for You through the Secrets of Personality Type* by Paul D. Tieger and Barbara Barron-Tieger. An excellent book (recommended earlier in this book) to help explore your interests and passions using personality type.

For each participant, the result from completing and scoring the Keirsey Sorter was a four-letter combination representing 1 of 16 personality types. For example, my personality type is ESTJ: Extrovert, Sensing, Thinking, and Judging. Interestingly, the true power we found in applying personality type to team building was not just in the 16 types. We found tremendous insight in an extension of personality type called *temperament*. According to David Keirsey, *temperament* is a set of inclinations that each of us is born with; it's a predisposition to certain attitudes and actions. I think of *temperament* as a particular style or approach. Your temperament is determined by identifying one of the following four two-letter combinations in your personality type: SJ, SP, NF, or NT. As shown in Figure 9.2, these four two-letter combinations correspond to the following Keirsey Temperaments:

■ Guardian™ (SJ)
■ Artisan™ (SP)
■ Idealist™ (NF)
■ Rational™ (NT)

Guardians are task-oriented and thrive on procedure. They are responsible, trustworthy, stabilizing leaders. They are valued by their teammates for being dependable and hardworking, and for keeping things running smoothly.

FIGURE 9.2 The Keirsey Temperaments

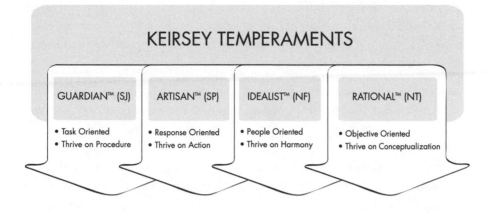

Artisans are response-oriented and thrive on action. They want to be where the action is and will go boldly down roads that others might consider risky or impossible. They are spontaneous and adaptable, which positions them as excellent troubleshooters or negotiators on a team. *Idealists* are people-oriented and thrive on harmony. They are gifted at helping others find their way, often inspiring them to grow as individuals and to fulfill their potential. They can also demonstrate high ethnical standards and acts of goodwill and kindness. You want them on your team because of their ability to work with people and bring out their best. Finally, *Rationals* are objective-oriented and thrive on conceptualization. They yearn for achievement and have an insatiable hunger to accomplish whatever they set their mind to. They are excellent problem solvers, bringing logic, analysis, rigor, and a thirst for knowledge to any team.

Think about all the steps necessary to plan for and execute your business plan. At the conceptual stage, when you are brainstorming different possibilities, you would benefit from the strengths of Rationals to understand the problem your product or service solves and establish a vision to bring a solution to the marketplace. Once the objectives have been set, you will certainly need Guardians to focus on the nuts and bolts of what needs to get done. When unexpected events arise, as they are certain to in any business, you can count on Artisans to handle the situation capably. Lastly, at every step along the way, Idealists will help ensure harmony among the team, including the members' individual and collective growth and development.

Like personality type, each temperament represents a preference. It is likely that you embody aspects of each temperament, yet have a preference for one. Because my personality type is ESTJ, my temperament is that of a Guardian (SJ).

I have found the temperament framework (and others like it) to be extremely helpful in determining certain contributions I can make to a team, the contributions that others can make, and how to coordinate a team's overall efforts to achieve a common goal. The following are some additional ideas to keep in mind as you look to build your team:

- *Identify your team's strengths and limitations.* It is just as important to know what your team is good at, as it is to know areas where your team could improve. First look at the needs of the company, then look at the skills your team brings to the table. Then ask the following questions: Are we lacking in certain areas? How can we make sure those areas are still being addressed? How can we strengthen our team in those areas in the future?

- *Recognize that team conflict can be good.* Not all conflict is bad. Conflict often results from differences in perspective. But those differences, when channeled properly through discussion and a genuine desire for understanding, can lead to better ideas, better solutions, and better teams. Conflict is bad when it causes dysfunction or negative feelings among teammates. Conflict is good when it promotes deeper levels of understanding and is rooted in mutual respect for one another.

- *Make an explicit effort to diversify your team.* Our world is becoming increasingly diverse. Companies that reflect that diversity will be more responsive to the marketplace. I strongly believe that diversity is a strength that can be leveraged as a competitive advantage but it doesn't happen by accident. Diversity includes differences in thought, age, ethnicity, gender, physical ability, sexual orientation, religion, and much, much more. Be mindful of these dimensions of diversity as you round out and grow your team.

- *Foster greater awareness of your style and your team's style.* Over the several years I have worked with my four main business partners I have seen, firsthand, the benefits of working on a team where we are all familiar with each other's leadership style. Through regular and ongoing discussions among each other about how to approach work and a perspective on leading and managing, we continue to deepen our understanding of one another. This allows us to assign responsibility, delegate tasks, and work together more effectively. The better you know your teammates, and the better your teammates know each other, the better you can work together to build your company.

- *Promote camaraderie and teamwork.* Dedicate time to organizing team-building activities that promote camaraderie and collaboration. This could include something as simple as eating dinner together. It could be something as elaborate as spending an entire weekend during the summer participating in icebreakers and games, along with strategic planning and business-development discussions.

While temperament has been a useful framework in building our team, naturally, other factors should also be taken into consideration when building your team. Some examples include the areas of expertise, major field of study, interests, and experience of your colleagues. The takeaway is not to be haphazard, but, rather, to think strategically about placing the right people in the right job at the right time.

CAMPUS CEO CHECKLIST

After reading Chapter 9, take these steps toward creating a strong team:

- ☐ Identify your strengths and weaknesses, and those of your colleagues, to determine what can be done to improve the team.

- ☐ Create a list of benefits that your firm has to offer those who work with you.

- ☐ List the various forms of capital (human, social, financial, etc.) and sweat equity found among your team.

- ☐ List three people you know who could be interns, employees, or partners in your venture.

- ☐ Write job descriptions defining the roles and responsibilities for each position in your company.

- ☐ Visit the career placement center to review other student résumés for potential employees.

- ☐ Visit one of the online Web sites offering consultants, experts, contractors, part-time assistance, and freelance talent to see what it has to offer.

- ☐ Learn more about your personality type and temperament, and foster an awareness of these characteristics among your team.

PROFILE OF A CAMPUS CEO

■ **Name:** Jeffrey Gut

■ **Business:** CollegiateMall

■ **Web site:** *www.collegiatemall.com*

■ **Founded:** 1999

■ **His Story:** Jeffrey Gut started the Internet retailer CollegiateMall.com after getting frustrated by the process of acquiring beanbag chairs and other trappings of college life. He took a year off from school at Boston University to launch his business, returned to school, and has watched the business grow ever since. CollegiateMall.com originally targeted college students who needed to furnish their dorm rooms or apartments. In recent years, though, the business has evolved to service a much larger marketplace. Now CollegiateMall.com helps individuals and corporate buyers in a wide variety of industries. The company's client list includes the U.S. military, schools and other educational institutions, government facilities, and travel and leisure facilities such as hotels and condominiums. All these customers simply log onto the Internet, and with the click of a button select the furnishings they want—whether it's for a living room, bedroom, kitchen and dining area, home office, or study area. What's more, CollegiateMall.com has thrived even when other competitors, such as CollegeClub.com and The DormStore, went out of business over the years.

■ **Advice for Student Entrepreneurs:** "I wish I had known how important it is to write a business plan. I always felt, as with my first business, that if I do something that is successful I won't need a business plan, because it's successful and therefore everyone will be interested in it. Yet it was still very hard to create investor interest. In today's world, you really do need a strong business plan, and I didn't do that until eight months after we were up and running."

—**Jeffrey Gut** to the *New York Times* (October 22, 2000)

Take It, It's Yours—
Leveraging Campus Resources

10

As a high school, college, or gradate student, you're probably familiar with the many academic resources available at your school. But what you may not be as familiar with are the multitude of resources that can benefit you as an entrepreneur. In Chapter 1, we talked about what to look for when choosing a college or university, but once there, it's up to you to leverage all the resources available. You're already paying tuition and fees, so you should take full advantage of these resources when launching and running your business. The good news is that there's absolutely no additional cost to you!

■ CAMPUS RESOURCES

Campuses are well known for centralizing quite a number of resources in one place. The items I'll highlight in this chapter include the following:

- Student business advisory committees
- Entrepreneurship and small business development centers
- Business incubators
- Technology laboratories
- College residential programs
- Student organizations

- Lectures and seminars
- Libraries and institutes

Sometimes these resources will be available at your school, and in other instances at a neighboring institution. Because you're a student, with a student ID, it may be possible to make a short trip to take advantage of a resource that's located nearby. If you keep your ear to the ground on all these offerings, you or a friend at a neighboring school can usually get hold of whatever it is you need for next to nothing or even at no additional cost.

Student Business Advisory Committees—Helping Navigate Rules and Regulations

First and foremost, heed this warning: To avoid having any problems at your school, such as an administrator challenging your right to even do business as a for-profit enterprise, make sure you consult with the appropriate entity at your institution concerning the rules and regulations that govern student businesses. Some campuses have *student business advisory committees* or related groups. If your campus does, it may be worth your time and energy to reach out to the head of that committee and/or its members. If you encounter red tape in starting or running your business on campus, the chair of the student business advisory committee may be able to help you navigate tricky issues and perhaps tell you about loopholes that can work in your favor.

Additional rules for operating your business may be detailed in your campus's student handbook. Harvard's student handbook states: "Harvard permits undergraduates to undertake modest levels of business activities on campus, subject to the Harvard Business Advisory Committee." Certain people may interpret "modest levels of business activities" differently, so obtaining authorization for your efforts is crucial. In certain instances, you may encounter obstacles in forming a business on campus, depending on how hospitable your school is to entrepreneurship. Sometimes, gaining approval just to operate on campus can be as simple as setting up a post office box off-site, so you don't tax the campus mail system with your business mail. That's what I did when I used my mother's home address as the official mailing address for MBS while at Rutgers. In this instance, it is far better to cover all your bases by researching your school's rules and regulations concerning campus businesses, instead of launching your company only to find out that you're in violation of a university policy. Still, another way to keep work in proper perspective—and to make sure you don't incur the ire of campus faculty or staff—is to adhere to the rules governing campus enterprises, or at the very least know the rules well.

Entrepreneurship and Small Business Development Centers— Coming to a Campus Near You

I've previously discussed *entrepreneurship centers* and *small business development centers* in Chapter 1, but they are so important that they are worth mentioning here again. Entrepreneurship centers present a variety of resources such as connections to business mentors, internships, venture capital firms, newsletters, business plan competitions, general advice, and more. For example, Mississippi State University is home to the Thad Cochran Endowment for Entrepreneurship, which is an organization that promotes entrepreneurship among MSU faculty, students, alumni, and Mississippi businesses and augments the university's entrepreneurship certificate program for engineering students. The endowment sponsors a business plan competition, provides business planning support and mentors, and awards monetary grants to support start-ups. If your school does not have an entrepreneurship center, you can find out if there is an entrepreneurship center at a neighboring school by contacting the National Consortium of Entrepreneurship Centers (NCEC) (*www.nationalconsortium.org*).

Similarly, small business development centers (SBDCs) are often housed on college and university campuses so there may be one on your campus or one nearby. SBDCs work with small businesses, providing training, counseling, loans, and other types of assistance. Contact the America's Small Business Development Center Network (*www.asbdc-us.org*) to learn more about an SBDC near you.

Business Incubators—Growth Accelerators

No doubt, one of the best resources many colleges have to offer for entrepreneurs is a *business incubator.* Start by asking an administrator whether your college has one. If there is one located on your campus, I recommend introducing yourself to its director. He or she may wear any number of hats—director, manager, vice president, or whatever—but what is key is that he or she knows all the ins and outs of the campus resources that are available to student start-ups. The following is a partial list of potential services you can receive from a business incubator:

- Below-market and low-cost rent
- Flexible office space and configurations
- Shared conference rooms and meeting rooms
- Legal assistance
- Administrative assistance (i.e., mail, fax, copy, notary)
- Business-development assistance
- Grant-writing assistance
- Networking with other entrepreneurs
- Financing
- Business plan feedback
- Internship opportunities
- Work-study students and student teams
- Computer, Internet access, and e-mail accounts
- Visitor reception and telephone answering service
- Use of campus facilities (i.e., gym, cafeteria, library)

I love business incubators because they can help you really bootstrap a business when funds are tight. For example, if you're just launching your enterprise and are not really flush with cash, an incubator can give you very flexible, affordable options for office space. Your choices may include below-market and low-cost rent, as well as yearly or even month-to-month leasing. Office space can range from a single cubicle at minimal cost for small operations to entire office suites for more established firms. Another big plus of a business incubator is that you're rubbing shoulders with other like-minded entrepreneurs, so you get the chance to network with a group of up-and-comers as well as established business owners.

You should also ask whether the business incubator on your campus specializes in any particular area. Some focus on helping with financing needs; others specialize in business counseling services; and still other incubators focus on giving you feedback on your business ideas or your business plan. Whatever the focus, though, you'll benefit from the supportive environment of the incubator. It's a place you can ask questions (even what you may feel are basic ones), learn a lot, and do some exploration, testing, and more before you later get your own business up and running. Rather than launching your company in an incubator, you may also choose to work or volunteer for a company located in an incubator to observe first-hand the inner workings of a start-up firm. Some incubators allow their companies to engage students or student teams at little to no cost.

As I mentioned earlier, after a few years of being housed in the equiva-lent of a garage, we moved my management, technology, and policy consulting company, BCT Partners, to the Enterprise Development Center (EDC) (*www. njit-edc.org*) on the campus of the New Jersey Institute of Technology (NJIT).

■ The National Business Incubation Association (NBIA)

There is support for business incubation at every level—from local colleges and chambers of commerce to international agencies that support entrepreneurship. Perhaps the best-known group and leading advocate for business incubation is the National Business Incubation Association (NBIA). Headquartered in Athens, Ohio, NBIA offers conferences, training seminars, publications, and research for budding entrepreneurs. The group also provides opportunities for professional development and various forums for advancing the industry. The NBIA membership is comprised of incubator developers and managers, including incubator professionals overseas. You can also search NBIA's national (and international) database, which is organized by state, to find an incubator near you. For more information on this group, visit *www.nbia.org*.

Technology Laboratories—High-End Tools at Low-End Prices

Another resource you can take advantage of is the *technology laboratory* or *multimedia laboratory* on your campus. There you can gain access to the latest hardware, software, peripherals, and equipment without having to purchase them for your company, or at a student discount. Just as important, you have access to the laboratory staff who can assist you in areas such as desktop publishing, graphic design, Web site design, scanning, imaging, printing, and more.

We took full advantage of the Digital Media Lab at Rutgers. A friend, Anthony Emmanuel, was a guru with desktop publishing and graphic design and worked in the lab. We used that lab extensively to design our brochures; to create our logo, Web site, and catalogs; and to print information about our business. Anthony helped us free of charge. And as technology-savvy students, we learned how to use some of the software applications ourselves. In the Rutgers digital media lab, Anthony was the go-to guy who everyone consulted if they had a technology problem. He was definitely worth his weight in gold in terms of the value he provided to our business, and he really helped get us off the ground—all at absolutely no cost.

College Residential Programs—Living It Up

Something of particular interest to student business owners is the growth of so-called *college residential programs* focused on entrepreneurship. A handful of colleges across the nation offer these environments, which double as a place to live and a place to run your business. You have to apply for these programs, and they're usually competitive, but well worth your efforts.

At the University of Maryland, for instance, the Hinman school runs the Hinman Campus Entrepreneurship Opportunities or "Hinman CEOs" program, which it bills as "the nation's first living-learning entrepreneurship program." Launched in the year 2000, the program puts entrepreneurially minded students from a host of academic backgrounds into a shared setting in which they live and learn from each other and their professors, as well as visiting lecturers. They also network with successful entrepreneurs and other business leaders via a weekly speaker series. According to Hinman, the mission of the program is "to foster an entrepreneurial spirit, create a sense of community and cooperation, and positively impact the way that students see their career opportunities." And just to make sure that students can develop and run their businesses effectively, participants are supplied with meeting rooms, a business center, and work spaces in the residence hall.

Babson College, meanwhile, offers an "E-Tower" to allow nearly two dozen student entrepreneurs who are either developing business plans or launching start-ups to rub shoulders every day, while living on the same floor. The idea is to allow the students the chance to benefit from each other by bouncing ideas off their peers and sharing their successes as well as their failures or frustrations. And Oregon State University has the Austin Entrepreneurship Program, where students live, dine, and work together 24-7. The program, housed in Weatherford Hall, is capped off by the presence of a College of Business faculty member and visiting professionals who actually live in the hall with the students, providing them with exclusive (and, of course, free) access to these experts, who help the students' business dreams become realities.

You should be able to find out if your school has a similar program by placing a simple call to an administrator at your institution's department of campus housing or residence life.

Student Organizations—Membership Has Its Privileges

In addition to access to incubators and residential programs, a student entrepreneur can also become a member of various *student organizations,* including groups focused specifically on entrepreneurship.

I am a huge proponent of student involvement in campus organizations. Serving as a student leader—from the committee chairperson of a fundraiser to the president of an entire organization—can help you develop valuable skills that sometimes aren't taught in the classroom. The benefits, both from a business standpoint and beyond, are abundant. For example, as a student leader you can learn how to effectively:

- Run meetings
- Work on a team
- Manage a budget
- Develop an agenda
- Manage time
- Lead others
- Negotiate contracts
- Delegate responsibility
- Write proposals
- Network
- Speak publicly and give presentations
- Manage projects

Look at this list and ask yourself which of these skills could help you start or run a business. The answer is that all of them can help! I mentioned earlier that in addition to my participation on the track-and-field team at Rutgers, I was heavily involved in the Rutgers Chapter of the National Society of Black Engineers (NSBE), the largest student-managed organization in the country. Through NSBE, I acquired all these skills by serving as a committee chair, chapter president, and regional and national executive. So it should come as no surprise that my first experience working with my business partners, Lawrence, Dallas, Jeffrey, and Aldwyn, specifically, was when we served on the Rutgers NSBE executive board together! It was through NSBE that we came to know each other professionally, worked together as team, and executed tasks, all while running the organization. When we launched MBS during my senior year, it was a seamless transition for us to be working together because we had done so previously, and had done it well.

Beyond involvement in general student organizations, there is also the opportunity to become involved with student groups specifically geared to entrepreneurs. In earlier chapters I mentioned a number of such organizations:

- Collegiate Entrepreneurs' Organization (*www.c-e-o.org*)
- Students In Free Enterprise (*www.sife.org*)
- Future Business Leaders of America (*www.fbla.org*)
- Delta Epsilon Chi (*www.deltaepsilonchi.org*)
- Business Professionals of America (*www.bpa.org*)
- Emerging Social Entrepreneurs Network (*www.eonfire.org*)

All of these organizations have a presence on various college campuses. Then, of course, school-specific organizations such as various entrepreneurship clubs, business associations, endowments, and new venture groups may be located on or near your campus. California Polytechnic State University's Entrepreneurship Club is one of many examples—with programs, services, and activities that are free for students, faculty, alumni, and professionals. Even when such a membership isn't free, it's usually relatively low-cost and you could reap dividends well above what you pay for the membership.

Of course, this is just one program. Whether you're in Tennessee or Texas, Maine or New Mexico, you should also investigate whether there are entrepreneurship clubs, groups, or organizations you can join free of charge. To find out about these networks, ask your professors about them, visit your school's student activities center, or get information from the entrepreneurship center on your campus.

Lectures and Seminars—Listen and Learn

Attending lectures is nothing new for students. But if you're interested in learning more about the business world, you should regularly check your school's calendar of events because there may be a series of *lectures and seminars* to which you should pay special attention. These events have names such as the "Entrepreneurs' Lecture Series," at North Carolina State University, "Dean's Business Forum," at Gonzaga University, or "Chief Executives' Roundtable," at Texas Tech University's Rawls College of Business. No matter what the name, however, these are campus-sponsored events where local entrepreneurs, and sometimes nationally known business experts, are brought in to speak to the student body. If you attend such lectures, you'll be doing yourself a favor in the long run. This is your chance to learn from someone else's mistakes, to tap his or her brain about industry trends or historical events, and to ask questions about any business challenges or obstacles you may be facing. And don't feel shy about approaching a speaker—no matter how well known the speaker or how "minor" you might believe your question is. The people who come to speak to students in business-lecture series are frequently generous with their time and advice; they genuinely want to give back to young and upcoming entrepreneurs. Consider volunteering to help and you may end up being their escort! You never know what can develop after you simply introduce yourself to a guest lecturer and tell her or him a little about yourself and what you'd like to do. The networking benefits and business opportunities that you can derive from these events can be priceless.

Libraries and Institutes—Infinite Information

Of course, you shouldn't forget one of the most critical and useful resources at your fingertips at school: the library—or to put it more accurately in most cases, the *libraries* and various *institutes* that are housed on your campus. At colleges and universities in particular, there are often multiple library centers based on many different academic programs and disciplines. Take the University of Pennsylvania as a case in point. Need a good reference on emerging opportunities in China? No problem. You're certain to find volumes in Van Pelt, one of Penn's 16 libraries. Penn is a researcher's delight, with more than 160 centers and institutes on campus, ranging from the Abramson Family Cancer Research Institute to the Zicklin Center for Business Ethics Research. Chapter 3 presented specific business resources that can be found in these libraries and institutes such as:

- Industry reports
- Databases
- Government sources
- Business and trade publications
- Trade association information

Arrange a time to meet with the business librarian on your campus, and perhaps on neighboring campuses, to learn more about what's available in your area.

The Campus CEO Advantage

In short, if you had to pay cash to take advantage of the tools available to you at your high school, college, or university, it would cost a small fortune. You also have a wealth of information available at your campus libraries and research and business development centers or from on-campus incubator programs. Combine all these with the excellent technological and administrative support offered by the college environment and it's easy to see why all these offerings are truly invaluable.

CAMPUS CEO CHECKLIST

After reading Chapter 10, take these next steps to leverage your campus resources:

☐ Clarify what rules and regulations exist governing student businesses on your campus.

☐ Determine whether your school has an entrepreneurship center or visit the National Consortium of Entrepreneurship Centers (NCEC) online (*www.nationalconsortium.org*) to learn more.

☐ Find out whether your school has a small business development center or visit the America's Small Business Development Center Network Web site (*www.asbdc-us.org*) to find your nearest SBDC.

☐ Visit the business incubator on your campus or contact the National Business Incubation Association (*www.nbia.org*) to find the one closest to you.

☐ Learn more about the products and services available at your school's technology laboratory.

☐ Investigate whether your school offers a college residential program focused on entrepreneurship.

☐ Join an entrepreneurship-focused student organization at your school or create your own.

☐ Plan to attend at least one speech by a business-oriented guest lecturer in the next month.

☐ Research what facilities, resources, and business information are available through your campus's main library.

PROFILE OF A CAMPUS CEO

■ **Name:** Brandon Griffin

■ **Business:** FyeBye

■ **Web site:** *www.fyebye.com*

■ **Founded:** 2005

■ **His Story:** FyeBye, or For Young Entrepreneurs . . . By Young Entrepreneurs, is an online community for young and aspiring young entrepreneurs between the ages of 6 and 21. The company is the brainchild of 17-year-old Brandon Griffin, who is currently an 11th grade student in the academically gifted program at West Side High School in Gary, Indiana. An award-winning entrepreneur and motivational speaker, Griffin was a 2005 *Black Enterprise* magazine "Teenpreneur" Nominee, and was named Indiana Black Expo's 2006 Youth Entrepreneur of the Year. Griffin actually started his first business in 2002, at the age of 12. Back then, he ran a company that developed Web sites called Quality Web Solutions, even though he initially wasn't quite sure if young people were allowed to have their own businesses. To prepare himself for the venture, Griffin attended the NAACP Reginald F. Lewis Youth Entrepreneurial Institute at Indiana University Northwest for three summers. These days Griffin is working on publishing a new business magazine for young people, which is set to launch in early 2007. The magazine will be named, naturally, *FyeBye*.

■ **Advice for Student Entrepreneurs:** "Young people have a hard time earning the trust of adults. But if you present yourself as serious, they will take you serious."

—**Brandon Griffin** to the *Hammond Times* (November 19, 2004)

"Type A"—
Maintaining Good Grades and a Healthy Focus

❝*It is very difficult balancing the business, school, and varsity athletics. Something has to give, and right now I am lucky to have two partners with whom I can share the business load on a daily basis.*❞

—Nicholas Palazzo, Cofounder of *Stack* Magazine
in *The Harvard Independent* (November 31, 2002)

Even as you pursue your entrepreneurial endeavors, it's important to stay on top of your academic studies and not allow your campus-based business to let you fall behind educationally. Unfortunately, many students who work part-time or full-time (and I'm not even talking about working on their own businesses) wind up dropping out of school or seeing their grades suffer. A variety of strategies—from working in study groups to preplanning for heavy course loads—can help Campus CEOs achieve both academic excellence and business success, regardless of whether or not you have a "Type A" personality.

Sometimes your parents may be the first ones to voice an objection to you starting a school-based business. They may be under the mistaken impression that your grades will automatically suffer if you launch a new enterprise. Fortunately, my mother was very supportive of my entrepreneurial endeavors—perhaps because I received mostly As. So by the time I was a senior and had earned a string of consecutive 4.0 semesters, she had little to no concerns about my business compromising my academic performance. I'm extremely proud of the fact I completed my undergraduate studies with a 3.9 grade point average, while competing on the track-and-field team, maintaining active involvement with a student organization, and launching my first business venture. But it didn't come easy. In the evenings and on the weekends, I usually worked on the business about two to four hours a day, taking care of everything from record-keeping and accounting to inventory management.

■ MAINTAINING GOOD GRADES

Even to this day, I'm still often asked the question: how did you manage to do so many things in school and also maintain good grades? The immediate answer is simple. The most important lesson I learned about being a good student was *to be a student of being a good student.* Stated differently, I realized that if I wanted to master my studies I would have to learn the best way for me to learn, and that meant addressing three areas:

- Studying and test-taking techniques
- Time management
- Stress management

Usually during my semester breaks, I read books and publications about all these topics (I'll recommend my favorites later) and basically studied the best way for me to study. I've always believed that my busy schedule in college was a blessing because it forced me to develop good time-management skills. Also, the fact that I was a college athlete necessitated that I receive regular exercise. And make no mistake, yes, I still made time to have a social life, spend time with friends, and go to parties. In fact, if you ask anyone who attended Rutgers during my years there they will tell you I threw some of the best parties on campus! I just had to make sure I was taking care of my other responsibilities.

Not surprisingly, one of our most popular seminars for students at MBS Educational Services & Training was called "The Real Deal on Academic Excellence: How to Get a 4.0 GPA." It was infused with a number of strategies I had picked up and used to maintain consistently good grades in undergraduate and graduate school. Following are some of the basic tips we shared in the "Real Deal" workshop (Source: MBS Educational Services & Training).

General Tips

Observing a few general guidelines can improve your grades (and student experience), no matter what your major.

Basic advice:
1. Talk to people in your major, inquire about classes, professors, and general advice.

2. Participate in class as much as possible; in some classes it is automatically a part of your grade. Professors and teaching assistants will commonly award better grades to students who actively participate in class.

3. Utilize the SQ4R (Study, Question, Read, Record, Recite, and Review) reading method for textbooks and other reading assignments. You can learn more online or by reading *Effective Study* (referred to later in this chapter), which first introduced the method.

4. Study with a group when possible. Have your friends quiz you.

Papers:

1. Start as early as possible; avoid waiting until the last minute to write papers.

2. Visit your professor or teaching assistant to clear up *any* questions you have about content, expectations, or format.

3. Determine what the professor or teaching assistant is looking for. Often the key to getting good grades is figuring out what the professor or teaching assistant wants.

Problem sets:

1. Prepare topic summaries for each chapter. Learn the precise meaning of each term (i.e., matter, mass, weight, etc.).

2. Memorize all formulas precisely, including the units associated with each quantity. Use mnemonic devices (a trick for memorizing something) as often as possible (i.e., acronyms, rhymes, groupings, associations, etc.).

3. Do all assigned problems over and over until you can do them without assistance.

4. Visit your instructor or a tutor to clear up *any* questions you have about concepts, procedure, or problems.

5. Concentrate on relations between concepts; make a concept map of the material. Use mental visualizations and imagery wherever possible.

Studying and Test Taking

No matter what your major, you will have quizzes and exams. And knowing how to prepare for a test can be the difference between a great grade and an average one.

Pretest strategies:

1. Create note/flash cards you can review until the test.
2. Determine what topics lend themselves to essays (i.e., certain topics to describe and discuss, certain points to list, etc.).
3. Take quizzes seriously; prepare for them as you would a test. Keep in mind that this information may appear on the final exam.
4. Read directions and questions carefully, paying particular attention to the number of points awarded for each question. Budget your time accordingly.
5. Save your study notes and quizzes for the final examination.

During-test strategies:

1. Write important formulas on the back of the test before you begin (where applicable).
2. Read the directions carefully! Read the entire test before you begin; answer the easiest questions first. Budget your time.
3. Show all work for partial credit. Do not leave any answers blank.
4. Verify that all answers make sense. Check your answers if time permits.

Post-test strategies:

1. Do not discuss the exam with other students immediately after it is over. You will only depress yourself.
2. When you get the exam back, analyze it thoroughly. Make sure that you understand why you missed the questions you missed, and why you were correct on the ones you got right.
3. Save all exams for use in studying for the final examination.
4. Do not let old test scores paralyze you with anxiety.

Professors and Teaching Assistants

Professors and teaching assistants (TAs) are some of the greatest assets you'll find on campus. They are academic pros and they are there to help you!

1. Get to know the instructor personally by meeting with him or her during office hours and help sessions.
2. Visit the TA during office hours on a regular basis; he or she often has input into the final grade assignments in a course.

3. Always visit the instructor prior to an examination to ask for any study hints or tips she or he might suggest.

4. Always arrange an appointment after an examination to go over any missed items.

Time Management

Ever hear the expression, "Work smarter, not harder"? There's a reason for it! If you feel like you're spinning your wheels, working yourself into the ground without noticeable results, you may not be managing your time as efficiently as you could be.

1. *Identify your goals.* What are your major goals? What are the most important things for you to do? What would you like to accomplish this semester?

2. *Prioritize your actions.* What do you need to do this month (or this week) to accomplish your most important goal?

3. *Plan, plan, plan.* Whether you use a notebook or a PDA, take the time to plan your time. Schedule important appointments such as study time and business meetings, while making sure to leave some quiet some for yourself. Failing to plan, is planning to fail.

4. *Distinguish between urgent tasks and important tasks.* Urgent tasks require immediate attention such as a text message that just arrived or your cell phone ringing. Important tasks are the ones we truly value, such as time with family and friends or studying. A key to time management is dedicating time to what's important and not urgent (i.e., eating right, exercise, quiet time, etc.).

5. *Create "time zones."* Identify fixed events or those activities you must do during the week (i.e., go to class, go to work, etc.), then create your own "time zones," or regularly scheduled periods of time for other tasks that are important. Plan your time; don't let your time plan you.

Stress Management

Sound mind = sound body. And college should be the best time of your life (thus far). By learning how to balance work and play, your experience will be that much more fulfilling.

1. *Develop a positive attitude.* According to *Managing Stress* from Krames Communications, stress is defined as "the way you react—physically or emotionally—to change." Accordingly, it is not the changes in our life that cause stress, it is the way we *react* to these changes. Developing a positive attitude simply helps change your perspective so that things that may have caused stress in the past no longer do so.
2. *Distinguish between positive and negative stress.* Believe it or not, stress can be positive or negative. Positive stress can lead to increased focus and attention, such as working more efficiently to meet a pressing deadline. Negative stress can lead to physical, emotional, psychological, and behavioral strain, such as anxiety or headaches.
3. *Practice relaxation techniques.* These include deep breathing, getting a good night's sleep, meditation, yoga, and stretching, to name a few.
4. *Live a healthy lifestyle.* The basics apply here: eat right, exercise, and try to get as much sleep as needed. The key is to make these habits part of your daily regimen. Check with your physician before beginning any exercise program or lifestyle change.
5. *Recognize yourself for your accomplishments.* When you have accomplished something that you set out to do, or achieved a milestone during the course of the semester, do something nice for yourself!

I'm certainly not the only Campus CEO to have fared well academically while running a business. In an interview for *Campus CEO,* Matt Lauzon of Babson College said, "I think there's a correlation between the business activities and your grades. The more time you put in, the better the grades you have. That was the case for me." While that might sound counterintuitive, Lauzon explained that being a student business owner was actually good for his studies because when you have a business venture, "You become more organized. You have to," he says, "because of the demands on your time."

■ MAINTAINING A HEALTHY FOCUS

Launching a campus-based business, as with starting any new enterprise, can be an exhausting, mentally draining initiative. The pitfalls of becoming too consumed by work are many. For this reason, any Campus CEO should really strive to adopt healthy habits—such as eating right and exercising at defined times—or break unhealthy patterns, such as ignoring friends and family. The point of all this is to create a healthy and happy lifestyle by balancing your work, social, and academic lives.

> ### ■ Excellent Books on Academic Excellence
>
> There are four books on academic excellence I frequently recommend to students:
>
> 1. Studying and test taking: *Effective Study* by Francis Pleasant Robinson
>
> 2. Time management: *First Things First* by Stephen R. Covey, A. Roger Merrill, and Rebecca R. Merrill
>
> 3. Stress management: *Managing Stress* by Krames Communications
>
> 4. Academic excellence: *Guaranteed 4.0* by Donna O. Johnson and Y. C. Chen
>
> In my opinion, these four publications cover all the important ground for those of you who would like to become students of being a student and bring the same level of rigor to their schoolwork as they do to their business. I myself used them during my 12 years in academia, and I truly believe that student mastery led to business mastery.

I certainly didn't always balance my studies well. I had a challenging transition from high school to college. I was largely motivated my first semester of college by fear. Rutgers School of Engineering is known as an extremely challenging and rigorous academic program. Many upperclassmen at Rutgers had a lot of war stories about how hard it was. I heard more about failure my first semester than I did about success, and it put fear in my heart. Therefore, I overstudied for two reasons: I was scared, and I believe it takes me longer to understand what I've studied. I still feel like I don't work very quickly.

My freshman year, I would study from approximately 6:30 PM to 2 AM, after a full day of classes and practice. It was total overkill and an unhealthy level of academic activity. I don't recommend it. After my first semester, I learned how to put less time into my studies yet still maintain my grades. But at graduate school at MIT, I had to relearn how to study. MIT didn't want me to regurgitate information; they wanted me to apply what I learned. By working closely with my TAs and a tutor, I eventually learned how to see the broader applications of each concept. From that experience, I further developed an ability to adjust to the rules of the game academically. Following are some simple ways for you to adapt to the constant demands of school and business.

Don't Take Yourself Too Seriously

Just because you're over the age of 18, you have a credit card, or perchance you actually are running a business and you feel "all grown up" doesn't mean you can't enjoy your youth and still laugh at yourself. It's important to maintain a good sense of humor because sometimes crazy things will happen and you should just laugh about them. It certainly beats crying! At the time, these odd or frustrating situations might not seem so funny. But later, trust me, you'll be able to look back at even the most trying of times and find some comic relief.

Don't Try to Do Everything

This is a lesson that most business owners learn much further along in their careers. But you might as well start practicing this habit now: learn to delegate. No matter how talented you are, you cannot possibly handle all the functions associated with running your enterprise, including finance, sales, marketing, customer service, and so on. So don't stress yourself out trying to be a business superperson. Let others pick up the slack. Work with your partners as a team, and empower your employees, interns, volunteers, and others connected to your business to make decisions and act, if necessary, without you having to chime in on every single issue that comes up.

Know Your Limits

As a student entrepreneur, it's important that you recognize your capacity. In other words, understand and respect what you can and can't do and be sure to set realistic and achievable goals that do not outstrip your capacity. You will be pulled in many different directions and your ability to stay on top of your game will depend on how well you recognize your limitations. After my first semester in college, I dropped my credit load because I was overwhelmed with the workload. Consequently, it took me five years to graduate, but the workload each semester thereafter was well within my limits. When you're juggling school, your business, personal relationships, extracurricular activities, and the like, it's critical that you avoid taking on more than you can handle. Your time is not without limits and sometimes you simply have to say "No" and make adjustments.

Focus on Results, Not Necessarily Hours

Many of you may have committed to spending a specific number of hours each day or each week on your business. For instance, you may devote—for no particular reason—two hours a day to your venture, or it could be five hours or even eight hours daily. The number is not what is important. It's largely arbitrary. So don't impose such artificial time limitations on yourself. A better strategy is to think about the work that must be done from a results standpoint. Some initiatives will require you to work all hours of the day and still burn the midnight oil. But other tasks just need to get done—and the sooner the better. If they take an hour, that's fine. You may be able to just work one single hour and call it a day. My point is that if you focus on the results you want to achieve, and you find that you're constantly hitting those targets, then you'll know that you're progressing and spending enough time dedicated to your business, as opposed to simply thinking: I spend 20 hours a week on my venture, so I must be doing something right. Think results—or quality—instead of quantity.

Place a High Value on Your Time

As I've mentioned earlier, the right people are your most valuable asset. But at the same time, *time is your most precious commodity.* As it is often said, "Time is money and money is time." So if you're wasting time, you're wasting money.

Over the course of my brief career, I've also come to recognize that valuing one's time is really a skill. We're all busy people. But you should consider how to value your time. You no doubt have a lot of demands on your time. There are classes to attend, papers to write, and exams to ace. You have friends, family members, and social contacts who you need to stay in touch with. You may also be a member of a sports team, sorority or fraternity, or a student organization. And last, but not least, you might be running a campus business, dealing with all the challenges that being an entrepreneur entails. So when another person asks you to do something for him or her, attend social or professional events, or give advice or help in some way, there's a value you can ascribe to the time it takes to honor that person's request.

While I'll always dedicate time for family and friends, and continue to give very generously of my time to groups and organizations whose missions I support, as I've gained more experience as an entrepreneur I have become much more discerning with how I spend my time and how I value it. When my team fields invitations and other inquiries soliciting me, my services, or my attendance at various events, I always ask: "What's the value of me personally doing this?" This is an empowering and introspective question for many reasons. First, it begs the question: "What are you good at?" If someone is asking you to do something beyond the scope of your expertise, you're probably better off saying "No"—at least until you become comfortable in that area or get a little more experience under your belt. After all, saying "Yes" to every opportunity means you'll be away from the office or away from clients, and there's an opportunity cost associated with the fact that while you're doing something else, you can't take care of your own business interests.

This is not to say that outside activities and events can't support or tie into your entrepreneurial endeavors. As I'll discuss in Chapter 12, sometimes being in the right place and networking with key players can make a world of difference. But at the same time, take my word and place a premium value on your time because it is indeed a precious commodity.

Do Some Soul-Searching

If and when times get tough, take some time to reflect on what it is you're doing and why you're doing it. If it helps, remind yourself of why you wanted to become an entrepreneur. Or think about your aspirations and how your work is leading you to make them a reality. These simple exercises can help you stay focused at times when you're wondering why you're up at three o'clock in the morning, while your friends are fast asleep. We're constantly thrown curve balls. Your job is to catch those balls and throw them back.

■ COMBINING SCHOOLWORK WITH COMPANY WORK

When I earned my PhD, I did something that I believe every Campus CEO should aspire to do: I used my schoolwork as a basis for launching a business. More specifically, the focus of my doctoral dissertation—the role of technology in building community—eventually became a focal area for our consulting practice at BCT Partners. Furthermore, the software application I designed for my PhD project, the Web-based Creating Community Connections system, became the first product marketed by the company. Leveraging my schoolwork in this manner served two purposes: it met my academic needs and personal goals by helping me attain the PhD. But it also supplied me with critical information I needed to build BCT Partners.

One of the reasons it's smart to launch your business venture based on a class assignment or research project is that you'll get valuable feedback from your professors. Moreover, you'll glean the added insights and constructive criticism of your peers. Hopefully, all this input will help you determine whether an idea you have is truly worthy of being a business. For most Campus CEOs, it is possible to take advantage of academic assignments and course requirements (even those that are already completed) and use those studies as the launchpad for a commercial enterprise. In light of that, here are some opportunities that you may be able to take advantage of on your campus:

- Focus a term paper on a business issue of relevance to your company.
- Request an independent study to conduct research related to your business.
- Assist a professor with his or her research, especially if it could inform your venture; there may be promising intellectual property, such as new technologies, that you could help commercialize for the marketplace.
- Seek out work-study or internship opportunities with local start-ups (i.e., business incubator companies).
- Sign up for courses that require projects with area businesses.

Campus CEOs around the nation point time and time again to the connection between their entrepreneurial work and their schoolwork. Some stories are legendary. For example, while I'm sure you'd all like to get As on your assignments, even if you don't get top marks for your class projects, don't let that deter you from taking an idea to market. Just think of what would have happened to Frederick Smith, the founder of FedEx, if he had been deterred by the decidedly average grade—a C—that he received on his class project for starting a rapid package-delivery service. You can also have an in-class project where you consult for an outside business—all the while getting credit, of course.

During my studies at MIT, I had a class called Entrepreneurship Lab. The sole focus of this course was to work with start-up companies. Throughout the course of the semester, we learned the different challenges that start-ups faced and helped develop a plan for how they could address a particular problem. I was fortunate in that the company I was assigned to work with, Child's Play, developed computer and Internet skills among children. This was closely related to work we would eventually do at BCT Partners in education and technology. In short, you simply can't put a price tag on things like that, which is why leveraging student projects and turning them into businesses is so very effective.

Perfect Your Pitch

Many entrepreneurship classes require you to complete a final project, which will then become an original business plan for a start-up, either a hypothetical business or a real one. Depending on the instructor, and the level of coursework you are taking, you may have to write a paper anywhere from 10 to 50 pages in length as your business plan. The more detailed you make this project, and the more effort you devote to taking it seriously, the better it will be for you—especially if you're in a class where you have to get up and verbally explain or defend what's in your business plan. Needless to say, not everyone is comfortable speaking in public, whether it's in front of a small group or an audience of 500 or more. But to the extent that you can push yourself to do something that may be a bit out of your comfort zone, it is great practice to turn those written projects/business plans into verbal pitches. You already know that you have to develop an "elevator pitch," or a quick, informative description of your business in just a few sentences. Consider this a chance for you to expand on that pitch, enough so that you can properly deliver perhaps a five- or ten-minute oral presentation of your business idea and plan. Don't wring your hands over the process. Yes, you will be critiqued by your classmates and professors—and consider that a good thing. The practice you get from standing before this crowd will be invaluable and will give you more confidence when you stand—perhaps with sweaty palms—before a bank loan officer or venture capitalist to obtain corporate financing at some point in the future. Besides, polishing your public speaking skills will serve you well in countless life scenarios.

Book Smarts vs. Street Smarts

During Season 3 of *The Apprentice*, the teams squared off in a contest of book smarts versus street smarts. As a result, people often ask me: "Do you think one area helps you more in business?" I believe they complement one another. On one hand, experience is the best teacher. Gaining practical experience, going through the process of trial and error, finding out new ways to approach situations in real life is invaluable. On the other hand, academic experience is indeed another form of experience. In the best school environment, you get exposed to a host of entrepreneurial theory as well as practical applications of the lessons you learn in the classroom, while also recognizing there is no substitute for actually running a business.

It's extremely valuable to learn the fundamentals of entrepreneurship, such as sales, marketing, and management, from books, courses, and lectures, because at some point you'll be able to apply what you've learned. For example, case studies in the classroom are great to learn about the successes and failures of other businesspeople, but their added value comes when you're able to use what you've learned from their stories in real time. So there's obviously a role for book smarts and academic business training. At the same time, and most people probably wouldn't suspect this from me—a Rhodes scholar with five academic degrees—there's also a certain intangible edge to having street smarts that you can't get solely from a book or from school. As I stated earlier, practice what you preach as early and as often as possible: get as much exposure as possible to entrepreneurship. But also make sure you maximize the campus experience and learn as much as you can in the classroom. Studying at a high school, college or university represents a once-in-a-lifetime opportunity. As a Campus CEO you can have the best of both worlds—book smarts and street smarts!

CAMPUS CEO CHECKLIST

After reading Chapter 11, take these steps toward balancing academics and business:

☐ Become a student of being a student by reading a book or article on academic excellence.

☐ Choose three studying and test taking tips that you can put into practice for your next exam.

☐ Create a time sheet calculating how many hours you spend each week on schoolwork, business work, social activities, and other endeavors. Determine how balanced (or out-of-balance) your schedule presently is.

☐ Identify sources of stress in your life and understand how you respond under those circumstances. Commit to incorporating at least one new technique that can help alleviate the most prevalent stressors.

☐ Write down three business tasks that you can delegate to someone else.

☐ Consider whether any term projects or papers you must complete for class can double as assignments to advance your business.

PROFILE OF A CAMPUS CEO

■ **Name:** Jaime Mautz

■ **Business:** Pacific Ink

■ **Web site:** *www.pacificink.com*

■ **Founded:** 2000

■ **Her Story:** Jaime Mautz created Pacific Ink, an online printer ink retailer based in Southern California, out of a business plan she wrote for a graduate thesis at San Diego State University. She cofounded the company with her brother and financed it using $12,000 in credit cards and student loans. Pacific Ink sells everything from inkjet paper to original and remanufactured ink cartridges. It also carries more than 500 different products for a wide variety of printers such as HP, Epson, and Lexmark. Since the company's inception, Pacific Ink's sales have reportedly doubled annually and now top $7 million. In November of 2005, Mautz also launched a new venture centered on recycling, raising money for community groups, and employing the developmentally disabled. And in 2006, Mautz, who earned an MBA from San Diego State University, was named a recipient of a Charles Lamden Rising Star of Business Award, which recognizes—from thousands of recent graduates of SDSU's College of Business—those individuals who are on the fast track to becoming leaders in the business industry.

■ **Advice to Student Entrepreneurs:** "[Use] all the case studies—you learn from other people's mistakes."

—Jaime Mautz to *Entrepreneur* Magazine (July 2006)

Networking Works—
Profiting from Professors and Mentors

*It gives me a great base to interact with great entrepreneurs.
I get to play a role and lend my expertise to many great companies
instead of jumping into one venture.*

**—Alex F. De Noble, Professor of Entrepreneurship at San Diego
State University in *Inc.* Magazine (May 2000)**

12

Being a student means having a unique opportunity to tap into a deep and wide brain trust found on most college campuses—professors—as well as the opportunity to forge relationships with professionals as mentors. Let's examine the ways that the entrepreneurially minded Campus CEOs can benefit from one-on-one consulting from some of the most brilliant minds on the planet. For example, the head of the marketing department can offer tips on how to successfully reach new target markets. A law professor can advise you on specific legal considerations. If you need help evaluating uses of technology for your company, a faculty member in engineering or information technology can assist you. Lastly, a local, successful entrepreneur can certainly offer powerful management solutions and advice on how to run your business.

Of course, all this wisdom and advice from professors comes at no charge, because this is what they do all day. For business mentors the challenge is, of course, finding someone who isn't too busy to lend a helping hand. So from a department chairperson to a serial entrepreneur who just happens to run a business in your area, you should make it a point to try to profit from all their collective insights and that means you must network. In short, now is the time to think about how you can get valuable consulting and professional guidance from faculty, adjuncts, administrators, and businesspeople with ties to your campus community. This chapter presents tips and strategies for establishing and strengthening a relationship with these individuals, as well as how to network and make the right connections for your company.

■ MENTORING

As a Campus CEO, you have virtually unfettered access to consultants, in the form of professors and administrators, as well as the opportunity to meet and interact with local professionals. Above all, their relationship to you could become that of a business *mentor*. A business mentor is someone who assists you in your entrepreneurial pursuits by providing expert advice, general business advice, encouragement, or connections. Maybe you've noticed that I've mentioned professors and mentors a number of times throughout this book. Because I've had some great professors and mentors in my life, this shouldn't be a surprise. My mentors have helped me in all aspects of my life—professional and personal. Mentors are great sources of information, contacts, wisdom, and advice.

Your first step in identifying a business mentor is determining exactly what kind of assistance you're looking for and, therefore, the role you're hoping she or he will play. The second step is identifying and researching someone who could possibly fill the role. As shown in Figure 12.1, professors and business mentors potentially play one of four candidate roles: *industry expert, business expert, coach,* and *sponsor.* The successful Campus CEO will benefit from having all these roles filled at some point in the life cycle of his or her company. As you review them, bear in mind that each of these represents a role and, therefore, it is possible that one person could fill all four roles, or four different people could each fill a different role. Also shown in Figure 12.1 are some tips on finding professors and professionals who best meet your needs.

After identifying which of these roles is most appropriate given your needs and identifying someone who could potentially fill the roles, your third step will be to conduct some basic research to make sure it's potentially a good fit. Fourth, you'll have to arrange an initial meeting or discussion. Figure 12.2 provides some tips on both counts.

Fifth, you'll want to make sure you are prepared for the meeting and have a specific idea about the assistance you're seeking. If you're looking for some initial, general advice, then have your questions prepared. If you're hoping he or she could review your business plan, make sure you have a copy of it already on hand. The key is to be prepared but not presumptuous. It is possible the professor may not have the time, expertise, or wherewithal to help, but it never hurts

FIGURE 12.1 Four Roles of a Business Mentor

Role	Benefits	Finding Professors	Finding Professionals
Industry expert	*Industry experts* are entrepreneurs or business professionals with *specific* experience in your company's industry or closely related industries. They can provide you with insider information about competitors, effective strategies, and pricing, and can be helpful in identifying your market or understanding your customer.	Look in the academic department that is directly or closely related to your industry. For example, a professor of biology may be able to advise you on a life sciences venture.	Find someone who has been in the industry for years to make a recommendation. Also consider reaching out to industry and trade associations.
Business expert	*Business experts* are entrepreneurs who know the *general* process of starting and growing a business. They are distinguished from an industry expert in that they may not know your industry or market very well. However, they will be able to assist you with general business assistance such as reviewing your business plan, revamping your marketing efforts, etc.	Look in the business school or inquire in other departments about faculty members with past business or entrepreneurial experience.	Explore alumni mentoring programs or inquire through small business assistance organizations such as an SBA office, SCORE office, or SBDC.
Coach	A *coach* is someone who can provide motivation and encouragement throughout the ups and downs of entrepreneurship. Here, it's important that he or she is someone you trust and are comfortable with. Coaches don't have to have to be business experts or industry experts. They just need to be a person who can coach you through difficult situations and be a sounding board for your ideas and issues.	Consider the professors you have had for class, or come highly recommended by peers, that you believe could make a good coach.	Reach out to local professional organizations as well as past supervisors during part-time job assignments or internships.
Sponsor	A *sponsor* is an important source of contacts and connections. Sponsors are interested in helping your business to succeed. Sponsors help expand your network, broker introductions to decision makers and potential clients, as well as open doors to new opportunities that can help grow your business.	Nurture relationships with professors who help you as industry experts, business experts, and coaches, so that their role may evolve into that of a sponsor. Network at events on campus.	Nurture relationships with mentors who help you as industry experts, business experts, and coaches, so that their role may evolve into that of a sponsor. Network at events off campus.

FIGURE 12.2 Tips on Researching Mentors and Arranging a Meeting

	Researching a Potential Mentor	**Arranging an Initial Meeting**
Professors	■ Sit in their class ■ Read their research or books they've written ■ Talk to students who've taken their class ■ Review course evaluations	■ Call or send a short e-mail or letter requesting a meeting ■ Approach them after class, or visit during their office hours, then schedule a separate appointment to meet
Professionals	■ Research their company and its products/services ■ Research their professional background online (if possible)	■ Call or send a short e-mail or letter requesting an informational interview

to ask. Jeffrey Robinson, Professor of Entrepreneurship at New York University and cofounder of BCT Partners, offers this advice: "Taking a professor's class is one of the best ways to get the discussion started. If you don't have the professor for a class, send him or her a polite e-mail or possibly show up during office hours, introduce yourself, and then ask to schedule a time to meet later so you are mindful of his or her time." Robinson cautions students not to send any written documents until there is a mutual agreement that they will be reviewed. Because of the volume of papers, business plans, and PVAs that professors sometimes receive, he or she may only be able to review a few chapters of your executive summary. He adds, "Leverage our referrals. Professors know a lot but we don't know everything. However, we are certain to have former students, colleagues, and other alums that could be helpful to you."

Sixth, and finally, if you are fortunate enough to establish the beginnings of a business mentor relationship, you should explore ways you can maintain and strengthen the relationship. Here are a few suggestions on how to accomplish this:

■ Learn more about his or her past experience
■ Discuss any projects or research he or she is working on
■ Discuss current events in his or her field or industry
■ Ask to meet others who can advise you on specific topics
■ Discuss the attributes of successful entrepreneurs
■ Discuss books or articles on topics of interest
■ Solicit recommendations on courses, seminars, articles, and books

Business mentors can make a major impact on your venture. Not only can their advice take your venture to the next level, but business mentors can also play active roles in the future of your venture. For example, some mentors become members of advisory boards, members of boards of directors, and even investors. While there is debate as to whether professors should serve in this capacity, it is well within reason for a professional or practicing entrepreneur to do so. No matter how you cut it, *identifying a mentor can be a key milestone for any Campus CEO.*

Mentoring Works

Ever since I started my PhD program at MIT, I've considered my doctoral advisor, Professor Mitchel Resnick, a friend and mentor. For me, earning a PhD was a means to an end. It's not like I needed it to have my own business or to turn BCT into a multi-million-dollar enterprise. In fact, I honestly believe that I could've been successful without the doctorate. But there's no question that the degree itself has afforded me heightened credibility, visibility, and, just as important, the opportunity to establish a meaningful

> ### ■ Online Mentoring
>
> An alternative to in-person mentoring that is growing in popularity is online mentoring and one of the leading Web sites is MicroMentor (*www.micromentor.org*). MicroMentor provides online matching software to connect protégés and mentors from within similar business sectors or industries.

mentoring relationship. After all, it was during my tour as a PhD candidate that I was able to establish some of my strongest business ties and Mitchel had a lot to do with it.

On a few occasions, Mitchel asked and encouraged me to serve as his proxy when he couldn't attend certain conferences and events. As a result of standing in for him, I was able to mingle with corporate executives, foundation and nonprofit leaders, government officials, and other high-profile individuals. A number of these individuals would eventually become partners or clients of BCT. In that sense alone, Mitchel's role as a sponsor and coach was absolutely priceless.

Needless to stay, you really never stop growing—at least not when you're a business owner—so there is always a role for a mentor. Even now, I still try to soak up all the wisdom I can from my mentors and others who know more about different subjects than I do.

■ **Profiting from Peers—The Extreme Entrepreneurship Tour**

Your professors and mentors aren't the only ones who can teach you skills, ideas, and business strategies that matter. You can also learn a lot from your peers, especially from others who are business owners and from students who possess the entrepreneurial mindset.

One very impressive student I've met in my many travels to schools across the United States and abroad is a young man named Michael Simmons. Simmons is a 2005 graduate of New York University who was 16 years old when he started his first business—building Web sites—with a friend. Although this company, called Princeton Web Solutions, was in operation for three years, it ultimately went out of business. In an interview for *Campus CEO,* Simmons said he was glad that he experienced "failure" with Princeton Web Solutions, because it prepared him for future entrepreneurial endeavors. "I met lots of people through the business. I gained tons of knowledge, and I realized what I was passionate about," Simmons says. His latest business, started in 2003, is called Extreme Entrepreneurship Education Corporation. The goal of the venture is "to help spread the entrepreneurial mindset on campus" by helping students identify opportunities and tangible goals they can accomplish. In the fall of 2006, the company launched a three-year campaign called the Extreme Entrepreneurship Tour (*www.extremetour.org*), to encourage students nationwide to consider becoming business owners. In all, Simmons and some of the country's best and brightest young entrepreneurs—from best-selling authors and millionaires to award-winning social entrepreneurs—will visit 150 schools nationwide, reaching more than 100,000 entrepreneurial college students. So keep your eye out for the Extreme Entrepreneurship Tour—soon it may be coming to your campus.

■ NETWORKING

Networking is a cornerstone of entrepreneurship. It is about establishing, maintaining, and nurturing meaningful relationships. It is also the way you increase and leverage your *social capital* (a concept that was introduced in Chapter 2). The majority of jobs are found through networking (according to one study, as high as 74 percent) and, I believe, the majority of business opportunities are found through networking as well. Networking is also about give-and-take, because there is always the possibility that you could be of benefit to someone or someone could be of benefit to you. What I've quickly learned as an entrepreneur is that almost any interaction you have with other people is an opportunity to network. This is both the challenge and the opportunity of networking—it can always be happening. In fact, sometimes I have to shut down my natural instinct to network, network, network, because, as an entrepreneur, I am so accustomed to doing it. That's probably why when I'm on vacation it's so hard to leave my business cards at home!

Another interesting fact about networking is that your most valuable contacts are often the people who know you the least. Why? Because the people you're close to tend to know the same people you do, while the people you're not close to tend to know people you don't know. Therefore, it's the people you don't know that have a higher likelihood of knowing people and opportunities you're not aware of. So *you should constantly seek opportunities to network both on campus and beyond campus to continually expand your network.*

Building Your Network

As a Campus CEO there are a host of opportunities for face-to-face networking such as seminars, symposia, conferences, social events, student organization activities, and even career fairs being held right on your campus or at neighboring schools. Here are some of my tips for turning any in-person networking function into an opportunity (Chapter 13 presents tips for maximizing the use of social and professional networking sites):

- *Print dual-purpose business cards.* Print business cards for informational purposes and marketing purposes. Nowadays, business cards are easy to obtain. Include all relevant contact information, but also include something descriptive about your products and services, even if that means placing this on the back of the card. People can easily forget what you do and placing this information on the card ensures that they will remember. Separate personal e-mail and business e-mail and, if possible, separate personal voice mail from business voice mail.
- *Practice entering, maintaining, and exiting a networking conversation.* Work with a friend to practice your handshake (a firm one), entrance (do not interrupt others), introduction (be sure to introduce yourself to everyone), listening skills (follow the "flow" of the conversation; don't change the topic abruptly), body language (look comfortable but confident), eye contact (direct), and graceful exit ("It was a pleasure meeting you. Do you mind if I have your business card so we can stay in touch?").
- *Prepare an "elevator speech" on your proposed venture or company.* I never understood why they call it an "elevator speech," because people rarely

talk on elevators! It is because in an elevator you have a captive audience for a brief, focused period of time so you must be clear, to the point, and, hopefully, memorable. One of the most popular questions at any networking event is "So what do you do?" You should always be prepared with an elevator speech, that is, a quick and simple description of your background, your company, and what makes it unique. My elevator speech for MBS was as follows: "I am a senior at Rutgers University majoring in electrical engineering. Along with two of my roommates I also recently launched a new company, Mind, Body & Soul Enterprises. We have two divisions, one that retails compact discs on campus and another that offers workshops, lectures, and seminars for students and other young professionals." I also tried to end my elevator speech with something that opened the door for advice such as, "Would you happen to know of any organizations that might benefit from our services?"

- *Work the room; don't let the room work you.* Try to meet as many people as possible without curtailing conversations too abruptly. Time tends to go by quickly, and because networking is so powerful you want to make as many connections as you can. Do not just talk to friends or isolate yourself. If you practice, it should be easier, and the more you do it, the more comfortable you will get. Learn more about others and try to find areas of common interest. Look for opportunities to sell yourself and your business, but don't force it.

- *Don't just collect business cards, manage and use them strategically.* Write down where, when, and under what circumstances you met someone on the back of his or her card. In certain circumstances, consider writing this information on the back of your cards before you give them to someone who may be already inundated with cards. This will increase the likelihood that he or she will remember you. Now that I've become a bit of a celebrity, I've noticed people using this tactic at networking functions I've attended. Also develop a way of organizing your business cards; otherwise they can become unmanageable. Develop a database of business cards using technology tools such as a spreadsheet and/or card scanner to categorize cards by their potential uses such as "potential customer" or "investor" or "press/public relations." Don't wait until you have piles and piles of cards to do this.

- *Do unto others as you would have others do unto you.* Always follow up if you say you're going to follow up (this gets back to keeping your word, which is paramount in business). Send thank-you e-mails or thank-you notes when others have been helpful to you. Reach out to others just to check in or update them on your progress. Don't just take from your network; also be willing to give. Effective networking is about give-and-take.

I often tell people, "You are your *word*, your *work*, and then your *network*." You can build a lot of credibility, and build up trust with your team members and clients, if you can say what you mean and mean what you say. Your work is really the *quality* of the work that you produce. It's reflected in your company's product or service, the capabilities you demonstrate, accomplishments you've achieved, sometimes in your grades or your GPA, or in various awards you've received. Good news travels fast, and great news travels even faster, so don't be afraid to share your accomplishments with others. Your network goes beyond people you know in school or in business. It also is built largely on the strength

> ### ■ Network with Young Entrepreneurs
>
> Mind Petals (*www.mindpetals.com*) is an online community for young entrepreneurs geared toward networking, sharing ideas, and producing content such as blogs, books, newsletters, and conferences that promote entrepreneurship. Your Success Network (*www.ysn.com*) offers self-assessment, discussion forums, mentoring, tools, and resources for young professionals, leaders, and entrepreneurs.

of the people that believe in you and are willing to support you. A key indicator of whether you're running your business correctly is whether others are willing to lend you a hand. If you've never been able to convince someone to assist with your venture, you're probably doing something wrong. When you deliver on your word and you deliver on your work, it all helps to expand your network.

Networking Works

While operating MBS Educational Services & Training, a number of administrators on the Rutgers campus helped us to network. One was Dean Donald Brown. He was the advisor for our National Society of Black Engineers chapter. He was also a member of the Equal Opportunity Fund Professional Association (EOFPA), a New Jersey–based organization of EOF programs that work with students throughout the state. He connected us with the head of that organization and it eventually became a client. We facilitated workshops at EOFPA's annual Student Day conference.

Rutgers administrators also pointed us in the direction of high schools and nonprofits that could use our education and training services. Jack and Jill of America, a national organization, became a client through these connections. In various ways, experts of all kinds at Rutgers were connected to higher education institutions, student development organizations, or corporations, and they got us introductions and connections that we would have never established otherwise.

We also worked with the career services office to help direct us to corporations or internship programs that might need our services. By working through their campus chapters or affiliates, we also reached out to groups that had national counterparts such as the Society of Women Engineers (SWE), the Society of Hispanic Professional Engineers (SHPE), and various fraternities and sororities.

These are just a few examples of how networking accelerated my business pursuits. Similarly, you can use these strategies and the previously mentioned tips on networking and mentoring to spur your business toward expansion and growth, which is the subject of the remaining chapters.

CAMPUS CEO CHECKLIST

After reading Chapter 12, take these steps to network and reach out to your professors and potential mentors:

☐ Ask at least two professors in different areas (such as marketing and finance) and an experienced entrepreneur to act as business mentors for you during this school year.

☐ Visit MicroMentor (*www.micromentor.org*) to establish an online business mentoring relationship with an expert in your sector or industry.

☐ Hold a brainstorming session with your business-minded friends, student peers, and employees/partners to strategize about solutions to a business problem or challenge you face.

☐ Identify and plan to attend at least one networking event within the next month.

☐ Make sure your business cards include both company contact information and information about your company's products and services.

☐ Practice entering, maintaining, and exiting a networking conversation with a friend.

☐ Create an elevator pitch —of no more than 20 seconds—that succinctly describes your business and what you do in an interesting way.

☐ Develop a database of your business cards using a spreadsheet and/or card scanner; categorize each card according to its potential use.

PROFILE OF A CAMPUS CEO

■ **Name:** Michael Simmons

■ **Business:** Extreme Entrepreneurship Education Corporation

■ **Web site:** *www.extremetour.org* and *www.successmanifesto.com*

■ **Founded:** 2003

■ **His Story:** Michael Simmons cofounded the Extreme Entrepreneurship Education Corporation with his wife, Sheena Lindahl, while both were students at NYU. When it comes to Campus CEOs, he ranks among the top young entrepreneurs in the country and has won many major awards, including honors from the National Foundation for Teaching Entrepreneurship, Fleet Bank, and the National Coalition for Empowering Youth Entrepreneurs. Simmons says that now, even at age 24, he has benefited tremendously from having an entrepreneurial mindset. While he was a student at NYU, Simmons participated in the incubator program, took advantage of the expertise of faculty mentors, and obtained pro bono strategy and legal assistance and a team of MBAs to help him. He also won the school's undergraduate business plan competition in 2004 and was president of NYU's Entrepreneurial Exchange Group. As a result of being so tied in to the campus community, Simmons was able to leverage his relationships and get his company's products and services—including his books and speaking services—to his alma mater. "NYU was one of my first customers in terms of bulk purchase sales and speaking," Simmons says. Today, his Web site receives 100,000 page views per month, and he has written several books. "I think what stops a lot of people from pursuing their goals is fear," Simmons says. "But I think you can help people let go of their fear or take control of it. For example, I'm not naturally outgoing. But through the business, I've learned to work a room or do sales calls or speak to a large audience. So through entrepreneurship, I've let go of my fears," he adds. And you may let go of any fears you have of entrepreneurship, if students such as Simmons have their way.

■ **Advice for Student Entrepreneurs:** "There's almost no better way to get business experience than starting a business, whether it fails or succeeds. The biggest mistakes students and potential entrepreneurs make is that: (1) they don't get started; and (2) they don't keep going when it's not working out the way they expected."

—Michael Simmons

■ PART 4

Growing Your Business

Why You Must Tell Everybody—
Marketing and Public Relations

13

If you want to really grow your business, word-of-mouth advertising is critical. When a loyal customer is enamored with your product or service, that person is more likely to refer business your way when a friend or colleague is looking for something you offer. For this reason, make sure you always treat your customers in a manner that makes them want to give you repeat business and tell others about you. This means offering a fair price, a fantastic product or service, and exceptional customer service. Do these things and you'll find that your reputation grows slowly but surely as positive word of mouth about your company begins to spread.

But are there other ways to let people know that your company exists and what it has to offer? You bet there are. It's through marketing and public relations, and the best place for you to start is by tapping into the rich array of resources that are right at your very own high school, college, or university.

Practically every college in the nation has a campus newspaper (as do most high schools), and many colleges and universities also have their own radio and TV stations. Each of these media can be of tremendous value to promoting the operations of a Campus CEO. And guess what? In some cities, the campus radio station is also the town or city's major radio station. For example, WHUR, out of Washington, D.C., is heard out of Howard University's campus. It also serves as one of the top radio stations for the tristate area in D.C., Virginia, and Maryland. This gives you great exposure and helps build "buzz" about your business beyond the campus environment. And because there are more than 1,500 daily newspapers and more than 8,000 weeklies published in the United States, in addition to countless radio, TV, and Internet outlets, you've got a lot of other potential targets.

In addition to publicity generated by media channels, there are a number of traditional approaches to marketing your business such as newsletters, flyers, and discount or incentive programs, and various other creative marketing strategies, including Internet marketing, speaking, and publishing. These strategies can enable you to establish your brand in the marketplace, build credibility, and cultivate stronger relationships with your customers. In this chapter, I'll share these and other no-cost or low-cost ways to market you or your company and generate positive publicity about your business activities.

■ TOOLS OF THE TRADE FOR MARKETING AND PUBLIC RELATIONS

First and foremost, you must make sure you possess all the tools you will need for your marketing and public relations efforts. These may include some combination of the following items:

- Logo
- Business cards
- Stationery (i.e., letterhead, envelopes, etc.)
- Brochures
- Web site
- Marketing kit/press kit

When seeking opportunities to promote your company, you'll want your materials to have a clean, professional look. This means ensuring that all your correspondence, marketing collateral, and online materials reflect the image you want your company to project. A *logo* may be worth the investment for there are very reasonably priced options that are available to you. A well-designed logo, which is integrated into the other items, can make a tremendous difference in how your company is perceived. Having *business cards* and *stationery* printed is very easy to do nowadays. Given

> ### ■ Got a Logo?
>
> Check out the Logo Loft (*www.thelogoloft.com*) to obtain a good logo at a low cost, or Logoworks (*www.logoworks.com*).

the completely free options, there is no excuse for not having these available and ready, not to mention that business cards are a must for networking opportunities. The same is true for a *Web site.* There are free, easy-to-use, Web-site builder tools at your disposal that make it easy to produce a good-looking, fully functioning Web site (see Chapter 5 for a list of these options and tools to optimize and register your Web site with search engines). And if a full-blown Web site is too heavy a lift, then a dedicated profile page for your company on MySpace.com, Facebook.com, or another net-

> ### ■ Free Printing and Stationery
>
> You can obtain free business cards, postcards, notepads, magnets, announcements, and low-cost brochures, flyers, and more for your business from VistaPrint (*www.vistaprint.com*). A related site is Best Printing Best Price (*www.bestprintingbestprice.com*), which highlights some of the best deals at VistaPrint.

working site may suffice. Regardless, you should have some online destination where interested parties can learn more about your company, the products and services being offered, and how to contact you for more information. A *brochure* may also be warranted and, again, there are low-cost ways you can have one produced (see "Free Printing and Stationery"). This may depend on the extent to which you expect to rely on printed materials as a significant method of outreach. Nowadays, it is possible, particularly in certain lines of business, to use Internet marketing and other forms of electronic marketing as your primary channel. Last, but not least, you should consider developing a *marketing kit* or *press kit.* This would include some or all of the following items, placed in a portfolio:

- Business card
- Company overview
- Description of products and services
- Client list
- Brochure
- Noteworthy articles and press releases
- Biographies of key founders and members of the management team

You may present this kit to prospective clients, partners, and media and public relations representatives, or they may request it from you. Be sure you have a number of kits ready to be sent, and update the kit regularly to make sure it reflects the most up-to-date information about your company.

■ STRATEGIC MARKETING AND PUBLIC RELATIONS

There are a number of ways to be strategic in your marketing and public relations efforts. Here are seven tried-and-true strategies for marketing and promoting your business to customers through local, regional, and national channels, at various events, and in the media.

1. Pitch a Story—Not Your Service or Product

Probably the number one mistake that inexperienced business owners and others make when trying to get publicity is that they solicit the media based almost exclusively on the "merits" of their own products or services. Frankly, most journalists could care less about your new product launch or your one-of-a-kind service that no other business owner has yet discovered. Ask any reporter in the country, and he or she can tell you that he or she receives "pitches" all the time from rookie sources, many of them small business owners, who espouse the virtues of their products or services and swear up and down that it's "the only one of its kind." I certainly don't want to tell you that your business idea is not innovative, but most journalists won't believe it if you say so. They don't care about you and your business per se, but what they do care about greatly is meeting the needs of their readers, viewers, or listeners. So to the extent that you can succinctly explain how your product or service ties into a bigger story—one that would have interest to their audience—then you've got a chance at getting some publicity.

> ### ■ Free Online Marketplace
>
> CafePress (*www.cafepress.com*) is an online marketplace where you can create, buy, and sell your own products. On your behalf, the site manages all aspects of doing business online for free, including storefront development, site hosting, order management, fulfillment, secure payment processing, and customer service.

So what's a practical way to do this? The simple rule of thumb is to pitch a story, not a product or service. Let's say you develop a special suntanning lotion that can be used in all climates or that has special applications for use in tanning salons. You might pitch a local reporter a story on how "X" number of people use suntanning products each year, many of them in areas outside of the West Coast or the sunny locations such as in Florida. In the context of you pitching the story, you artfully demonstrate your expertise by giving the reporter industry facts and statistics, background information about the world of tanning, and so forth. Needless to say, you're going to state as well that your company markets the new "Suntanning Solution," which is designed to give users a healthy tan without exposing them to harmful sun rays. But in this way, you're really pitching a story into which you will be woven, as opposed to trying to give a reporter a hard sell about your product. Also be sure to target the most logical news organizations that would be likely to publicize information about your company. For instance, if you offer college prep services for high school students, target a media outlet whose demographic includes high school students preparing for college.

Lastly, to increase your chances of any coverage, cultivate relationships with on- and off-campus journalists. That includes the sophomore who writes for your campus paper as well as the local radio host in your region and the national TV producer you might meet. Call them up from time to time with interesting news and information. Send them clips of articles that might be of value to them. Take them to lunch and find out what stories they're working on. See if you can refer sources to them to help them complete their assignments. Most journalists will appreciate such efforts.

2. Become a Columnist or Regular Guest Expert

One surefire way to get your name in print, or to build face recognition on TV, is to become a regular media expert or "media darling." You can become a preferred expert in the eyes of the local—and even national—media players. So whenever a story breaks, and reporters, editors, show hosts, or producers need experts, they'll call you first. Even if there is no "hard news" to report, you can still generate feature story coverage if you go about securing publicity in the right way. For example, you can offer to write a column for your campus paper, your town's paper, or other industry publications. In this way, you get the opportunity to showcase your knowledge and expertise on a regular basis. If you become a biweekly columnist for your city's newspaper, you can have a tagline such as "Cindy Smith is the owner of XYZ business. Contact her at csmith@xyz.com" or something like that.

Many columnists develop a loyal following of readers. So if you have an interesting topic to write about routinely—and you also have good writing skills and the time to devote to a column—you can use this strategy to great effect. But even if you don't want or need to see your name in print every week or every month, you can still get publicity by being an occasional expert on the radio or TV. For instance, some topics are perennial favorites in the media; you can count on repeat coverage of anything related to self-help, health, finances, family, and career, to name a few subjects. Even if you write exclusively for your school newspaper, it'll be a boon to your business to be well known on campus.

3. Become a Speaker or an Author

Positioning yourself as a speaker or author of a book, manual, or even a short guide, can be a very effective strategy to market your company. To help you choose a topic for a publication or speaking opportunities, use your experience (or your company's experience) to identify areas where you bring unique or valuable insight. For example, if you run a graphic design company, you may be able to speak or write about creating visually engaging, high-impact marketing materials using examples from your firm's portfolio.

The benefit of speaking and writing is that it helps you establish credibility in the marketplace and exposes you and your firm to an audience of potential customers, partners, and vendors. Being a published author can lead to media coverage as well as speaking engagements. And given recent advances in technology, self-publishing has become a more viable option. Moreover, there are many events, workshops, seminars, symposia, conferences, conventions, and expositions taking place at your school and surrounding communities that are constantly looking for speakers, panelists, and moderators. Look locally first, but don't sell yourself short. Reach out directly to organizers of major events and pitch them on the valuable perspective you can bring to their next gathering.

> ### ■ For Speakers and Authors Only
>
> If you're looking to develop strong public speaking skills in a supportive environment, you should contact your local club of Toastmasters International (*www.toastmasters.org*). Similarly, if you're considering self-publishing you should obtain a copy of *The Self-Publishing Manual: How to Write, Print, and Sell Your Own Book* by Dan Poynter.

4. Send Out Press Releases Regularly

When you have major news to announce, a good idea is to send out a press release about it. What qualifies as "major" news? Certainly the launch of a new business, the development of a critical product, a partnership with a major company—all these scenarios and more would be reasons to tell the world about important happenings at your company. Three channels for distributing press releases are:

- PR Web® (*www.prweb.com*). Fortunately, there is a way to broadcast your message free of charge to all who are willing to listen—by using a service such as PR Web. (According to officials at PR Web, this is the only newswire service on the Internet that provides free global news distribution. When you submit a press release for distribution through PR Web, it sends your press release right to the in-boxes and databases of more than 100,000 media contacts, industry analysts, and freelance journalists. PR Web also guarantees that your press release will be included in the databases of the major search engines.)

- BusinessWire (*www.businesswire.com*). Bought in 2006 by billionaire Warren Buffett's Berkshire Hathaway holding company, BusinessWire allows you to target your news to select audiences based on your geographic and industry market needs. Although the company is headquartered in San Francisco, BusinessWire's delivery network includes roughly 60 major news agencies, financial and information providers, and Web-based news services around the globe. It can deliver your news release and photos online, via e-mail, or by fax.

- PR Newswire (*www.prnewswire.com*). The chief competitor for Business-Wire, PR Newswire is also a trusted source in the commercial press release distribution business. Journalists especially like PR Newswire's ProfNet site (*www.profnet.com*), which allows reporters to put out queries when they're working on stories and get feedback from a variety of professionals, including experts in business, academia, or politics. You might want to consider signing up for ProfNet as an expert. That way, when a reporter is seeking a source in your industry, you'll instantly be notified. Like BusinessWire, PRNewswire allows you to distribute electronic content, photos, and video.

One creative way to get a lot of press coverage is to get written up in a newswire such as the Associated Press (AP), United Press International (UPI), Reuters, or Dow Jones Newswires. These outlets may pick up your press release, or reporters within these organizations may just write about you. The benefit of such coverage is that content from these wire services could be picked up by their member papers. The result: a story about you could be carried in hundreds of newspapers. Imagine the response you'd get from that kind of publicity! So any time you have something newsworthy, don't forget to send out a press release.

5. Seize Opportunities to Create Media Attention

There are a variety of ways you can seize opportunities to generate positive media attention for your company, such as the following:

- *Sponsor something worthy and newsworthy.* If you sponsor the local Little League team or donate money, services, products, or even just your time to a worthy cause, sometimes your philanthropic gesture will attract media attention. It's not only the right thing to do, but your corporate largesse could wind up making the local news—and attracting more customers in the process.
- *Write op-ed pieces or quickly respond to "spot" news.* Express your views about various recent news events in letters to the editor of your paper or opinion-editorial (op-ed) pieces.
- *Show the media a trend.* One quick way to get a reporter's attention is to call him or her up and say, "Here's a trend that no one else has written about yet," and then briefly explain an ongoing phenomena or trend you've spotted that is interesting and newsworthy. In the minds of most reporters, if an event has happened three or more times in the recent past, it points to a trend or at the very least an emerging trend. Being in the forefront of a trend can really work to your advantage because your competition is limited. Naturally, your business is one of those high-lighted in the story as "proof" that such a trend exists or is emerging.
- *Create a photo opportunity.* Think creatively about whether there is a photo op you could offer to a local reporter that might intrigue him or her. If you can't think of a single thing, there are a few standards that any business could use. You could have a "ribbon cutting" or a "grand open-ing." In small markets, sometimes just the launch or opening of a new enterprise is enough to bring out a local reporter and/or photographer. You could stage a contest and, for example, offer a "grand prize"—a desirable product or service from your company—to local residents or to people who agree to do something that is visual and that has a natural tie-in to your business.

6. Harness the Power of Internet Marketing

The Internet continues to evolve as a very powerful marketing tool. As men-tioned earlier, a *Web site* or a *profile page* at a networking site is an absolute must.

Make sure it is up-to-date concerning your company's products and services and post new information regularly. Include your Web address in all of your marketing materials and mention it in your interviews or speaking engagements for those seeking more information about your company. Also, contact the webmaster at Web sites that are likely frequented by potential customers of your company and explore the possibility of *bartering links,* that is, placing a link to your site on their site and vice versa.

Networking via *social and professional networking sites* is also an excellent way to spread word-of-mouth advertising, cultivate relationships, and identify new customers. The key to leveraging these sites (see Chapter 5 for a complete list) is to treat your online network like you would your offline or in-person network. The same rules apply to building relationships and helping others as you look for others to help you. From a marketing perspective, you can use these sites to generate buzz about your product or service, but you must be very deliberate in your networking activities:

- Convey what is interesting and unique about your company
- Send personal, not generic, invitations for others to join your network
- Make specific requests from others in your network, such as referrals
- Be explicit about asking others to pass the word on about your company

Lastly, in terms of general marketing, consider publishing an *electronic newsletter* to your own e-mail distribution list or posting regularly to a *blog* (see Chapter 5 for tools). Build your distribution list by scanning business cards and giving visitors to your Web site the ability to opt in. These approaches can prove valuable to your customers, such as providing information about industry trends, and can keep your company fresh in their minds as they make purchasing decisions.

7. Market and Sell Deeper into Existing Customers

While it's important to pursue activities that market your company to the widest possible audience, there's also tremendous value in marketing and selling deeper into existing customers.

As Figure 13.1 shows, your goal is to cultivate relationships with clients beyond that of a *prospect, suspect,* or *customer,* to the point where they regard themselves as a *partner, advocate,* or *former customer.* One way to do this is *market segmentation,* or establishing specific marketing strategies for specific groups.

FIGURE 13.1 Customer Relationship Marketing Stages

Stage	Description
Suspect	Has been introduced to your company
Prospect	Understands how your company could benefit him or her
Customer	Has purchased a product or service from your company
Partner	Regards himself or herself as an extension of your company
Advocate	Recommends your company to others
Former customer	Brings repeat business to your company

For example, to market and sell deeper into customers, partners, advocates, and former customers, you may consider offering discounts or gift certificates for repeat business; incentives for referrals; targeted mailings or e-newsletters; special outreach via e-mail, telephone, or in person; and gifts as tokens of appreciation. Lastly, look for ways you can solicit feedback from clients (i.e., surveys or questionnaires), with incentives, so you can constantly improve your products, services, and customer service. Your customers are your best source of information to make your business more successful.

■ START SMALL, THINK BIG

In conclusion, don't buy into the notion that because you're young, or because you only have a "small business," or you're only doing something local, etc., that you should only pursue marketing and public relations opportunities via campus, small, or regional channels and media outlets. If you, your company, or your story is a good fit, go ahead and pursue opportunities with the big guys, too. Now, I'm sure you are already aware that everybody is angling to get the attention of these major media outlets or be a part of the agenda at a major event, but don't be afraid to take your best shot at them, too. From national newspapers, magazines, radio and television stations, to large conferences, conventions, symposia, and expositions, it can't hurt to toss your hat into the ring—especially if they're looking for someone just like you. Wouldn't you love the opportunity to be on *Oprah* or *Today?* Or see your name on the front page of the *New York Times* or the *Washington Post?* Or speak at the Jacob Javits Convention Center in New York City? That kind of exposure is often golden—and it's not outside your reach. The entrepreneur's mindset suggests that you keep these options open at all times. Then it's you and your team's job to make sure you're prepared to handle the potential onslaught of new clients!

CAMPUS CEO CHECKLIST

After reading Chapter 13, take these steps to develop your marketing and public relations initiatives:

☐ Design your company's marketing kit/press kit.

☐ Develop your company's Web site or profile page.

☐ Make a list of the local print, online, and broadcast media you could target for publicity.

☐ Call two local reporters and two national journalists and introduce yourself as an expert in your field. Give them your contact information so they can call or e-mail you whenever they need a source.

☐ Join a public speaking organization or read a book on self-publishing, if appropriate.

☐ Distribute a press release about something significant your company has done, or about the launch of your venture, and submit it to various media or a free press release service.

☐ Read your campus newspaper regularly and offer to write a column related to your business, an op-ed piece, or an article highlighting a trend in your industry for your campus newspaper. Weave the name of your business into your submission.

☐ Strategize to create a newsworthy sponsorship, event, or photo opportunity that could get you free publicity.

☐ Implement an Internet marketing campaign for your company using blogs, e-mail, e-newsletters, or social and professional networking sites.

☐ Develop a marketing program aimed at existing customers (discount, incentive for referrals, etc.) and a mechanism to solicit feedback (surveys, questionnaires, etc.).

PROFILE OF A CAMPUS CEO

■ **Name:** Blake Robertson

■ **Business:** Alertus Inc.

■ **Web site:** *www.alertus.org*

■ **Founded:** 2002

■ **His Story:** Blake Robertson and Jason Volk met at the University of Maryland, when the two were part of the school's Entrepreneur in Residence program at Hinman. Together, they created Alertus Inc. and developed a device to provide vital information in the event of emergencies such as terrorist attacks or severe weather to people in large buildings such as those on university campuses. The Alertus solution was developed at the University of Maryland beginning in 2002 after a deadly tornado killed students on campus and threatened thousands of other students, faculty, staff, and visitors. In the aftermath of the tornado, the Alertus research team thoroughly studied the emergency warning process and, with funding from the state of Maryland, developed a sophisticated emergency warning system. Alertus's emergency warning system lets public officials, along with police, fire, and rescue units, disseminate localized, custom text alerts to wall-mounted beacons. Just like a fire alarm, each beacon has strobe lights and a siren, but also contains a text LCD display. Alerts are quickly transmitted in just seconds to all beacons or to specific areas and buildings using a reliable radio frequency communication. In the event of an emergency, the Alertus solution offers audible and visual signaling coupled with text information so that people can respond quickly and appropriately to any threats. The ultimate goal is to save lives, minimize property loss, and decrease business interruptions. Alertus is now commercializing its technology and offering it to campuses and institutions across the nation.

■ **Advice for Student Entrepreneurs:** "Real-world experience is priceless."

—**Blake Robertson** to the *Christian Science Monitor* (November 2, 2004)

Take It to the Next Level—
Expanding Beyond Your
Own Campus

It's one thing to launch a business at the University of California, Los Angeles (UCLA), but it's another matter entirely to have business operations going at all ten schools within the University of California system. This leads to multiple streams of income and a way to really power your business full steam ahead. In this chapter, I'll share with you some ideas about how you can leverage a business built on your home campus to the fullest extent—by taking that business elsewhere, to neighboring schools, to new marketplaces, to other educational institutions within your campus system, or even cross-country.

The first way to expand beyond your campus is to replicate your business in other geographic areas, including other schools. For instance, smart entrepreneurs based on one Ivy League campus, such as Brown, can develop networks with their peers at another Ivy League school such as Cornell. Similarly, a business on one Historically Black College or University, such as North Carolina A&T State University, could be expanded to another HBCU, such as Morehouse, Spelman, or Howard. An enterprise launched within a given state's college system can be taken system-wide, and so forth. The second way to expand beyond your campus is to extend your products and services to the general population, not just to students. For example, a company delivering food to dormitories could possibly broaden its services to include residents in the same vicinity. Or a business that sells used furniture to students could also look to sell those products to consumers in the area. It is important to distinguish whether you are replicating your business in other areas or extending your products and services to the general marketplace, or both, because each objective calls for a different set of strategies.

■ REPLICATING ON OTHER CAMPUSES OR IN OTHER AREAS

Referring back to Chapter 2, replicating your business on other campuses, or in other geographic areas, is the same as moving from a *lifestyle company,* for example, with a single location, to a *growth company* with multiple locations, as shown in Figure 14.1. This means breaking out of the confines of your own campus to other schools or other regions. Regardless of whether your company focuses on students or the general marketplace, establishing a base of operation or a presence on other campuses may provide avenues to expand the customer base you've secured on your campus. The key is to determine whether market conditions exist on other campuses or in other areas that are similar to yours:

- Is there a similar or related product or service being offered there?
- Do students on those campuses, or consumers in those markets, have the same needs as they do on your campus and in your market?
- Can you make your product or service available quickly enough to capture the market?

To answer these questions, you should apply the same market research, competitive analysis, and business planning techniques that were discussed in Chapter 3 for the preliminary venture analysis. If a PVA, or even a revised business plan, suggests that your product or service has the same, if not greater, potential at other campuses than it did on your campus, then expanding your business may be something to explore. If you're willing to put in the work, conduct the proper due diligence, and solicit the necessary resources, you could be rewarded for your efforts in a huge way.

Just look at Spencer Lewin, for instance. He started Soapy Joe's in 2003 as a laundry service in the D.C. area, servicing students at both Georgetown and George Washington University. Back then, Lewin was a senior at GWU. Since that time, Lewin has branched out to the West Coast and now has operations at the University of Southern California in Los Angeles too. His strategy for obtaining customer business rested not on convincing students to let him pick up their dirty clothes. That was the easy part. (Do you know any students who actually *enjoy* doing laundry?) Instead, Lewin recognized early on that getting

FIGURE 14.1 Replicating in Other Areas/On Other Campuses

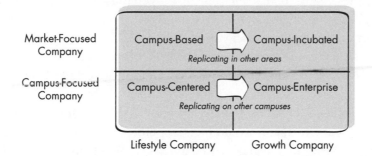

buy-in from university officials was the key to making his operation fly. So he struck savvy deals with universities. In exchange for them letting him operate on campus grounds, Lewin uses a revenue-sharing model, by which the universities get a cut of his sales. "Everyone wins," Lewin says of the arrangement, which has helped him snag more than 40,000 orders since 2003. Lewin is also offering other entrepreneurs the chance to own Soapy Joe franchises to serve campuses nationwide.

A number of other high-profile businesses originally started out on one campus or within a campus system. One of them is Cluck-U Chicken®, which was founded at Rutgers University in 1985 by Robert Ilvento, who was then a 20-year-old college sophomore. Ilvento dropped out of Rutgers to pursue his business interests and was later joined by J.P. Haddad, a graduate of the University of Maryland in College Park. According to the company, Haddad and his brother, Simon, both of whom had engineering degrees, jumped into the Cluck-U franchise with vigor because they were so inspired by their shot at being entrepreneurs.

Over the past 20-plus years, Ilvento and the Haddad brothers have built the Cluck-U Chicken brand into a formidable franchise. There are now more than 75 Cluck-U restaurants in the United States, including 25 in Maryland. Company officials say their goal "is to have a Cluck-U Chicken restaurant near every college campus and in every city in the United States, and later, the world."

Strategies for Replicating on Other Campuses or in Other Areas

If you have a *lifestyle company*, either campus-based or campus-centered, here are three ways you can replicate your business to other campuses or other areas and work toward becoming a *growth company:*

1. *Market your company directly to students at neighboring schools.* This includes high schools, colleges, or universities. Use flyers, brochures, blogs, profile pages, and other advertising materials to let students at other campuses know that you exist!

2. *Hire student workers or interns from other schools to represent your business on their campus.* You don't have to do all the legwork. Just because you want to have a presence on another campus doesn't mean you have to physically be there. Enlist the assistance of other students who attend a school at which you would like to operate. After all, they'll know the campus better than you do, and may even have a better feel as to where, when, and how to best market your offerings.

3. *Set up affiliate programs at sister campuses.* Encourage other people to sign onto your business as affiliates. Offer a sales commission to those who promote or sell your services or product. Or perhaps you can barter and exchange something of value with others who land you business. Whatever you do, if you set up an affiliate program, just be clear with all parties involved what is expected and what will be received in return.

Student Advantage, a leading integrated media and commerce company focused on the higher-education market, is a classic example of replicating on other campuses. Founder Ray Sozzi is profiled at the end of this chapter.

■ EXTENDING TO THE MARKETPLACE OR NEW CUSTOMERS

But what if you want to take your business beyond the student scene? Regardless of whether your company is a lifestyle company or a growth company, there is the possibility of extending your product or service beyond the high school or college population. Once again, referring back to Chapter 2, extending from students to the marketplace is the same as moving from a campus-focused company to a market-focused company, as shown in Figure 14.2. Here, the most important consideration is realistically assessing whether there is indeed a market for your company beyond students. After all, many things students like, want, or need may or may not be of interest to the general public.

- Is there a sizable nonstudent population?
- Is the demand sufficient to justify the costs needed to expand your operations?
- What changes to your product or service may be required to market to this group?

FIGURE 14.2 Extending to the Marketplace/New Customer Base

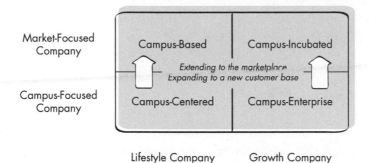

Once again, to answer these questions you should utilize a PVA, perhaps leading to a revised business plan. Should you find that it makes sense to market to a larger demographic, you may need to tweak your business model to ensure maximum appeal to those outside the college environment. Your mentors, faculty members, and others may be able to give you guidance about how to best adapt your campus-focused business to a general market-focused business.

Strategies for Extending to the Marketplace or New Customers

If your company is *campus-focused*, that is, a campus-centered or campus-enterprise business, and you would like to become more *market-focused* or expand to a new customer base, here are three strategies for doing so:

1. *Market directly to residents/consumers.* You can use e-newsletters, e-mail blasts to customers who opt in at your Web site and give you permission to market to them, direct-mail literature, or door-to-door salesmanship to let customers know about your product or service.
2. *Enlist faculty, administrators, and staff as referrals.* They aren't students and can perhaps lend credibility and help you tap into a wider network of potential clients.
3. *Advertise in media outlets that reach beyond campus.* You can find low-cost advertising opportunities in small newspapers and some free classified ad spots online. Do a Google search using the phrase "free classified ads" for some leads.

At MBS Educational Services & Training, we were able to transfer our success working with students into opportunities to work with new hires, young professionals, and seasoned professionals. At the company's peak, we were training full-time managers at General Motors. As we became more experienced, we greatly extended our reach into the marketplace—and enjoyed increased business as a result of our expansion.

■ MANAGING GROWTH

Business growth can be exciting but can also present challenges and growing pains. When preparing for or experiencing growth, first you should be sure to revisit your business model, the economics of your business (i.e., fixed costs, variable costs, etc.), and their underlying assumptions (discussed in Chapter 3). You'll want to make sure you understand the elements of your business model and operations that must scale or expand to accommodate increased activity. You'll also need to understand what aspects of your finances may necessarily need to change as you scale up.

- Will you need to hire more staff?
- Will you need more office space?
- Can your suppliers handle an increase in demand?
- Do certain fixed costs, such as your rent or Web hosting, become variable costs because you're now conducting more business?
- Does an increase in sales change your profitability?
- Do you need to adjust your working capital needs?

By reevaluating many of the same questions that were posed when developing the business plan, you can make sure that your company is prepared for anticipated growth. As I always tell our team at BCT: growing pains are indeed painful, but they're a good problem to have!

The Value of Strategic Alliances

One of the best strategies for any small or growing company to use is to find a larger company that is arguably as good or better than you are, and team up with it. But you have to present such potential alliances in terms of their value. In some cases, you'll need to first do your homework to find out exactly what the value proposition might be for a larger company to join forces with you in some way. Maybe you can work as a small, minority-owned or women-owned business that fulfills a subcontracting require-

ment need. In other instances, you may bring something very specialized—a unique customer list, knowledge about a niche demographic, agility to respond to opportunities, and so forth—that the larger enterprise doesn't currently have.

The single largest contract my company, BCT Partners, has been awarded to date stemmed from just such a partnership. The deal was for an approximately $4 million, four-year contract signed in 2003 with the U.S. Department of Housing and Urban Development, the federal housing agency. That contract was based on the strength of our performance with a previous $850,000 contract, in which we partnered with a much larger company, Lockheed Martin Corporation, on a total contract valued at $22 million.

Franchising As a Means of Expansion

Whether you're going beyond your own campus environment, or beyond just the student marketplace, you should investigate whether or not the smartest method of building your business might be franchising. Franchising your business (the franchisor) generally involves granting other individuals or legal entities (the franchisees) the ability to sell your goods or services, under your company name, for an initial fee and ongoing royalties paid to your company.

Some of the advantages of franchising are the ability to expand your customer base quickly and minimize reliance on your own financial capital to fuel growth. Some of the disadvantages of franchising are the need to put extra measures in place for training, quality control, and legal considerations. If you're considering franchising as a means to expand, visit Entrepreneur.com's Franchise Zone (*www.entrepreneur.com/franchises*) for more information, and be sure to consult an experienced franchise attorney.

Joe Keeley found franchising to be the magic formula for his company's success. After a stint as a nanny to a family with three kids, Keeley launched College Nannies & Tutors while he was a student at the University of St. Thomas. Now, for $52,000 to $115,000, others can start their own College Nannies franchises, and receive all the necessary training, support, and marketing materials necessary to make their businesses successful. College Pro Painters, founded by student Grieg Clark in Thunder Bay, Ontario, is another successful

> ### ■ Looking for Franchising Opportunities?
>
> The International Franchise Association (IFA) Web site (*www.franchise.org*) offers a database of over 1,000 franchise opportunities, in addition to news, publications, and information on where to obtain franchising assistance.

example of growth via franchising. The company, which solicits motivated students to establish their own franchises performing exterior home painting, is now the largest student painting company in North America.

Expanding to International Markets

And what if you *really* want to expand beyond your own campus—in fact, beyond your country's borders? Any business owner aiming to go global has to take into account a host of considerations, from currency differences to language barriers to cultural norms that are probably different from what you've experienced. So make sure you do your homework in all these areas. Get feedback and help from your on-campus resources, such as exchange students who are already on your campus and international business professors who teach at your school.

You can also get better educated about this arena by visiting the Centers for International Business Education and Research at *www.ciberweb.msu.edu.* CIBERs operate branches at 30 different universities in the United States, ranging from USC, UCLA, San Diego State, and the University of Washington on the West Coast to the University of Connecticut, the University of Pennsylvania, and the University of Maryland on the East Coast. CIBERs were created to increase and promote the nation's capacity for international understanding and economic enterprise. The CIBER program is administered by the U.S. Department of Education and aims to supply the information and manpower needs for students, business owners, and academics in need of international education, language training, and research.

Lastly, you should also connect with the U.S. embassy's office in the country where you are considering doing business. There is usually an officer responsible for commerce who can advise you on how to do business there. Links to embassies' Web sites can be found at *http://usembassy.state.gov.*

■ Thinking of Going Global?

The Office of Commercial and Business Affairs (CBA) in the Bureau of Economic and Business Affairs under the U.S. Department of State Web site offers information on doing business in international markets at *www.state.gov/e/eb/cba/.*

■ BUSINESS LIFE AFTER GRADUATION

Two students who founded GlobalComm Suppliers—Dennis O'Donnell who graduated in 2005 from Georgetown and Eric Griffin-Shelly who graduated the same year from Villanova—know firsthand about the power of shifting strategy to appeal to a larger customer base. In 2003, the two partners started out selling high-end cell phones on eBay. It didn't take them long to discover that the bulk of their clients weren't actually cell phone users, but other eBay sellers who wanted to sell the phones to their customers. The result of this market knowledge led the duo to shift their business model almost exclusively to wholesaling instead of selling cell phones one or two at a time on eBay. That turned out to be a great decision: 2006 revenues for the company are expected to top $4 million.

More important, perhaps, O'Donnell and Griffin-Shelly were proactive in preparing themselves to run the business after graduation. They'd operated the company for two years while studying at their respective campuses. But they started strategizing in 2004 about how the business would function once they were no longer students. One step they took, for example, was to procure office space in King of Prussia, Pennsylvania, where the business is now headquartered.

If you want to expand beyond your campus environment and keep your enterprise going after graduation, remember to plan accordingly as well. It can be a bit of a shock to go from the nurturing, supportive environment of the campus system—where free resources abound and loads of professors are on hand to help you at every turn—to the "real world" where you may feel a bit like you're truly "on your own." But if you've followed the strategies recommended throughout *Campus CEO*—particularly with regard to networking, getting feedback from thought leaders and experts, and so forth—even this transition will be manageable.

By thinking ahead about my postgraduate life, I was able to create the business I wanted and ensure that it would be financially strong enough to support me. For instance, during my last semester of my PhD program at MIT, I accelerated my business development activities, while simultaneously completing my dissertation. My goal was to close enough deals so that the revenue generated from those deals would be enough to be my parachute, that is, pay my salary. I also timed the receipt of my scholarship money to near perfection. My scholarship funds were allocated on a semester-by-semester basis. At the beginning of the fall semester, in September, I received my scholarship check and I timed the completion of my dissertation so that I had the majority of the work completed in September. Thus I could live off my scholarship for the remainder of the semester—until December—and chase after opportunities for BCT without having to worry about where my next meal would come from. The plan worked, and soon after my scholarship money ran out, I officially hit the payroll on January 2, 2002, at BCT Partners.

Begin with the End in Mind

All these questions about whether to become a lifestyle company or a growth company, or a campus-focused company or a market-focused company, or even a global company beg the following question: What is your ultimate goal? Earlier in the book, I talked about knowing your passion and the importance of beginning with the end in mind. Never is it more important than now to think about where you want to take your business after graduation—if anyplace—so you can begin preparing today. The sooner you know what your ultimate vision is, the better you can align your marketing and sales efforts, networking activities, partnerships, and the like. For those of you who want to pursue entrepreneurial activity without actually starting a business, this is the time to think about your ultimate objectives as well. You may want to improve social conditions, address a problem in your community, or play a supporting role in another entrepreneur's venture. Whatever your interests and objectives, if you want to operate with the entrepreneur's mindset, you should be thinking today about where you would like to see yourself tomorrow.

CAMPUS CEO CHECKLIST

After reading Chapter 14, take these steps to expand your business beyond your campus:

☐ Network with students on other campuses. Consider how some of these students may become partners or ambassadors for your business at their respective schools.

☐ Develop a revised PVA or business plan that examines the feasibility of offering your company's product or service in other geographic regions and/or the general marketplace.

☐ Identify three potential allies or larger companies with whom you might strategically align your business or some aspect of your operation.

☐ Visit Entrepreneur.com's Franchise Zone (*www.entrepreneur.com/ franchises*) or Franchise.org (*www.franchise.org*) to evaluate franchising your company.

☐ Contact the Centers for International Business Education and Research (*www.ciberweb.msu.edu*), the U.S. Embassy (*http://usembassy.state. gov*), or the Office of Commercial and Business Affairs (CBA) (*www. state.gov/e/eb/cba/*) to learn more about doing business internationally.

☐ Write down your professional goals for your postcollege life. Does your plan include maintaining your campus business? If so, jot down some ideas about how you will continue to run your venture.

PROFILE OF A CAMPUS CEO

■ **Name:** Ray Sozzi

■ **Business:** Student Advantage

■ **Web site:** *www.studentadvantage.com*

■ **Founded:** 1992

■ **His Story:** Ray Sozzi is the founder of Student Advantage, the nation's largest student discount program. Sozzi had the idea for Student Advantage while a student at Dartmouth College, where he had already established several businesses, including a disc jockey company, a cake-and-balloon delivery service, and a published guide to Dartmouth. He was even able to pay for his senior year in school with the earnings. After graduating in 1990, Sozzi worked briefly as a management consultant for two years before leaving to launch Student Advantage. He financed the company initially by selling his car and his apartment, borrowing money from family and friends, and using credit cards. Sozzi then acquired four different businesses from college students or recent graduates who had built up small discount programs on their campuses. "In looking to grow, we faced a chicken-and-egg dilemma. It was hard to convince corporate partners to provide valuable services and discounts without a large group of students as members, and it was hard to get students to join unless we had significant value-added services. We were able to resolve this challenge and grow to scale quickly by rolling up similar businesses." Another benefit of Sozzi's growth strategy was that most students running the businesses he acquired decided to join his team. "It was a phenomenal source of talent. In fact, many of them ended up staying with the company for five to ten years," says Sozzi. In 1997, Student Advantage received its first round of financing and two years later went public via IPO. In 2002, Sozzi took the company private again, and in November 2005, sold it to The CBORD Group, the world's leading supplier of campus card software and systems.

■ **Advice for Student Entrepreneurs:** "When you're in college it's a very unique and opportune time to take a risk with nothing to lose. But I've talked to too many students who have great ideas and even write the business plan, but never take the next step of launching the business. Go ahead and take the leap because there is no better time."

—**Ray Sozzi**

Ten Mistakes Every Campus CEO Makes—
And How to Avoid Them

Mistakes in the business world are inevitable, and no aspiring entrepreneur is immune to them. Many of the business missteps that Campus CEOs make are operational, such as mismanaging money, or strategic in nature, such as hiring the wrong people. It's my aim in this chapter to keep you from doing things that can sink your business venture. After all, what good is it to team up in business with your best friend or roommate if he or she has absolutely nothing to offer the enterprise? And what purpose will it serve if you launch your business out of your dormitory, only to realize that you've violated a university policy? If either scenario unfolds, your business will suffer and may even cease operations. This chapter highlights the most common business pitfalls that Campus CEOs face (many of which I have encountered myself), and explains how to fix any errors that may have already been made. The sentiment of this chapter is also a quote from Malcolm Forbes, publisher of *Forbes* magazine, who said, "Failure is success if we learn from it," which means that practically every mistake is a step along the road to success in school, business, and life, as long as you learn from it.

Here's my list of the Ten Mistakes That Campus CEOs Make . . . numbered but in no particular order.

Mistake #1: Not Having the Infrastructure to Support What They're Advertising

You never get a second chance to make a first impression. So when you lack the infrastructure to deliver the product or service you're advertising, you risk losing a potentially valuable customer forever. For example, don't plaster posters everywhere about your business and spread the word about your company on every list group, chat room, and blog known to mankind and then fail to have the capacity to handle a rush of business. And don't blast your toll-free 800 number to a 50,000-person e-newsletter if you're the only one available to answer the phones. Scale your marketing and advertising efforts to be commensurate with the volume of business you can reasonably handle and expand thereafter. Prepare for the long term by ensuring that inventory is on hand to meet customer demand (product) or that enough employees or consultants are ready to handle new business (service). Even though it can be extremely tempting, learn to say no to opportunities that you know will outstrip your capacity. Be honest with yourself about what you can and cannot do now versus what you hope to do later—otherwise you risk damaging client relationships.

Mistake #2: Not Knowing the Value of What They're Offering

If I had to do it all over again, one of the things I would've changed would be to have a better appreciation for the value of our services at MBS Educational Services & Training while I was in college. We bought into the myth that because we were students and young people, we should charge less than what was being charged by older, more established people. Aldwyn always pushed the envelope and wanted us to charge more for our services. In retrospect, I wish we had heeded his words more often. I recall one instance in particular when we developed a proposal to organize a conference, and Aldwyn's recommendation proved extremely valuable. We were shooting in the dark on this proposal, because we hadn't yet benchmarked the competition in terms of pricing. Up until that point, we'd been charging just under $5,000 for our conferences. Aldwyn thought: What do we have to lose with throwing out a larger number? At first JR and I, both being more conservative than Aldwyn, thought it was too risky. Eventually, after a good amount of persuasion, we agreed with his suggestion and priced our proposal at more than double our previous rate—$10,000—thinking that was a huge amount of money. That week, I sat down with a corporate vice president and the program's coordinator to discuss our proposal. The first question they asked me was: "Have you ever done a conference for $10,000?" I answered: "No, but I know for a fact that it will be worth it." You know what happened? We got the assignment!

Despite our excitement, we may have still left some money on the table—that day and others as well. But Aldwyn taught us a valuable lesson nonetheless: know the value of what you're offering. It's terrible when you're a student and you have no concept about pricing and you sell yourself short. Nobody pulls you aside to tell you: "Hey guys, you're way off the mark. We have a budget that's three times the amount of your bid." Do your homework and you will avoid making the mistakes that we made.

Mistake #3: Being Afraid to Pursue Business at the Highest Levels

Many aspects of my collegiate entrepreneurship days were great fun. It was also very exciting. It felt like we were years ahead of our time. I recall Lawrence, Dallas, JR, and I doing a six-figure contract with General Motors when we were 23 and 24 years old. We would sit down with people who were twice our age or older and negotiate. Even though we made some mistakes, we weren't scared to step into the ring with executives of any rank. And you shouldn't be either. Don't be afraid to enter arenas dominated by people more seasoned or older than you are. Sometimes ignorance is indeed bliss as you may one day look back, like we do, in amazement at what you were able to accomplish at such a young age. By the same token, know your limitations and try to learn everything you can when you're in these situations.

Mistake #4: Neglecting to Explore Funding and Other Support from Family and Friends

Too many times entrepreneurs fail to tap into sources of help that are just waiting to come to their aid. I know that in my case, we were initially gun-shy to ask for other people's money to play with. In our early years, I don't think we had the confidence to go to family and friends as potential investors. We didn't even consider it an option and that was a mistake. And because we lacked any money whatsoever, we initially weren't able to be as strategic as possible in our business. When you have money at your disposal, you can decide what kind of opportunities you want to create.

Mistake #5: Being Reluctant to Bootstrap Their Company

If you visit many campuses where entrepreneurship is hot, you'll find that a lot of students get far too focused on being successful in business plan competitions, obtaining venture capital, or winning over angel investors. And if they don't win, they think there's no way they'll get financing for their businesses. As mentioned in Chapter 6, an alternative and sometimes equally effective strategy for launching and running your business is to combine whatever financial capital you can—using personal savings, credit card debit, etc.—and use creativity to leverage other forms of capital (i.e. human, intellectual, social, and cultural) along with pure sweat equity to push your business forward. Bootstrapping is the most common way to finance a business. We used this approach with MBS, by pursuing contracts instead of investors. We then reinvested all our profits back into the company to fuel our growth. In retrospect, we will never know whether or not we could have raised money. What we do know is that bootstrapping worked for us. For those of you who find yourself in a situation where you do not have access to financial capital, it is a growth strategy you should strongly consider instead of throwing in the towel.

Mistake #6: Not Knowing Their School's Rules and Limitations Concerning Campus Businesses

In business, it's often better to just do something—and ask for forgiveness instead of permission. But many schools have very strict policies about campus resources for commercial enterprises. A student may have a popular business, then other students start talking about it, with the student entrepreneur only ending up having to shut it down because he or she has violated a campus rule or regulation. Your best bet? Avoid getting run off campus because of these technicalities. "When a student wants to start a business on campus, he or she should talk to someone in the law school, the technology transfer office, and/or or the business development office," says Desiree Vargas, a specialist in collegiate entrepreneurship at the Kauffman Foundation, one of the country's leading organizations in the area of campus entrepreneurship.

DCSnacks (profiled at the end of this chapter), formerly known as CampusSnacks, is one such company that ran afoul of campus rules. Founded by in 2003 by Matthew Mandell while he was a student at George Washington University, the company delivers late-night snacks and other products to people in a niche location of the Washington, D.C., area—anyone within one mile of the White House. But when the university found out that he was operating a business out of his residence hall, campus officials threatened to shut the business down. Mandell moved his location to the Foggy Bottom section of the city and DCSnacks remains a viable, growing business to this day thanks to the founder's ingenuity and perseverance.

Mistake #7: Being Far Too Rigid in Their Concepts about How the Business Should Be Run

If you have tunnel vision, and you believe that your business can only operate a certain way, or only reach a certain market, or only use certain sales channels and so forth, you're not being as flexible as you should be. The result is that you may not recognize offshoots or other potential areas in which your company could function successfully. In other words, don't be so tied to one unique business idea or model that you miss other opportunities for that business. Remember the entreprenuer's mindset and the fact that the best entrepreneurs are creative and visionary; they don't yet subscribe to the misconception that there is only one way to get something done or one way to achieve success.

Mistake #8: Being Blind about Course Selection

Students in liberal arts or the hard sciences often mistakenly think that they need to get business degrees to become business owners, or that entrepreneurship is about taking a litany of management, accounting, and finance-related courses. You can pursue a degree in any major and still be entrepreneurially minded. Students in fields as diverse as nursing, environmental studies, and art history can make just as good entrepreneurs as those studying finance. There's certainly no requirement that you only take business-specific classes. In fact, you'll get a more well-rounded education and learn a variety of approaches and philosophies if you take a range of courses in the humanities and social sciences, as well as in the hard sciences. An entrepreneurship course can fill required courses or be an elective, while also killing two birds with one stone— getting good grades while devoting time to developing your business.

Mistake #9: Bringing On Board the Wrong Employees, Volunteers, Interns, or Partners

As I stated earlier, having a friendship with someone is not a sufficient basis for going into business with or hiring that person. The key to finding the right talent to work with you is to have alignment with the company's mission, vision, and values, a clear understanding of what each person brings to the table and what each person expects to get out of the business relationship, and finding people who can separate business from personal issues.

Mistake #10: Undervaluing the Importance of Networking

Your enterprise will grow faster, and your experience as an entrepreneur will be more fruitful and rewarding, if you deliberately take the time to network with people. And I mean dedicating time to establishing meaningful and productive *relationships* with people. Your goal shouldn't be all about boosting your own fortunes. Take the time to learn about other people's interests, ambitions, and goals. Find out what they enjoy and see if you can be of help to them. Relationships are about give-and-take. As a student, you may be wondering, "What do I have to give?" The answer is "A lot," especially for aspiring or practicing student entrepreneurs. Among other things, you can provide insight to the student marketplace, a fresh perspective on business opportunities, and access to your network of other students and emerging professionals.

Extracurricular activities, having a social life, your own private time— they're all important. But you still must take the time to network, particularly with faculty members, experienced entrepreneurs, and potential investors. Unfortunately, a lot of students graduate and don't have meaningful references. You should know at least three professors in your major who would be able to write a strong letter of recommendation for you or vouch for you in some way. For example, to apply for a Rhodes scholarship you must provide at least four letters of recommendation from professors that have taught you in the classroom. These must be people that actually know you and can attest to your strengths and abilities. So also get to know people who work in your field or industry, and make sure they know you as well and what you're trying to accomplish. Ironically, career fairs, student recruitment events, and summer internships are all great opportunities to expand your network for the purpose of later starting a business.

Obviously, there are tons of other mistakes you could make, but these are the most prevalent and resonant for many. Just for good measure, here's a bonus item to consider. Are you guilty of this one?

Mistake #11: Being Paralyzed into Inaction

Some college students can be procrastinators of the worst kind. You know you have a test next week, but you'll blow it off until the night before the exam and then cram like crazy. Ever done that? I'm sure some of you have. Everybody procrastinates now and again. But constant procrastination can be a real killer in business, causing you to never get anything substantive done! A few cases in point: Some student entrepreneurs seem to work on their business plan for all four years of their undergraduate education. What's with these people? Get it done already! Others research their industry or target market to death, and never put anything into use in the real world. Still other student entrepreneurs will talk your ears off about the "best business idea ever"—one that they've conceived, naturally—but that they never quite bring to market.

Ramit Sethi is a graduate of Stanford University. He operates "I Will Teach You to be Rich," a free blog on personal finances and entrepreneurship. In one blog post he presented "8 Stupid Frat-Boy Business Ideas." It's meant to be a humorous critique of business ideas that college students have come up with, including those offbeat concepts dreamed up after one-too-many beers. Some of the ideas Sethi mentions are, in fact, really funny—at least in the light in which he casts them. But at a certain level, I don't think there's really a "stupid" idea you could come up with: it might be ill-conceived, it might lack market potential, or it might be something that's already in existence. However, if you're letting your entrepreneurial mindset flow, don't be afraid to just go for it and dream big when it comes to a potential business idea—no matter how outlandish it might initially seem to others. The key here is: don't curb your natural enthusiasm. If you have a passion for something and it leads you to a potential business idea, or some type of entrepreneurial endeavor, pursue it with gusto and see where it takes you. Sometimes the only "stupid" thing you can do in business is to do nothing at all.

CAMPUS CEO CHECKLIST

After reading Chapter 15, take these steps to avoid common pitfalls:

☐ Write down this statement: "Failure is success if we learn from it." Put it someplace visible to remind yourself that mistakes represent learning opportunities along the pathway to success.

☐ Have a conversation with supportive family members and friends about your desire to launch and/or grow your business. Ask who might be willing and able to invest in your venture if necessary.

☐ Think about a hobby or personal interest you have that may or may not be related to your business. Review your class catalog to see if there's a course offered that you could sign up for to expand your knowledge of this subject and broaden your horizons.

☐ Identify something related to launching or growing your business that you've been procrastinating on, and commit to a firm deadline for completing the task.

PROFILE OF A CAMPUS CEO

■ **Name:** Matthew Mandell

■ **Business:** DCSnacks

■ **Web site:** *www.DCSnacks.com*

■ **Founded:** 2003

■ **His Story:** During his junior year at George Washington University, Matthew Mandell took about $1,000—money from his own savings and a loan from his parents—and bought soda, bottled water, cookies, muffins, and other things he thought students would want during the wee hours of the night. It didn't take long for word to spread on campus that when you needed a caffeine jolt to stay up studying all night or just had a case of the munchies, you could simply log onto the Internet, place an order for whatever you wanted, and within 20 minutes or so, a delivery person would be at your doorstep. Back then, the business was called CampusSnacks, reflecting its focus solely on college students at GWU. Over time, however, the business began serving a wider customer base, including people in homes and apartments, as well as individuals burning the midnight oil at different local businesses. If you're within roughly two miles of the White House, Mandell's company will take care of your late-night needs between 8 PM and 4 PM. As a result, CampusSnacks has now become DCSnacks. The business originally carried about 50 items for delivery. Now it offers more than 800 products, ranging from ice cream to condoms to cold and flu medicine. Although Mandell is tight-lipped about his company's revenues, the U.S. Business Directory estimates that DCSnacks sales top $1 million annually.

■ **Advice for Student Entrepreneurs:** "The most important thing is to realize the amount of time and effort it takes to run a business. In many ways, it's very much like having a child. It's a lot of responsibility. You never sleep. And the business is something that most people will come to identify you with—for better or worse."

—Matthew Mandell

Final Advice—
Seven Universal Lessons for Every Entrepreneur

66 *Keep going until you break through that wall.* 99

—Russell Simmons, Founder of Rush Communications
in *MBA Jungle* Magazine (December 2000/January 2001)

16

Let me share with you seven universal lessons I have learned that can help you achieve entrepreneurial success. Based on my experiences thus far, these are things I would tell myself if I could somehow go back to the time when I was an aspiring Campus CEO.

Lesson #1: Work with a Team, but Know Your Position and Play Your Position

The importance of creating teams and working with teams has been said in a million ways, a million times: "There is strength in numbers." "Two heads are better than one." "I am my brother's keeper." "A chain is only as strong as its weakest link." "All for one and one for all." All these sayings are true. But what these quotes fail to mention is that it's not only important to work with a team, it's also important to know your position on the team and play your position. Now what do I mean by this?

Knowing your position means defining your specific role, which hopefully plays to your strengths. You can't and shouldn't do everything. Football is a good analogy here. The linemen block; the running back runs; the quarterback throws; the receivers catch, and so forth. With MBS Educational Services & Training, my role and JR's role were first to find business opportunities (i.e., to find work, to make rain, to lead our marketing and sales efforts). For Lawrence and Dallas, their primary role was to manage getting the work done. Some refer to this as the "inside-outside" game. JR and I were focused on what happened outside the office, while Lawrence and Dallas were focused on what happened inside the office, and it worked well for us.

Once your role is defined, playing your position means making sure you are in the right place at the right time, and that the team can depend on you to be there. Going back to football, I've never played the organized sport, but I know enough to know that when they run a play, it works best when everybody is in the right place at the right time. Let's take a pass pattern as an example. The linemen block in a certain way. The quarterback falls back to a certain position. And most important, the quarterback throws the ball to a certain location with the expectation that the receiver will be there to catch it. When things go wrong, the quarterback ends up throwing the ball into empty space or, even worse, into the hands of the opponent for an interception. So the lesson here is that I encourage all of you, especially those who have or will pursue something entrepreneurial, to form a team, define your role based on your strengths, and play your position to the best of your ability.

Lesson #2: Take Risks and Accept Uncertainty

At the very beginning of *Campus CEO*, I told you that I hoped to help you develop an entrepreneurial mindset. Part of that mindset involves the healthy realization that if you're going to be a business owner, you'll have to take risks from time to time. Unfortunately, not everyone is comfortable taking risks, even calculated risks. But the truth is, business success demands it. It requires it. In my role as chairman and CEO, I take risks every day. I've taken personal loans to cover employee salaries during slow months. I've "maxed out" credit cards to pay company bills. I've committed company dollars to marketing or advertising efforts when there was no guarantee they would work. But that is the name of the game. No risk, no reward. No pain, no gain. No struggle, no progress. No test, no testimony.

Though we founded MBS Educational Services & Training while we were in college, our vision at the time was to pursue the venture full-time. After we graduated from college, we ran the company part-time for six years from 1993 to 1999. We had no full-time staff as each of us pursued graduate degrees or took positions in corporate America. We basically worked evenings and weekends.

The trend over our first six years from 1994 to 1999 was that we approximately doubled our revenues each year, but there was no guarantee that trend would continue. At the end of 1999, we were faced with a critical decision: whether someone should leave their comfortable job or graduate school to work for MBS full-time and, if so, who and when.

I remember the day we met to make the decision. Without a doubt, the underlying question for the discussion was the following: To what extent were we willing to take a risk and live with the uncertainty of leaving our current, secure environments? To make a long story short, Lawrence and Dallas ended up leaving their jobs at Merrill Lynch and Lucent Technologies, respectively. I continued part-time with MBS while pursuing a dual master's in electrical engineering/MBA at MIT while JR, who just completed his master's at Georgia Tech, continued part-time with MBS, while working full-time at the pharmaceutical giant Merck & Co. Aldwyn and Raqiba eventually left the company to pursue other priorities.

Guess how much we made in 2000? We tripled our revenues! And keep in mind this is all from educational services and training, and we were engineers. None of us had academic backgrounds in educational services or training, but we were able to learn the industry, a principle I'll revisit in lesson #5.

> ### ■ Join a Global Community of Entrepreneurs
>
> Once you grow your company to revenues of $1 million or higher, you can join the global network of business owners known as the Entrepreneurs' Organization (EO). The EO has 120 chapters and peer groups worldwide within 40 countries throughout North America, Latin America, Asia, and Europe. The organization offers direct peer-to-peer learning, once-in-a-lifetime experiences that involve learning or social events, and connections to business experts. You can learn more at *www.eonetwork.org.*

Lesson #3: Be Persistent and Learn from Mistakes

Because lesson #2 was to take risks and accept uncertainty, lesson #3 should come as no surprise. Any time you take risks, you're going to make mistakes. That simply comes with the territory. And as mentioned in the previous chapter, the key is that every mistake must be seen as a learning opportunity. Dealing with failure—that is, learning from it—requires you to be persistent and never allow failure or setbacks to discourage you.

On the subject of persistence, Calvin Coolidge said:

Nothing in the world can take the place of persistence.
Talent will not, nothing is more common than unsuccessful men with talent.
Genius will not, unrewarded genius is almost a proverb.
Education will not, the world is full of educated derelicts.
Persistence and determination alone are omnipotent.

Persistence is never giving up and never giving in, because sooner or later the man or woman who persists will succeed. In school and in the workplace, I can't tell you how many times I've seen talented individuals outperformed by others who were willing to go the extra mile—outdone by others who were unwilling to accept failure. So, indeed, you are talented, but that talent means nothing if you're not willing to get up after you've been knocked down, because you will be knocked down. *If you desire success, failure is unavoidable.*

After we tripled our revenues at MBS in 2000, we made the strategic decision to move beyond just educational services and training and begin leveraging our backgrounds in engineering by starting a new division focused on information technology consulting. So you figure things were looking pretty good now, right? If we doubled or even tripled our revenues again in 2001, we stood to do millions of dollars in sales and we were all still in our 20s. That was huge for us!

Well, maybe not. Let's think back to 2001. The economy had already begun to decline in the fall of 2000, which was around the time of the dot-com bust, also known as "dot bomb." This was also around the time that JR and I were both deep into our PhD programs. In fact, I was completing my doctorate that year. So for both of us, our ability to do marketing and sales was somewhat limited. Last, but not least, as we are all well aware, that fall we witnessed the terrorist attacks of September 11. All these factors translated into a very difficult year for everyone. And, furthermore, we made plenty of mistakes. We waited far too long to catch the technology wave. We had a few breakdowns in communication and clarification of expectations. And we made a sizable investment in a marketing campaign that largely failed. So, given all of that, guess how much we made in 2001? Instead of tripling our revenues or even doubling our revenues, our revenues were cut in half! Sadly, we were faced with potential layoffs.

But looking back, I appreciate the fact that we made these mistakes, because they gave us the opportunity to learn from them. And I know it sounds a little crazy that failure is a good thing. I mean, could you imagine coming home for the semester with a report card of straight Fs and telling your parents, "Mom, Dad, don't be upset. I didn't fail, I learned a lesson." For some reason I don't think that would fly! But again, the lesson in business, not necessarily school, is to make sure you learn from your mistakes. If you look at the careers of successful businesspeople and entrepreneurs, they have undoubtedly experienced one setback after another. But they never allowed setbacks to hold them down or hold them back. Along those same lines, we were set back in 2001, but we continued the fight in 2002. We made a series of positive changes, which I will discuss in the context of the next lesson.

Lesson #4: Reinvent Yourself When Necessary

While running MBS as students, we went from a dorm to a living room to a garage, and eventually to a business incubator. This series of transitions meant that my business partners and I were gradually reinventing ourselves to deal with new working conditions, new opportunities, and a changing business environment. While at Rutgers, I did my internships at AT&T. After Oxford, I worked for AT&T, which later split into AT&T and Lucent Technologies. When I got a dual degree in the MIT Leaders for Manufacturing Program, that two-year, double master's program required an eight-month internship with a corporation, which I performed back at Lucent most of my second year. It wasn't until the summer before I started my PhD program in 1998 that I worked as a full-time summer intern at MBS Educational Services & Training with Dallas, one of my business partners.

As mentioned earlier, two years later, Dallas and Lawrence, another business partner, decided to leave their full-time jobs to become the first full-time employees at MBS. This was around the same time as the economic downturn of 2000 and the tragic events of September 11, 2001, both of which presented considerable challenges for the company. Soon after, it seemed as if the business crumbled almost overnight. We started immediately losing clients who called to say they were cutting back on their educational initiatives. When budgets got cut, training was the first thing to go. At first we still had major clients, but within two weeks of September 11, they all canceled contracts. That month, almost every single major account called to say it was cutting its budget for conferences and training. And just like that, the business for MBS dried up. We hardly threw in the towel though. The end of MBS actually marked the birth of my current company, BCT Partners.

As it turns out, at the end of 2000, MBS had already established a new department called our technology consulting division. It wasn't something we'd pursued with any great level of effort. But by the time we saw the writing on the wall for the demise of the educational and training component of our business, we realized that companies were much more interested in technology and ways in which they could be smart in utilizing it in the new economy. Therefore, what began as the same legal entity that sold CDs and tapes out of my dorm room and then morphed into MBS Educational Services & Training wound up being the entity that today is BCT Partners. We simply did a name change. All this occurred while I was still a student at MIT. BCT grew sufficiently enough in that year so that by the time I finished my PhD in the fall of 2001, I was able to join BCT Partners full-time on January 2, 2002, focusing initially on technology consulting and later expanding to include management consulting, policy consulting, organizational development, and strategic planning. This was the ultimate case of us reinventing ourselves and adapting to the market as necessary.

> ### ■ The Entrepreneur's Mindset
>
> Two good books on the entrepreneur's mindset are:
>
> - *The Entrepreneurial Mind* by Jeffry Timmons
> - *The Entrepreneurial Mindset* by Rita Gunther McGrath and Ian MacMillan

Lesson #5: It's Not What You Know, It's What You Can Learn

You've probably heard the expression, "It's not *what* you know, it's *who* you know." But you may not have heard this next truism: namely, that it's not *what you know*, it's *what you can learn* that often matters most.

We live in a world where the only thing constant is change. Therefore, anything we learn can become obsolete very quickly. At least once a month at BCT we hold a knowledge review session during which a team gives a presentation about a project they have worked on to share the lessons learned, or to highlight the latest trends, the latest technologies, or the latest developments in our industry. The purpose is to disseminate that knowledge throughout the company. Why? Because, as an organization, we must never stop learning. Lifelong learning is a must. And, fortunately, that is where college can be a big help. In college, you're not just learning, you're also learning how to learn.

Lesson #6: It's Not Who You Know, It's Who Knows You

In addition to believing that "it's not what you know, it's who you know," I also believe that "it's not who you know, it's *who knows you*." With all the forms of communication we have at our disposal—U.S. mail, electronic mail, voice mail, and then telephones, mobile phones, pagers, PDAs, the Internet, and let's not forget face-to-face contact—we live in an incredibly networked society, which is why your social network is so important.

According to Earl Graves, an accomplished entrepreneur who founded *Black Enterprise* magazine, "Networking is a social first, business second activity." To that point, one of the changes we made in launching BCT that we didn't do well at MBS was to make sure we were at conferences, trade shows, receptions, conventions, social events, etc.—to be networking, networking, networking as much as possible so people knew who we were. A good example of how that paid off was our first six-figure opportunity at BCT with a municipal government. It all came about through networking.

I attended a fundraiser for a small nonprofit organization where I met the mayor of a local city, who was one of the speakers that evening. He invited me to his office to meet and discuss business opportunities. I later found out that a friend of mine who was familiar with our company worked for the city. She was willing put in a good word for us. By the time I got to the meeting, the mayor was already putting opportunities on the table for us to do business with the city!

In building your network, where does it all begin for you? It begins right on campus. In fact, it started before you even arrived on campus. To the extent that you are involved in campus organizations and activities and are establishing good relationships with your classmates and professors, people who are getting to know you as someone they can trust to get things done, then your time is well spent. I guarantee that your track record and those relationships will serve you well in the future.

Lesson #7: Stay True to the Entrepreneur's Mindset

Aspiring entrepreneurs must embody the entrepreneur's mindset of creativity, resourcefulness, courage, vision, and perseverance in almost every facet of their businesses. Sometimes problems occur that you can't throw money at to fix—simply because you don't have the money! But even if you did, at times mere dollars alone won't suffice. As an entrepreneur, you're invariably trying to maximize resources—everything from interactions with students and faculty to information on the Internet. The entrepreneur's mindset is a must in all these endeavors.

Students often embody the mindset naturally. So don't let the influences of the world take it away from you, as it is a core trait needed by every entrepreneur. Embedded in the MBS story, as you can tell, are lots of twists and turns and maneuvering—among partners, the focus of the business, and so forth. At times, we had to figure out certain problems: Now that you're in school in another state, how can we make this work? Or now that you can only devote a modest amount of time to the business, are we still configured the right way? Creativity and adaptability helped us find our way. This is the art of entrepreneurship at its finest.

■ FINAL LESSON—HAVE FAITH

While it's inevitable that you will make mistakes as you launch or build a business, I want to leave you with some parting thoughts that will help you overcome adversity and deal with whatever challenges—personal or professional—you may face in the future.

My final questions to you are the following: What are your hopes? What are your dreams? What are your aspirations? And what would they be right now, right at this very moment, if I completely removed whatever inhibitions you have about what you *think* you can't do? Or what you *think* you shouldn't do?

Whether you aspire to become an entrepreneur or not, above all, you must have faith and believe that you can be successful at whatever you set out to do. Faith is the substance of things hoped for, the evidence of things unseen. And while I, along with my business partners, am a spiritual person, this is not a principle reserved for the religious alone. Faith also means believing in yourself, believing in those you work with, and believing that there is something inside

■ Additional Resources for Campus CEOs

Following is a list of organizations, not previously mentioned, that can provide ongoing support and resources to Campus CEOs and entrepreneurship educators:

- Impact (*www.impact.org*)
- Institute for Entrepreneurial Leadership (*www.ifelnj.org*)
- United States Association for Small Business and Entrepreneurship (*www.usasbe.org*)
- Entrepreneurship Education Consortium (*www.entre-ed.org*)

- Roundtable on Entrepreneurship Education for Scientists and Engineers (*http://ree.stanford.edu*)
- National Association for Community College Entrepreneurship (*www.nacce.com*)
- National Institute for Urban Entrepreneurship (*www.ni-ue.org*)

For a comprehensive and up-to-date list of all the programs, organizations, and Web sites mentioned in *Campus CEO*, please visit: *www.CampusCEO.com*.

you that will enable you to reach your goals, even if you don't know exactly how you're going to get there. I believe that faith is a guiding principle of business success, which can also be interpreted as an acronym, F.A.I.T.H.: Feeling As If Things Happened; or Having F.A.I.T.H.: Having Full Assurance In The Heart.

We have eight values at BCT that guide our day to day activities. They are balance, integrity, innovation, growth, excellence, entrepreneurship, teamwork, and last but not least, faith. From Mind, Body & Soul Enterprises to MBS Educational Services & Training to BCT Partners, our faith has constantly been tested. We've lost valuable partners. We've failed to deliver on certain contracts. We've watched as competitors beat us in obtaining new opportunities. But we've grown and evolved from a small dormitory operation to a multimillion-dollar enterprise because we continue to believe that the sky is the limit—and so should you. Sorrow looks down, and worry looks back, but faith looks up. Staying true to the entrepreneurial mindset as a Campus CEO means you should *always* look up!

CAMPUS CEO CHECKLIST

After reading Chapter 16, take these steps to assess your business and its progress:

- ☐ List three major risks that you face in your business. Now write down three ways you can mitigate those risks.

- ☐ Think of the biggest mistake you've made (so far) in your business. Reflect on what lessons you learned from the situation.

- ☐ Take a fresh look at the primary aspects of your business. Does anything need to be revamped or reinvented? Is your Web site up-to-date? Is your marketing plan still effective? What about your corporate image—is it reflective of what you want to project to the marketplace? If not, retool things as necessary.

- ☐ Analyze your business know-how. Do you need to hone any skills, such as your technological proficiency, your public speaking skills, or your ability to make sales calls? If so, write down what steps you will take and give yourself a reasonable deadline to enhance your skills in any area you may be weak.

- ☐ Keep the faith! Don't let minor setbacks or adversities cause you to give up on your dreams. Maintain the entrepreneurial mindset and know that you can persevere and succeed.

PROFILE OF A CAMPUS CEO

- **Name:** De'On and De'Juan Collins

- **Business:** Collins Capital Investments

- **Web site:** *www.collinsinvestments.net*

- **Founded:** 2005

- **Their Story:** These twin brothers launched their real estate investment company while undergraduates at Texas Tech University in Lubbock, Texas. The duo is currently enrolled in Texas Tech's Rawls College of Business, where they are pursuing degrees in finance with an emphasis on real estate. Their business, Collins Capital Investments (CCI), invests in undervalued and distressed real estate by purchasing and making improvements to the foundation, wiring, plumbing, and other physical attributes of the properties. CCI's goal is to provide quality housing in low- and moderate-income communities through acquisitions, property management, and asset management. One year prior to establishing CCI, they founded Collins Entertainment and Promotions. Leveraging their people skills and outgoing personalities, they hosted parties for fellow students by renting venues off-campus. "We learned a lot from our first business, such as networking and negotiation. Our professors also were extremely helpful in providing guidance," says De'On. Their parties did so well they were able to generate the initial start-up capital to launch CCI. "Our strong faith in God and our belief that entrepreneurship is a part of our destiny caused us to be creative in our approach to pursue our real passion, which is real estate," says De'Juan. Today, CCI maintains active operations in three markets across the state of Texas and continues to grow.

> - **Advice for Student Entrepreneurs:** "It may take awhile for certain aspects of your business to come to fruition, but be patient and, most important, be persistent. You never know how close you may be to a new or exciting opportunity, but if you keep trying, eventually good things will happen."
>
> **—De'On and De'Juan Collins**

Index